National Identity in Serbia

National Identity in Serbia

The Vojvodina and a Multi-Ethnic Community in the Balkans

Vassilis Petsinis

I.B. TAURIS
LONDON • NEW YORK • OXFORD • NEW DELHI • SYDNEY

I.B. TAURIS
Bloomsbury Publishing Plc
50 Bedford Square, London, WC1B 3DP, UK
1385 Broadway, New York, NY 10018, USA
29 Earlsfort Terrace, Dublin 2, Ireland

BLOOMSBURY, I.B. TAURIS and the I.B. Tauris logo
are trademarks of Bloomsbury Publishing Plc

First published in Great Britain 2020
Paperback edition first published 2021

Copyright © Vassilis Petsinis 2020

Vassilis Petsinis has asserted his right under the Copyright,
Designs and Patents Act, 1988, to be identified as Author of this work.

For legal purposes the Acknowledgements on p. viii constitute
an extension of this copyright page.

Cover image: Serbian flag in Novi Sad and City Hall tower in Novi Sad, Serbia.
(© Miroslav Jacimovic / Alamy Stock Photo)

All rights reserved. No part of this publication may be reproduced or
transmitted in any form or by any means, electronic or mechanical,
including photocopying, recording, or any information storage or retrieval
system, without prior permission in writing from the publishers.

Bloomsbury Publishing Plc does not have any control over, or responsibility for,
any third-party websites referred to or in this book. All internet addresses given
in this book were correct at the time of going to press. The author and publisher
regret any inconvenience caused if addresses have changed or sites have
ceased to exist, but can accept no responsibility for any such changes.

A catalogue record for this book is available from the British Library.

A catalogue record for this book is available from the Library of Congress.

ISBN: HB: 978-1-7883-1373-5
PB: 978-0-7556-3681-5
ePDF: 978-1-7883-1709-2
eBook: 978-1-7883-1708-5

Typeset by Integra Software Services Pvt. Ltd.

To find out more about our authors and books visit
www.bloomsbury.com and sign up for our newsletters.

Contents

List of Data-Tables and Figures	vi
Acknowledgements	viii
Glossary of Abbreviations and Acronyms	x

1. Introduction: Setting the Conceptual and the Theoretical Frames — 1
2. Vojvodina through Time: From the Habsburg Era to the Socialist Federal Republic of Yugoslavia — 29
3. Vojvodina in the 1990s: From the Termination of Autonomy to the Fall of Slobodan Milošević — 77
4. Vojvodina Going through Transition (the 2000s) — 171
5. Vojvodina Today: Between New Challenges and Opportunities — 209

Bibliography and Other Sources — 236
Index — 257

List of Data-Tables and Figures

Tables

1	The ethnic structure of the population of Vojvodina in 1921	44
2	Membership of the League of Communists of Vojvodina, 1953–8	71
3	Opinions concerning relations among nations and nationalities in Yugoslavia, in per cent	75
4	The ethnic structure of the autonomous province of Vojvodina according to the 1991 national census	92
5	The results of the Serbian parliamentary elections in Vojvodina, December 1992	100
6	The results of the Yugoslav parliamentary elections in Vojvodina, December 1992	100
7	The results of the early Serbian parliamentary elections in Vojvodina, December 1993	101
8	Electoral results by number of votes at selected municipalities in Vojvodina (including break-up by occupational, social and ethnic structure)	104
9	War-displaced persons accommodated in the territory of FR Yugoslavia	118
10	Colonists and refugees in Vojvodina (1948–96)	120
11	Number of refugees in municipalities with a dense or a majority Hungarian and/or other ethnic minority population (1996)	121
12	Electoral results by number of votes at selected municipalities in Vojvodina	158
13	The results of the Yugoslav parliamentary elections (September 2000) at the Vojvodinian electoral units	167
14	What should Vojvodina's administrative status be?	197
15	What kind of status should Vojvodina enjoy?	197

16	What should Vojvodina's administrative status be?	197
17	Vojvodina is denied the right to finance projects within its territory from the provincial budget. Would this be a good arrangement?	198
18	What kind of meaning does the term *autonomy* have for you?	199
19	What should Vojvodina's status within Serbia be (broken down in accordance with national affiliation)?	200
20	Should the Assembly of the Autonomous Province of Vojvodina comprise a Chamber of National Communities where the major national communities in the province will be equally represented (broken down in accordance with national affiliation)?	202
21	The results of the elections for the assembly of the autonomous province of Vojvodina (May 2012)	212
22	The results of the elections for the assembly of the autonomous province of Vojvodina (April 2016)	213
23	The ethnic structure of the population in Vojvodina (2011 census)	220

Figures

1	Vojvodina's regional flag and coat of arms favoured by SNS	215
2	Vojvodina's regional flag favoured by LSDV	215

Source

http://www.skupstinavojvodine.gov.rs/: The official website of Vojvodina's provincial assembly.

Acknowledgements

I would like to cordially thank the following individuals and institutions without the help of whom this piece of work would not have been completed successfully. First of all, I am highly indebted to the European Commission, the Marie Skłodowska-Curie actions in particular, and to the Johan Skytte Institute of Political Studies (University of Tartu). I am also indebted to the Centre for Baltic and East European Studies (Södertörns Högskola, Stockholm), Collegium Budapest (now Centre for Advanced Study at the Central European University), IESIR (Comenius University in Bratislava), New Europe College (Bucharest) and to the Herder Institute in Marburg. Then, I would like to thank my PhD supervisor Professor Judy Batt (CREES, University of Birmingham) for her steady and punctual supervision, as well as the helpful directions that she gave me while writing up my thesis on Vojvodina. In addition, I would like to thank CREES (University of Birmingham), the British Association for Slavonic and East European Studies and the coordinators of the ESRC-funded 'Fuzzy Statehood' project for offering me various kinds of financial support between 2000 and 2004. My thanks also go to Professor Hillary Pilkington (former Head of CREES), Professor Jeremy Smith and the secretaries of the department (Ms Tricia Carr and Mrs. Marea Arries) for offering me various kinds of assistance.

I would like to express my gratitude to Professor Martyn Rady (School of Slavonic and East European Studies, University College London) for offering me some preliminary hints in regard to the coordination of my field research. In Novi Sad, I would like to thank, first of all, Professor Saša Kicošev (Head of the GIS Centre, Geography Department, University of Novi Sad), Professor Zsölt Lazar (Sociology Department, Faculty of Philosophy, University of Novi Sad) and Professor Milan Prodanović (Department of Urbanism, University of Novi Sad/Belgrade University). The aforementioned individuals dedicated much of their precious time arranging interview appointments, in the course of my field research in Vojvodina. Also, Professor Kicošev let me make use of the archive collection at the Geography Department of the University of Novi Sad, whereas Professor Lazar offered me invaluable assistance with the sociological aspect of my research.

Then, my thanks go to Dr Ratko Bubalo (Director of the Novi Sad-based refugee NGO Humanitarian Centre for Integration and Tolerance) for offering me a variety of useful data, regarding the refugee question in Serbia, and helping me have a first-hand experience with the refugees accommodated in Vojvodina. My gratitude also goes to Dr Dubravka Valić-Nedeljković (Director of the Novi Sad-based media NGO Novi Sad School of Journalism) for offering me lots of useful information in regard to the state of the media and press in Vojvodina and allowing me to make use of the archive collection at the Novi Sad School of Journalism. The willingness of the personnel at the library of Matica Srpska to let me make use of the institution's vast archive collection is very much appreciated as well. In Belgrade, my thanks go to Ms Dubravka Vujošević at the Media Centre NGO and in Budapest to Mrs Iulia Chircu for letting me make use of the archive collection of the Central European University. I would also like to thank Dr Claudiu Mesaros (Philosophy Department, West University Timisoara) for helping me conduct my fieldwork in Timisoara. Last, but certainly not least, I would like to express my gratitude to all individuals interviewed in the course of my field research in Vojvodina and elsewhere (political party representatives, journalists, NGO representatives, academics, individuals employed in cultural institutions, representatives of the Serbian Orthodox clergy in Vojvodina) for the invaluable information that they offered towards my research objectives.

I would like to dedicate this piece of work to my parents for the psychological support that they have been continuously offering me throughout the years of my engagement in the academia.

Glossary of Abbreviations and Acronyms

AER	Assembly of European Regions (Brussels)
AVNOJ	The Anti-Fascist Council for the National Liberation of Yugoslavia
CPP	The Croatian Peasants' Party
CPY	The Communist Party of Yugoslavia
CUP	Popular Unity Candidacy (Spain)
DEPOS	The Serbian Democratic Movement
DKMT	The Danube-Maros-Tisa (or 'Banat') Euroregion
DOS	The Serbian Democratic Opposition
DPS	The Party of Democratic Socialism (Montenegro)
DS	The Democratic Party
DSS	The Democratic Party of Serbia
ERC	Republican Left of Catalonia (Spain)
FIDESZ	Hungarian Civic Alliance (Hungary)
GSS	The Civic Alliance of Serbia
HDZ	The Croatian Democratic Community
JNA	The Yugoslav National Army
JUL	The Yugoslav United Left
KLA	The Kosovo Liberation Army
Kosmet	Kosovo and Metohija
LC	League of Communists

LCY	The League of Communists of Yugoslavia
LDK	The Parliamentary Party of Kosovo
LSDV	The League of Vojvodina's Social-Democrats
NDH	The Independent State of Croatia
NPP	The National Peasants' Party
NRP	The National Radical Party
OSCE	The Organization for Security and Cooperation in Europe
PKK	The Kurdish Workers Party (Turkey)
RDSV	The Reformist-Democratic Party of Vojvodina
Republika Srpska	The Bosnian Serb Republic
RTS	The Serbian Radio-Television
SAP	Socialist Autonomous Province
SNP	Socialist National Party (Montenegro)
SNS	Serbian Progressive Party
SPO	The Serbian Renewal Movement
SPS	The Socialist Party of Serbia
SR	Socialist Republic
SRS	The Serbian Radical Party
UNHCR	The United Nations High Commission for Refugees
VANU	Vojvodina's Academy of Sciences
VMDK	The Democratic Community of Vojvodina's Hungarians
VMSZ	The Alliance of Hungarians in Vojvodina

1

Introduction: Setting the Conceptual and the Theoretical Frames

This book centres on the different layers of identity among the Serbs of Vojvodina and their implications for political preferences regarding the basic structure of the state, namely either for regionalization or for the centralized model of the nation-state. The main focus is on the period from the dissolution of the Socialist Federal Republic of Yugoslavia until present day. Nevertheless, this topic requires a historical background to set the Serbs as an ethno-national group in context. Particular emphasis is laid on the national identity of the Vojvodinian Serbs and the process of its formation.

The regional identity of Vojvodina is also set in historical context. This firstly sets out the regional concept of Vojvodina as a 'Serbian homeland', which was developed by the Serb nationalist elites and the Serb intelligentsia within the Habsburg Monarchy during the nineteenth century. Subsequently, in the Communist era, Vojvodina's regional character was redefined in terms of a socialist multicultural society and this requires a historical perspective. Reference to the broader historical context can clarify the complex relationship between centre and periphery and consequently the local understandings of the unitary model of the nation-state and the regionalist alternatives that have been proposed in Vojvodina since the year 2000.

The pattern of ethnic relations in this region is highly unique. Although Vojvodina hosts approximately twenty-five ethnic communities (including a sizeable and politically organized Hungarian minority), besides the Serbian majority, it is by no means an ethnically divided society. Alongside separate ethnic group cultures, a trans-ethnic cultural substratum, which manifests itself in the form of Vojvodinian regional identity, is present. Intercultural cohabitation has been a living reality in Vojvodina through time. This more 'integrated' pattern manifests through the lower impact of territorial segregation and ethnic distance, as well as the higher frequency of intermarriage in urban and rural settlements alike. This book explores in depth Vojvodina's intercultural realities and illustrates how these have facilitated the introduction of flexible and regionalized legal models for the management of ethnic relations in Serbia since the 2000s. This regional monograph also casts its focus on fresh developments (most notably, the recent arrival of war refugees from Syria and Iraq) and measures the impact that these have been exerting on social stability and inter-group relations in the province.

Most importantly, perhaps, Vojvodina is a region that not much has been written about, especially by Western academics and in the English-language academic literature (e.g. Stjepanović 2018). This has created a black hole in the study of the society and politics of Central and Southeast Europe, since Vojvodina is one of these 'small places with big issues'. The modern-day Serbian autonomous province of Vojvodina is situated exactly at the geographic area where the Balkan peninsula meets Central Europe. For centuries, this zone was the frontier that separated two contesting realms: the Ottoman and the Habsburg. Throughout the past century, the same area saw different political and administrative systems come and go. The combination of the aforementioned catalysts resulted in the, forced as well as organized, migrations of several ethnic groups towards modern-day Vojvodina and the subsequent formation of a varied mosaic of group identities in the region. This triggered the emergence of various political concepts regarding Vojvodina's regional character among its inhabitants, the Serbian majority in particular.

The first main object of this book is the question of identity definition among Serbs in Vojvodina. The Serbian community in Vojvodina comprises three segments with different historic origins: the so-called 'old Serbs' who trace their ancestry back to the days of the Habsburg Monarchy; Serbs originating from other parts of the former Yugoslavia, who moved to Vojvodina after the two world wars ('new settlers'/'colonists'); and the latest refugee waves from Croatia and Bosnia-Herzegovina (1991–5). Each of these groups has its own grassroots perceptions of identity and this book analyses the way that these perceptions are communicated on the political level. The sources that this book has relied on are electoral data, public opinion polls and parliamentary/governmental reports. Especially electoral data can prove very helpful in regard with the assessment of the political tendencies and voting patterns of each segment. At the same time, the relations among the three segments are set in comparative perspective. Particular emphasis is laid upon the integration process of the colonists and, more recently, the refugees into the Vojvodinian society.

The second main object of this book is the interaction between identity-formation and political preferences for the constitutional and administrative framework in Serbia. Since the mid-1970s, Vojvodina, as one of the two autonomous provinces of the Socialist Federal Republic of Yugoslavia (the other was Kosovo), enjoyed broad administrative, legislative and economic autonomy. The centralization process, which was undertaken during the 1990s, caused the resentment of quite a few Vojvodinian Serbs towards the regime in Belgrade. Consequently, quite a few projects which demanded the concession of an 'asymmetric' administrative status to Vojvodina within Serbia were drafted by certain political and academic circles in the province. These projects were and are still contested up to date by the proponents of various forms of a unitary arrangement, in Vojvodina and Serbia in general. Therefore, this book also assesses the dynamics of the two aforementioned trends in Vojvodinian society, with specific focus on the post-Communist era. With respect to the Serbian majority, the degree (if any) to which the inclinations of Vojvodinian Serbs for or against their province's asymmetric status within Serbia are conditioned by the segment that they originate from is assessed.

The third main object of this book is the theoretical definition of the pattern of multi-ethnic cohabitation that is observed in Vojvodina. In other words, an answer is sought to the question whether the Serbian majority and the numerous ethnic minorities form a coherent whole within the Vojvodinian society or if, on the contrary, social segregation along ethnic lines is the case. Particular emphasis is laid on the relations between Serbs and the most numerous and politically organized ethnic minority who live in Vojvodina, the ethnic Hungarians. Interethnic relations in the province are also viewed from a historical angle. In regard to its methodological scope, this book has largely relied on the notion of 'situational identity'. The meaning of the term is that the construction (or reinforcement; even transformation) of collective identities and loyalties is highly influenced by socio-economic and political factors.

This notion is a dynamic one, in contrast to that of 'fixed identity'. This mode of interpretation will help the reader comprehend the regional character of Vojvodina and the local standpoints for or against regional autonomy more adequately.

In the following pages, selected theoretical approaches with a direct relation to the scope and objectives of this book are outlined. Particular attention is paid to theoretical approaches that situate the operation of constituent myths of origin inside identity-construction processes (namely, *ethnosymbolism*) and to theoretical approaches in ethnopolitics beyond *groupism* and *groupness*. Then, the focus shifts to identity-formation processes under 'special' circumstances with a major stress on the cases of ethnic minorities and migrant groups. Finally, this chapter touches upon the subject-areas of regionalism and regionalization with case-specific references to Western Europe as well as to Central and Eastern Europe.

The 'nation' as a socio-psychological phenomenon

According to Anthony D. Smith, the modern nation can be summarized as 'a named human population, sharing a historic territory, common myths and historic memories, a mass public culture, a common economy and common legal rights and duties for all its members'.[1] In

---

[1] Anthony D. Smith, *Myths and Memories of the Nation* (Oxford: Oxford University Press, 1999), 11.

this section, particular reference is made to the common myths and historic memories of the nation. These myths and memories usually form part of the collective experience of the core group around which the nation-building process takes or has taken place (e.g. Hungarians in Hungary, Greeks in Greece). A core group, or *ethnos* in Classical Greek, can be defined as 'a named human population with myths of common ancestry, shared historic memories and one or more common elements of culture, including an association with a homeland and some degree of solidarity, at least among the elites'.[2] Perhaps the most powerful myths are those referring to the linear continuity of the group through the ages and also those pointing towards an older 'golden age' of the group. These myths acquire a poetic and mystical dimension when associated with an ancestral or 'sacred territory'.

The ultimate objective of myths of origin is to create an overriding commitment and bond for the group. Such myths aim to forge an imagined continuity of the group through the ages. Roughly speaking, there exist two types of myths of origin: myths that point towards genealogical descent ('biological continuity' myths) and myths that cite an ancestry of a cultural–ideological variant. 'Biological' myths generate high levels of communal solidarity, since they regard the national community as a network consisting of interrelated kin groups descending from a common ancestor. In this case, imagined blood ties provide the basis for a strictly primordialist sense of belonging and identity (e.g. certain currents of Basque nationalism).

The other, and perhaps the most common, type of constituent myths of origin are those that rest on the cultural affinity with the presumed ancestors. In this case, we have to do with a spiritual type of kinship, which seeks to trace a 'historical' link between the present ideals and aspirations of the group and those of its presumed ancestors. Cultural–ideological myths of descent stress the persistence of certain types of collective virtue (e.g. the heroic spirit) or other distinctive cultural qualities, such as language, religion and customs through the ages. They

[2] Ibid., 13.

also seek to draw a parallel between these old qualities and the present virtues and cultural qualities of the group in question. By locating the present in the context of the past of the group, myths of origin interpret social changes and collective aspirations in a way that satisfies the drive for meaning, by making up new identities that also seem to be very old. All myths of group descent have as focal point of reference an older 'golden age'. Some examples of such 'golden ages' are respectively Periclean Athens in Modern Greek nationalism and the Nemanjid dynasty in Serbian nationalism. The reference to a 'golden age' is always linked with a 'myth of decline'. The latter seeks to provide an explanation about how the community fell from its state of prosperity in the past, to its present state of alleged decay.[3] On such occasions, the 'golden age' serves as a model for the regeneration of the community.[4]

Myths of origin are always associated with specific ancestral territories. Hence the importance attached to 'sacred territories' in all types of nationalist imagery. 'Sacred territories' are added a poetic dimension: these are the territories where the group flourished during its golden age and which have to be defended by all means and at any cost.[5] To sum up, then, in Anthony D. Smith's words, constituent myths of origin serve the following purposes:

1. *They link past to present (or future) and act as models.*
2. *They possess external references of comparison, even implicitly.*
3. *They designate a space and time for action, a territorial programme.*

---

[3] For instance, nineteenth-century Greek intellectuals (Adamantios Koraes, in particular) bewailed the degeneration of their contemporary Greeks in comparison to the underlying genius of their community, as revealed in its purest form during the golden age of Periclean Athens (fifth century BCE).
[4] On some occasions, the need for the regeneration of the community may acquire rather mystical and semi-religious dimensions. A notable example is the notion of the 'Serbian Golgotha' in Serbian nationalist imagery. On this issue, see Dinko Tomašić, *Personality and Culture in East European Politics* (New York: George W. Stewart Publisher Inc., 1948), 30.
[5] Again, a characteristic example is the importance attached to the 'Saga of Kosovo' in Serbian nationalism. For an example of this kind see the article by the historian Milutin Garašanin in *Review of International Affairs*, 'Kosovo: Past and Present' (Belgrade, 1986).

4. They contain impulses for collective action, mobilizing people.
5. They are developmental, assuming the possibility of change.
6. They are partly voluntaristic, in that successive generations may add to the heritage and even regenerate themselves.[6]

Such core myths persist and are espoused through state rituals, even in states with a pronounced 'civic' character.[7] As far as their mobilizing power is concerned, this has mainly to do with the fact that these myths pertain to the non-rational domain of the 'nation'. Constituent myths endow the 'nation' with a near universality through the employment of certain images and phrases (e.g. home, forefathers, brothers, mother), which aim at forging a subconscious bond of integrity among its members. This is of vital importance for mass mobilization since, as Walker Connor phrases it, 'people do not voluntarily die for things that are rational'.[8] Even Marxist-Leninists have taken advantage of the mobilizing potential of constituent myths of origin, despite the philosophical incompatibility between nationalism and Communism.[9]

All these hint that the political and cultural–socio-psychological components of modern nations may in practice overlap with each other. The value of the *ethno-symbolic* approach (Connor 1993; Smith 1999 and 2000) for the purposes of this book consists precisely in that it seeks to situate the position of constituent myths of origin inside modern nations. This approach also positions the nationalist intelligentsias inside nation-building processes. The nationalist intellectuals are assigned with the task to recover each layer of the past and trace the origins and evolution of the nation from its rudimentary

---

[6] Anthony D. Smith, *The Nation in History: Historiographical Debates about Ethnicity and Nationalism* (Oxford: Oxford University Press, 2000), 82–3.
[7] A good example of this kind is the British state rituals (e.g. Remembrance Day). Zdzislaw Mach, *Symbols, Conflict and Identity* (English language edition) (Krakow: University of Krakow, 1989), 101–10.
[8] Walker Connor, *Ethnonationalism: A Quest for Understanding* (London: Routledge, 1993), 206.
[9] For example, Mao Tse-tung frequently stressed the 'family ties' among the Chinese people, and their descent from a common ancestor (Huang-ti, the legendary first emperor of China). Ibid., 199.

beginnings until present day. The intelligentsia responsible for creating the symbolic capital, from which a national culture is formed, derives from disciplines such as history, archaeology, linguistics, literature and folklore studies. Through its endeavours to elaborate core myths and create a standardized national culture, a rediscovered and authenticated past is 'scientifically' appropriated for present ends.

Ethnicity without groups and triadic configurations of ethnopolitics

Despite the academic value of *ethno-symbolism*, this book would also benefit from the complementary employment of an additional approach: one theoretical approach set beyond *groupism*. The term *groupism* addresses the tendency to view ethnic groups and identities as bounded, regards them as the leading protagonists of conflicts and treats them as the key units of social discourse. Of particular value for this book would be to rely on Rogers Brubaker's concept of 'ethnicity without groups'.[10] Ethnic conflict is obviously the conflict between ethnic groups. But these groups should not be perceived as compact entities or 'collective individuals'. Instead, group cohesion should be viewed as a continuous process that in some cases may be brought to completion but in others fail. Within this framework of interpretation, the notion of *categories* is of pivotal significance. For example, 'Serb', 'Slovak' or 'Hungarian' (as ethnic definitions) constitute categories but not groups. In order for these categories to generate a high degree of solidarity among a given number of people, become external markers and, ultimately, culminate into group cohesion (or *groupness*), a whole process is required.

The engineers of this process are certain actors, most commonly organizations, who claim to speak in the name of an ethnic group.

---

[10] Rogers Brubaker, 'Ethnicity without Groups', *Arch. Europ. Social.* XLIII, no. 2 (2002): 163–89.

These organizations may range from paramilitary formations and terrorist organizations to political parties and cultural associations. Consequently, the strategies employed by these actors in order to achieve groupness differ considerably from each other. They may range from armed operations to political engagement within mainstream structures. The common denominator, however, remains the endeavour to make good use of the historical background, collective myths, as well as an array of cultural and psychological catalysts, in order to cement group cohesion. An instrument for achieving this aim is violence. For instance, the attacks of the Workers Party of Kurdistan (PKK) and the Kosovo Liberation Army (KLA) against Turkish and Serbian security forces, respectively, resulted in state reprisals against the ethnic Kurdish and Albanian populations. This cycle of violence generated insecurity and increased group solidarity among ethnic Kurds as well as Kosovo Albanians. This was also the case in regard to the Kosovo Serbs and the Turks resident in the Kurdish-populated areas, respectively.[11]

At this point, attention should be paid to the cognitive dimension of ethnic conflict. In other words, what is it, specifically, that makes an armed or political conflict an ethnic one? The 'ethnic' quality is not intrinsic to ethnic conflict. It is up to organizations and a variety of individuals (e.g. government officials, political activists, journalists and others) to frame and, ultimately, constitute a conflict as ethnic. Framing an incident as a 'pogrom' or a 'riot' is not just a matter of external interpretation but an act of definition that can have important consequences.[12] The more an organization succeeds in constituting a conflict as ethnic or interpreting a governmental decision as detrimental to the group that this organization claims to represent, the more it succeeds in forging cohesion within the group. This success acquires a higher significance if the organization manages to internationalize its standpoints. For example, throughout the early 1990s, the primary

---

[11] Ibid., 170–3.
[12] R. Brubaker, M. Loveman and P. Stamatov, 'Ethnicity as Cognition', *Theory and Society* 33 (2004): 37 and 47.

concern of the Democratic Alliance of Hungarians in Romania was to portray certain policies of the Ceausescu era not as violations of civic rights but as a campaign of cultural genocide against ethnic Hungarians This successful lobbying not only put the Hungarian minority behind the party's platform; it also made a number of Western political analysts and NGOs sympathetic to the party's line.

Another particularly useful concept towards the objectives of this book, coined by Rogers Brubaker, is the *triadic nexus* theory.[13] According to the author, nationalism in multi-ethnic societies is often a dynamic interaction among the 'nationalizing state', the national minority (or minorities) living in that state and the minority's (or the minorities') external national homeland (or *kin-state*). A 'nationalizing state' is the one which subtly promotes the culture, language and political primacy of the titular nation within the state through the governing institutions. Each of these actors is not a static entity but a 'variably configured and continuously contested political field'. The interaction among these actors depends upon the relations and balances within each of them. Within this framework, the minorities' frequent response to the policies of the 'nationalizing state' is to push for more cultural or territorial autonomy and resist actual or perceived policies of discrimination. The external homeland's role is to monitor the situation of their co-ethnics in the state in question, protest alleged violations of their rights and assert the right, even the obligation, to defend their interests.

Rogers Brubaker's theoretical matrix becomes highly topical inside the context of numerous disputes over the collective statuses of ethnic minorities across Central and Eastern Europe during the 1990s. In light of the increasing significance of international institutions/organizations and supranational processes in Central and Eastern Europe, the prospect of European Union (EU)-membership started functioning as a powerful pole of attraction for most post-Communist states. This prompted several academic experts to reformulate Brubaker's triadic

---

[13] Rogers Brubaker, 'National Minorities, Nationalizing States and External Homelands in the New Europe', *Daedalus* 124, no. 2 (Spring 1995): 109.

nexus into a *quadratic* one, in light of the EU's eastward enlargement, and add the EU as a *fourth* actor inside the nexus.[14]

Identity-formation under 'special' circumstances: Ethnic minorities

The formation of ethnic minorities within European nation-states has been the result of multifaceted political processes. On some occasions, minority groups were included in new nation-states as a result of the dissolution of larger state formations. This was the case, for instance, with the Hungarians who found themselves within Yugoslavia and Romania after the dissolution of Austria-Hungary and, more recently, the Russian speakers who found themselves within Estonia and Latvia after the Soviet Union broke up. Often, the new borders divided one group from its fellow-ethnics who happened to be the dominant group in an adjacent state (e.g. the case of the Albanians of the former Yugoslavia in relation to Albania).

On other occasions, ethnic minorities were formed after the inclusion of small groups, whose external homeland was not an adjacent state, in a larger state (e.g. the cases of the Slovaks and the Ruthenes in the first as well as the second Yugoslavia). The main difference between these two cases consists in that, in the former case, the emergence of irredentist trends is possible under certain circumstances. The irredentist mini-nationalism of a minority group can be boosted in the event that the territory that it inhabits is a bone of contention, as a 'sacred territory', in the national mythologies of both the minority group (also its adjacent external homeland) and the titular nation in the state where the minority resides. This has been the case, for instance, with the Hungarian-Romanian dispute over Transylvania.

---

[14] Vello Pettai, 'Explaining Ethnic Politics in the Baltic States: Reviewing the Triadic Nexus Model', *Journal of Baltic Studies* 37, no. 1 (2006): 124–36; David Smith, 'Framing the National Question in Central and Eastern Europe: A Quadratic Nexus?' *The Global Review of Ethnopolitics* 2, no. 1 (2002): 3–16.

In international law, there is no universally accepted definition of ethnic minorities. In accordance to the definition by the Council of Europe (*Recommendation 1201*, 1993) 'a national minority is a group which: has been residing in a certain territory within a state; is numerically inferior and politically non-dominant; displays ethnic characteristics that differentiate it from the national majority; its members are conscious of their group-identity and strive to preserve and promote it'. For the purposes of this book, an ethnic minority can be tentatively defined as a segment, living within a national society, which differentiates from that society in a variety of ways. The differentiating factors may be collective historic memory, language, religion, customs or a combination of all these (i.e. the 'ethnic characteristics' of *Recommendation 1201*). Individuals belonging to minority groups have a specific legal relation with the nation-state where they live, that is they are recognized as its citizens and have been vested the right to political participation.

The function of the modern nation-state has highly relied on the homogenization of the linguistic and cultural trends within its territory. On such an occasion, two attitudes are usually encountered within the minority group. The first is the desire by some individuals belonging to the minority to transcend ethnic bounds and assimilate with the mainstream majority. In this way, they expect to gain certain advantages, especially as far as their professional and social life is concerned. The second tendency is the radicalization of the minority group or, at least, some segments within it. On such an occasion, the group tends to stress its identity even stronger and demand the concession of collective rights, even territorial sovereignty; in other words, political independence. The radicalization of minority groups is a common occurrence in states that pursue assimilative policies. On such occasions, ethnic minorities try to resist the cultural hegemony of the nation-state through the use of oral and unofficial tools of resistance, such as jokes, folklore and protests. This is so because the minority group does not possess the wide array of institutions available to the official state in order to construct its own history, culture and identity. However, as minority movements become better organized and better financed they begin to obtain some of the facilities initially available only to the official state (e.g. educational institutions).

Again, the key part is played by the intelligentsia within the group, assigned with the task to collect the orally transmitted group myths, appropriate them and give them a standardized form and meaning. The main motivation behind the actions of both the political and the intellectual elites within the minority is the desire to increase their power and privilege. By reinforcing the group's identity and advocating collective rights and autonomy, even political independence, these individuals expect to reach hierarchal positions, which are far more difficult to acquire in the more complex mainstream system. The question of 'unreliable minorities' generated political tensions within the states of Central and Eastern Europe throughout the interwar era. In this case, it was not solely the new elites that regarded the formerly dominant groups within their states with mistrust (e.g. the case of the ethnic Hungarians in Romania and Yugoslavia). It was also the mainstream societies that often did not possess much confidence with regard to their newly gained national sovereignty and were very suspicious of 'others'.

Nevertheless, even in the immigrant states of the new world, constituent myths of origin and ancestral homelands retain an emotive aura and provide materials out of which the group can construct an identity that corresponds to its present needs. Symbolic activities, such as the cult of ethnic saints, the veneration of historical heroes and the celebration of ethnic holidays, create boundaries with which a group stresses its uniqueness in a pluralist society. For example, in the United States there exist third-, even fourth-, generation ethnics who still designate themselves as Irish, Poles or Italians and try to communicate their ethnic sentiment in ways that suit their individual and small group needs.[15]

---

[15] On this issue, see Zdzislaw Mach's case studies on the cases of the American and British Poles in Mach, *Symbols, Conflict and Identity*, 207–21.

Migrant groups

The notion of a historical homeland possesses a focal position in all group myths. In the case of migrant groups, the spatial association of the group with its historic homeland has been disrupted as a result of a mass movement to another territory. There are two types of migration: voluntary migration and forced migration, or displacement/deportation. In the former case, individuals decide to leave their home base in search of a better future, usually for economic reasons. The land of the ancestors usually becomes idealized through the preservation of myths of origin in literature, art and folklore. The original homeland remains a part of the group's cultural worldview, a major component of their symbolic model of the universe. The migrants seek to reconstruct their group identity in the new environment by integrating the cultural images of their ancestral land with those of the new territory.

The other type of migration is forced migration or displacement. Some examples of this kind are the displacement of the Crimean Tatars and the Chechens by Stalin in 1945, on the charge of collaboration with the Nazis. Two more recent examples are the displacements in the former Yugoslavia (1990s), as a result of ethnic cleansing, and the latest refugee waves out of Syria and Iraq as a result of the ongoing warfare. The displaced migrants feel that they have been violently uprooted from their land base. Therefore, the symbolic construction of a new identity within the new environment is highly problematic, especially for the first generation of the displaced. This is particularly true when the new land considerably differs from the old one and in these cases that the new land has been previously organized by some other community reluctant to accept the newcomers. On such occasions, the migrant group becomes marginalized and alienated inside its new environment. Another interesting incidence is that of a displaced group that has been resettled into a new territory, currently or previously, inhabited by another group regarded as hostile. In such cases, the resentment of the displaced group is redirected against any indications of symbolic or material presence of the 'hostile' community.

Under such circumstances, the prospects for the creative integration of the displaced group into its new environment are seriously reduced.[16]

Regional identity and regionalism: The case of Central and Eastern Europe

A commonplace bipolar opposition in European states is that between the centre and the peripheries/regions. Centres within states can be briefly defined as 'privileged positions within a territory where key military/administrative/economic/cultural resource-holders most frequently meet; with established arenas for deliberations, negotiations and decision-making; with the largest proportion of the economically active population engaged in the processing and communication of information and instructions over long distances'.[17] Normally, a centre controls the bulk of transactions among resource-holders across a territory; it is nearer than any alternative location to the resource-rich areas within the territory; and is enabled to master the flow of communication through an array of consultative and representative institutions.

A minimal definition of the region is that it represents an intermediate territorial level between the state and the locality. Nevertheless, the establishment of regions in the Continent has been the by-product of a more complex process that involved the combination of geographic, historical, sociocultural, political and economic factors. On some occasions, regions are largely dependent on the centre, controlling at best only their own resources and more vulnerable to fluctuations in long-distance markets. Such regions are isolated from all other regions except the centre and do not contribute much to the total flow

---

[16] Zdzislaw Mach has demonstrated that the reintegration of displaced Poles from the former Eastern Polish territories that were incorporated by the Soviet Union in 1945, in Silesia (a Polish region formerly inhabited by a German community) was not very successful. Mach, *Symbols, Conflict and Identity*, 163–82.

[17] S. Rokkan and D. W. Urwin, *The Politics of Territorial Identity* (London: Sage, 1982), 5.

of communications. They are also often characterized by a marginal culture, which is fragmented and parochial. A good example of this kind is the cases of the Asturias and Galicia in Spain. This is not to say that peripheries are always marginal and impoverished backwaters. By contrast, certain European peripheries had not only pretensions to be more advanced than the capitals (wealthier, more developed, with a thriving intellectual scene etc.); they were also in some sense rivals to the capital in the nation- and state-building projects. Such were the cases, for instance, of the Banat and Transylvania in Romania and Piedmont in Italy.

Regionalism addresses a multitude of grassroots and political movements aiming towards the concession of 'special' administrative competencies to certain regions within a state. The popular bases of support, as well as the legitimization sources, of regionalist initiatives are remarkably diverse and have depended on the constitutional framework, the political history and the ethno-cultural heterogeneity (or homogeneity) of each state. Where the catalysts of geography, efficient economic lobbying, cultural distinctiveness, strong regional administrative institutions and territorial mobilization largely combine in space, we have powerful regional feelings and strong regionalisms (e.g. the Catalan case).[18] The most extreme shape that the combination of the aforementioned elements can acquire is an open separatist threat to the integrity of the state (e.g. the case of Basque militant ethno-nationalism in Spain). Most recently, the spectrum of Spain's economic crisis galvanized Catalan regionalist parties into a concrete bloc calling for independence via political means (referendum). Nevertheless, it is on rare occasions that regions seek to displace states or take over the state functions of social regulations and legitimization. Therefore, what we most commonly have to do with, on occasions of strong regionalism, is the appeals of

---

[18] Michael Keating, *Regions and Regionalism in Europe* (Cheltenham: Elgar, 2004), 'Introduction'.

a region (or more) to the centre for the concession of further political autonomy on grounds of economic, sociocultural, functional or other specificities.

During the Communist era, regional and ethnic identities were subordinated to the overarching principle of Socialist internationalism. Collective rights were allocated to minority groups but no autonomous regional institutions were established in most Central and East European states. The striking exception was the establishment of the socialist autonomous provinces of Kosovo and Vojvodina in SR Serbia, within the Socialist Federal Republic of Yugoslavia. The end of Communist rule was often accompanied by two parallel trends. The first was the endeavour by 'nationalizing states' to recentralize the state's administration. The other trend was the external pressures towards the democratization of the political order inside the frame of European integration. Those pressures also called for well-organized administrations capable of translating central government policies into action at the regional and local levels.[19]

The European Commission regarded the enhancement of administrative capacities, on the regional level, as an efficient trajectory for managing the anticipated transfers from the Structural Funds. In this light, regionalist political actors across Central and Eastern Europe sought to legitimize their endeavours through references to the necessity to oppose centralizing and nationalizing projects; counter-propose more efficient and regional alternatives which, at the same time, are compatible with 'European' standards and the EU guidelines.[20] To these, one may add the simultaneous endeavours by ethnic minority political actors towards the concession of ethno-territorial autonomy for their communities (e.g. the ethnic Hungarian parties throughout the Carpathian basin). Especially the persistence of ambiguities over

---

[19] Judy Batt and Kataryna Wolczuk, *Region, State and Identity in Central and Eastern Europe* (London and Portland, OR: Frank Kass, 2002), 8–9.

[20] On the case of Istrian regionalism, for instance, see J. Ashbrook, 'Locking Horns in the Istrian Political Arena: Politicized Identity, the Istrian Democratic Assembly and the Croatian Democratic Alliance', *East European Politics and Societies* 20, no. 4 (2006): 622–58.

questions with ethnic implications, plus the ongoing interest of *kin-states* in their minorities in neighbouring countries, have often rendered states in this macro-region rather insecure over their territorial integrity; quite suspicious vis-à-vis regional autonomy as such.[21] Therefore, an essential particularity of regional politics in Central and Eastern Europe is that they soon became subject to the political heritage(s) of the Communist era, post-Communist nationalization processes and European integration.

From identity to the form of the state: Centralization

There exist two standard strategies of organizing the relations between centres and peripheries. The one of them can be broadly defined by the term 'centralization'. Within the centralized/unitary state, the entire structure is built up around one focal political centre, which is economically predominant and pursues a more or less undeviating policy of administrative standardization. All peripheries are treated on equal terms and all institutions remain under the direct control of the state. The unitary model is in firm line with the classical liberal model of the modern nation-state.

Its proponents reject the establishment of regions with a special administrative status through reference to ethno-cultural or historical criteria.[22] Furthermore, pro-centralists resist the provision of special statuses to constituent regions, on instrumental grounds. In other words, they regard such initiatives as detrimental to the state's structure, financially over-demanding and time-consuming in regard to the execution of governmental policies. Especially when it comes to regions

---

[21] Michael Keating, 'Territorial Restructuring and European Integration', in *The Regional Challenge in Central and Eastern Europe: Territorial Restructuring and European Integration*, ed. Michael Keating and James Hughes (Brussels: P.I.E.-Peter Lang, 2003), 14–16.

[22] It should be added that in certain unitary states like France, the drawing of the state's regions itself has relied upon economic/'rational' criteria (e.g. the management of natural resources, the facilitation of inter-regional communication) rather than historical ones.

inhabited by ethnic minorities, whose loyalty towards the state is considered ambiguous, the unitary option is rooted in arguments over the protection of the state's integrity from secessionist trends. Therefore, on theoretical grounds, centralization is entrenched into the homogeneous concept of the nation.

Within the unitary state, the constituent regions are normally conceded the following competencies: regional administration (mainly the execution of regional sub-legal acts, in compliance with the state's legislation); management of regional income resources, always in accordance with the central government's budgetary planning; regional planning in accordance with the general developmental plan (e.g. public roads, railways, tourist industry); culture and education – the latter in accordance with the uniform state's curriculum; regional policing duties under the command of the central police administration. The administrative bodies granted to the region are usually a regional assembly and an administrative council. One more institutional provision is a regional magistrate and criminal court of justice, within a uniform judicial system. As it becomes apparent, the regions, under the unitary arrangement, are merely viewed as administrative units and not as territories with a *residual* political character. Moreover, in regard to the equal degree of competencies granted to all regions, the administrative structure of the unitary state is a symmetric one. In practice, several European states are constitutionally designated as unitary (e.g. France, Greece, Ireland, Romania and Bulgaria, to name but a few).

It should be noted, though, that, as far as the states formally designated as unitary are concerned, there exist two rather common slight deviations from the strict centralized pattern. The one of them is functional decentralization. In this case, ad hoc agencies with specific tasks are set up as an intermediary level between central and local governments. This is a move conditioned by functional necessities and, in some cases, may also be utilized by proponents of unitarism in an attempt to strengthen local government institutions within regions, as rivals to the potential anti-centralist trends of the larger regional governments. Regional agencies were used in Italy and in France in the 1950s and '60s, as well as Britain in the '70s, for economic development and planning. The other slight deviation from the unitary pattern is the deconcentration of the central government's organs. A good example of this variant is the system in force in France, where the regional prefect coordinates state functions at the regional level, as well as putting a check upon the work of the regional government through the General Secretariat for Regional Affairs. On theoretical grounds, both functional decentralization and deconcentration are attempts to find a balance between the homogeneous identity imperatives and the need for functional modernization.

Federalization

The other classical strategy for accommodating the relations between centre and periphery is federalization. In practice, there exist several varieties of political arrangements, which have been designated as federal. Across the Continent, the federal principle has been applied in states that consist of regions, which are inhabited by different national groups (e.g. Belgium, Switzerland); highly diverse on the basis of their historical heritages and identity (e.g. Germany, Austria). Therefore, federalism acknowledges historical differences within a nation, but also perhaps diverse national identities within an overarching civic-political union. The top objective in all federal arrangements is the achievement and maintenance of both unity and diversity. The equal importance attached to both unity and diversity is the main reason why federalization cannot be interpreted through the centralization-decentralization spectrum, but on a different continuum altogether, one that is predicated on non-centralization.

European federalism is anchored in an organic approach and it is orientated towards sharing power at the different levels of a society, instead of dividing it. The principle of separation of powers among the federal units is balanced by that of *subsidiarity*, especially in regard to economic administration.[23] In this context, federalism provides for 'a constitutional distribution of powers in which each level has its own guaranteed spheres of competence, and neither level is hierarchically superior to the other'.[24] In a genuine federation, all constituent units are equal before the federal constitution. Any conflicts of jurisdiction are to be resolved by a constitutional court, whereas the parliamentary structure comprises a Chamber of the Federated Units.[25]

Depending on the arrangement, the administrative bodies of the federated units enjoy a certain degree of 'independent' jurisdiction in regard to the enactment of legislation within their territories; fiscal management; judicial authority; maintaining contacts with foreign or international agents. Nevertheless, sectors such as national defence, foreign policy, social welfare, criminal law and central fiscal and monetary policy administration remain under the competency of the central government in almost all federations. Federalization represents one more form of symmetric organization. However, by contrast to the unitary state and its mono-centric structure, federalism advocates a polycentric system of organization.[26]

Regionalization: Asymmetric and symmetric

The most intriguing manifestation of the unitary state's transformation with the objective to accommodate regional demands, in contemporary Europe, is 'asymmetric regionalization'. This notion presupposes the concession of a special status to certain regions within the state. The

---

[23] Michael Keating, *The New Regionalism in Western Europe* (Cheltenham: Elgar, 1998), 114.
[24] Ibid., 113.
[25] In Germany, for instance, the second legislative chamber (*Budensrat*) is a committee of *Land* governments, voting by majority, with the larger *Länder* having more votes but not in proportion to their population. The governments of the federated units have representatives in the national capital and closely cooperate with federal ministries.
[26] Daniel J. Elazar, 'The Role of Federalism in Political Integration', in *Federalism and Political Integration*, ed. Daniel J. Elazar (Jerusalem: Jerusalem Institute for Federal Studies, 1979), 23.

latter decision is usually legitimized through reference to factors such as the ethno-cultural particularities of the region(s) in question; the different historical experience of the given region(s) in relation to the rest of the state; the consideration of the geographic as well as economic specificities of the region(s) with the aim to manage its/their economic and natural resources more efficiently; the growing dissatisfaction, encountered in certain peripheries, with the remoteness of the bureaucratic state and its inefficiency to meet the direct needs of those peripheries' citizens. Therefore, by contrast to the centralization's insistence on the homogeneous concept of the nation and the federalization's acknowledgement of historical–national differences within a predominant civic–political union, asymmetry is based on the recognition of specifics within a formally unitary structure.

The concession of asymmetric statuses to certain regions has formed vital part of the political bargaining in certain states, with the objective to appease centrifugal tendencies or reduce the popular appeal of militant secessionist movements (e.g. the ETA in Spain). More recently, the application of asymmetric policies had also been spurred by the impact of globalization and European integration. Especially the weakening role of the central state as the mediator in the transactions between EU institutions and certain regions had encouraged the latter, the richer ones in particular, to vigorously demand concessions in favour of more 'independent' economic policies on the regional level.[27]

The endowment of a region with a special status manifests on the institutional level through provisions such as legislative, executive and partially judicial authority. In certain cases, a regional assembly is established with the task to carry out the relevant legislative and executive functions. Moreover, in states where more than one region has been granted a special status the arrangement for a bicameral central

---

[27] There are plenty of inter-regional forums currently operating within the bounds of the EU. Some of these forums have sought to promote the cooperation among the more developed regions of the EU on economic issues. An example of this kind is the so-called 'Four Motors of Europe' initiative, which comprises the regions of Catalonia, Rhone-Alpes, Baden-Württemberg and Lombardy.

parliament, with a Chamber of Regions as its second body, can be one more provision. On this occasion, the adoption of a proportional electoral system may also be applied as a guarantee for the equal representation of the regions on the administrative macro-level. Another crucial provision is the concession of notable fiscal authority to the region(s). What is usually sought by the region(s) and the central government is a *modus vivendi* between the regional revenues spent on the improvement of regional infrastructure and the regional income channelled towards the centre or towards the reconstruction of the less-developed peripheries.

In the event that the region in question is characterized by ethno-cultural heterogeneity, steps are taken towards the accommodation of the demands of all groups involved. The usual provisions may range from the official use of minority language(s) in public administration and the right to education in the recognized minority language(s) to the establishment of an advisory body for the regions' minorities. In all of this, there exists a set of functions, which, in all European states where asymmetric policies have been implemented, remain in the competency of the central government. These are foreign policy, national defence and security, central fiscal and monetary policy administration, criminal law, social welfare and employment policies.

Although federalization and asymmetric regionalization rest on theoretically distinct premises, still the institutional provisions granted to federal units in the former case and the 'special' regions in the latter, make the practical distinction between the two concepts rather vague. The picture may become fuzzier, in the event that a greater number of regions within the 'asymmetric' state demand and gain equal or, at least, comparable status to that of the special ones. Therefore, as Michael Keating suggests, 'rather than making a sharp distinction between federal and [asymmetric] regional models of government, we can see the latter as a continuum from the strongest [e.g. the German and Swiss federal systems] to the weakest ones [administrative deconcentration and functional decentralization]'.[28] At this point, it

---

[28] Keating, *The New Regionalism in Western Europe*, 114–15.

would be useful to illustrate the theoretical discussion of asymmetric regionalism with two noteworthy examples, namely the Italian and the Spanish ones. Particular attention is paid to Michael Keating's work on these two cases (Keating 1988, 1998), which represents, perhaps, the most thorough treatise of questions of regionalization in the Continent.

The Italian case

Since the end of the Second World War, Italy underwent a process of decentralization. This process was triggered by the necessity to deal with centrifugal tendencies,[29] integrate the underdeveloped south and the nationally heterogeneous parts of the state (e.g. Southern Tyrol and Aosta Valley with their respective German and French-speaking populations) and respond to the phenomena of rapid economic growth, as well as migration from south to north, through more efficient regional planning.

Even though Article 5 of the Italian Constitution reads that 'Italy is one and indivisible', in 1970 some regions were granted a special status by certain constitutional laws, which took into consideration their 'geographic, logistical and historical particularities'. These regions were Sicily, Sardinia, Trentino-Alto Adige, Aosta Valley and Friuli-Venezia Giulia. The new accommodation granted the five regions with extended competencies over the arrangement of educational curricula, public health, agriculture, the management of income derived from regional taxes and the regulation of the revenues to be directed to the central coffers, and the enactment of regional legislation.[30] Moreover, any disagreements between the state-appointed commissioner and the

---

[29] D. V. Segre, 'Regionalism in Italy: An International Conflict Internalized', in *Federalism and Political Integration*, ed. Daniel J. Elazar (Jerusalem: Jerusalem Institute for Federal Studies, 1979), 137.

[30] These five regions cannot impose taxes on goods or people moving from one region to another, or restrict the right to work of any Italian citizen.

regional authorities are to be resolved by the Constitutional Court. The regions are to be administered by a *Presidente* and *Giunta* (executive council) elected by the regional legislative council. The regional councils can be disbanded by the president of the Republic but *only* after consultation with the Senatorial and Parliamentary Commission for Regional Affairs (bicameral arrangement).

Despite the formal concession of wide competencies, though, the five regions did not enjoy their special status in full. Instead of passing framework laws, allowing the regions to fill in the details, the Parliament continued to pass detailed laws transgressing the limits of regional competence.[31] Most importantly, the Italian elites often saw the devolved system as a trajectory via which to preserve political clientelism on the regional level, with no genuine intent to respond to popular pressures for regionalization or eagerness to modernize and reform the state.

The Spanish case

A distinctive feature of Spanish regionalization is the persistence of highly politicized core ethnic identities in the 'historical regions' of the Basque country and Catalonia. The concession of autonomous powers to Spain's 'historical regions' was seen by the Spanish elites as the main path towards the legitimization of the state's authority in Basque country and Catalonia, during the democratic transition. Therefore, Spanish regionalization had acquired an intrinsically political character from the very beginning.

At the same time, though, certain measures were taken, especially by the representatives of the Castilian elites, in order to ensure that the asymmetric status would be confined to the 'historical regions' and

---

[31] To this should be added that court decisions have often restricted the scope of regional jurisdiction. For more on this issue see Keating, *The New Regionalism in Western Europe*, 61–2; *State and Regional Nationalism* (Cheltenham: Elgar, 1988), 230–4.

the unitary character of the Spanish state would not be imperiled.[32] Consequently, Andalusia's attempts to make use of Article 151 and gain a special status proved fruitless. Nevertheless, following an aborted coup in 1981, a compromise was reached, which enabled Andalusia to gain an autonomous status.[33] Since 1982, two more regions, Valencia and the Canaries, were given more or less the same powers as Andalusia.

The 1980s saw a change in the policies of the central government vis-à-vis the question of autonomies. Instead of trying to restrict autonomy to the 'historical regions', Madrid would now try to place a check upon Basque and Catalan higher aspirations by harmonizing the statutes of all autonomous regions. This caused the discontent of the Basques and Catalans who saw their statuses imperilled. Consequently, these regions constantly appealed to the Constitutional Court against the central government throughout the 1980s. In the 1990s, though, both sides watered down their tones and sought a political compromise.

The Spanish constitutional provisions to the autonomous provinces are rather complex. Article 2 of the Constitution defines the state's order as founded upon the *unity of Spain* and the *autonomy of the nationalities and regions* integrated in it. This is a formal indication of a compromise between the unitarist Spanish/Castilian nation-statist positions and the Basque/Catalan asymmetric approaches. The unitarist component also becomes manifest in the absence of a Chamber of Regions in the Spanish parliament and the fact that, although drafted by the autonomous assemblies, the statutes need the approval of the central parliament to be effective. On the other hand, an autonomous statute cannot be modified without the region's approval, except in the event of a general constitutional reform. At the same time, autonomous regions enjoy a notable degree of decision-making capacity, through their institutions

---

[32] Keating, *The New Regionalism in Western Europe*, 68; *State and Regional Nationalism*, 223; Patricia Escobalherrero, 'Territorial Organization of the State', in *Essays on Regionalization*, Open University Subotica (Subotica: Agency for Local Democracy, 2001), 60.

[33] It has been assumed that this was a move that suited the political objectives of the ruling Socialists at that time. Andalusia was a Socialist stronghold and the then Socialist leader and prime minister, Felipe Gonzalez, himself, is an Andalusian native.

of self-government (a legislative chamber, a regional government and a president). Moreover, the languages of the 'historical nationalities' (Basque and Catalan in particular) are granted equal status with Castilian Spanish in public administration and education, within their autonomous regions. In regards to the economy, the Basque country retained its *concierto economico* and a similar arrangement was made for Navarra. As a result of successful lobbying by the Catalan government, Madrid, since 1996, concedes 30 per cent of locally raised income tax to the regions.

Spain's democratization provided the platform for the transition from an extremely centralized administrative matrix to a highly devolved one. The gradual extension of autonomy to seventeen regions literally speaks in itself. Therefore, many political analysts saw Spain as on the way to *de iuris* federalization. It might well be argued that the Spanish precedent confirms Keating's assessment of asymmetric regionalism as a political continuum, rather than a sharply contrasted model to federalism. Moreover, it might be argued that, at least until recently, the Spanish precedent has represented a fitting example of symmetric regionalization. This brief overview does not cover the new political realities that emerged in light of Spain's latest economic crisis and the Catalan referendum for independence (2017).

The chapter outline of this book is as follows:

'Vojvodina through Time: From the Habsburg Era to the Socialist Federal Republic of Yugoslavia': At the outset, this chapter outlines the development of modern nationalism among Habsburg Serbs (late eighteenth and nineteenth centuries). Then, the focus shifts towards Vojvodina's position within the Kingdom of Yugoslavia and the interethnic strife under Axis occupation. This chapter underlines the system of autonomy within the Socialist Federal Republic of Yugoslavia. Particular attention is paid to the constitutional provisions for Vojvodina and the implementation of socialist multiculturalism as a model for managing ethnic relations in the province.

'Vojvodina in the 1990s: From the Termination of Autonomy to the Fall of Slobodan Milošević': In the beginning, this chapter positions Vojvodina inside the context of Slobodan Milošević's 'anti-bureaucratic revolution' and the new wave of Serbian nationalism. Major attention is paid to the recall of regional autonomy for Vojvodina within the frame of the constitutional reforms. Then, the focus shifts towards the deterioration of the socio-economic situation in Vojvodina with the emphasis on the impact of Serbia's economic crisis and the influx of refugees from Croatia and Bosnia. This chapter underlines the politicization of Vojvodina's regional identity, since the second half of the 1990s, and its operation as a catalyst which provided a common ground for a variety of opposition forces in the province.

'Vojvodina Going through Transition (the 2000s)': This chapter places Vojvodina inside the broader spectrum of Serbia's regionalization since the year 2000. This consists in an overview which ranges from the inauguration of the *Omnibus* law (February 2002) to the adoption of the new statute for Vojvodina (2009). Simultaneous attention is paid to Serbia's regionalization as viewed from the perspectives of the political elites in the province. Then, this chapter sets in context the grassroots outlooks on regional identity and the state of interethnic relations in Vojvodina during that period. Of particular importance is to underline how the question of restituting Vojvodina's autonomous competencies became entangled into other crucial policymaking areas for Serbia, namely the developments in Kosovo and the readjustment of the Serbian-Montenegrin relations.

'Vojvodina Today: Between New Challenges and Opportunities': This chapter situates Vojvodina inside the context of the latest political developments in Serbia; namely the political predominance of President Aleksandar Vučić and the current prospects for Serbia within the trajectory of European integration. This chapter also casts its focus on fresh developments (most notably, the recent arrival of war refugees from Syria and Iraq and their concentration along the Serbian-Hungarian border) and measures the impact that these have been exerting on social stability and inter-group relations in Vojvodina. Of particular importance is to highlight whether and how Vojvodinian regional identity, as a trans-ethnic substratum, can withstand the new challenges and benefit from the new opportunities.

2

Vojvodina through Time: From the Habsburg Era to the Socialist Federal Republic of Yugoslavia

At the outset, this chapter outlines the development of modern nationalism among Habsburg Serbs (late eighteenth and nineteenth centuries). Then, the focus shifts towards Vojvodina's position within the Kingdom of Yugoslavia and the ethnic strife under Axis occupation. This chapter underlines the system of autonomy within the Socialist Federal Republic of Yugoslavia. Particular attention is paid to the constitutional provisions for Vojvodina and the implementation of socialist multiculturalism as a model for managing ethnic relations in the province.

The Habsburg era

This section outlines the Serbian historical presence in the Southern Habsburg lands. First, it sets in context the origins of the Serbs living within the Monarchy. Then, it introduces the institutional framework for the Habsburg Serbs and the emergence of modern Serbian nationalism. This section demonstrates that the Habsburg Serbs became caught between the traditional structures (Hungary and the sub-kingdom of Croatia-Slavonia) and the emperor's absolutist/centralizing tendencies. A third actor that entered the fore in the nineteenth century was the appeal of autonomous, later independent, Serbia to the Serbs of the Habsburg Monarchy.

The migration of the Serbs into the Habsburg lands

After the Ottoman defeat in Vienna (1688), the Habsburgs launched a counteroffensive which lasted sixteen years. The Habsburg monarch Leopold I appealed to the Serbs and the other Balkan Christians for help. In return, he promised them religious freedom, tax exemption and the right to elect their own *vojvode* (the Serbian equivalent of a military leader) and live by their own customs.[1] The Serbs responded to the emperor's call, armed themselves and Serbian *vojvode* were appointed in the Habsburg military ranks. In the beginning, the Habsburgs and their allies were victorious. On 6 September 1688, they captured Belgrade and a year later Skoplje. But the Ottomans commenced a successful counteroffensive and drove the invaders out of their territory. According to the Treaty of Karlowitz, signed between the two sides on 26 January 1699, in modern-day Sremski Karlovci, the Ottoman sultan surrendered Lika, Krbava, Bačka and parts of the Banat, Slavonia and Srem to Vienna.

Meanwhile, fearful of Ottoman reprisals, an estimated number of 35,000 Serbs led by the Peć Patriarch Arsenije III Carnojević followed the Austrian forces and retreated into Habsburg territory.[2] These Serbs originated from Prizren, Peć, Novi Pazar, Priština and other parts of Ottoman Serbia. They settled in the areas between the rivers Tisa and Drava, as far as Baja, Buda, Saint Andrew and Komarno. A small fraction, though, settled in Northern Hungary. The newcomers are mentioned in the Habsburg records as 'Servians' or 'Rascians'.[3] This massive movement is being referred to in Serbian historiography as the first '*Velika Seoba*' ('Great Migration').[4]

---

[1] Wayne S. Vucinich, 'The Serbs in Austria-Hungary', *Austrian History Yearbook* 3, no. 2 (1967): 11.

[2] Ibid. Mirko Mitrović, a historian from the University of Novi Sad, raises the total number of migrants to 40,000. Mirko Mitrović, 'Naseljavanje i kolonizacija Vojvodine (1690–1945)', *Godišnjak Društva Istoričara SAP Vojvodine* (1982): 197.

[3] Vucinich, 'The Serbs in Austria-Hungary', 9.

[4] Sporadic Serb movements out of the Ottoman Empire and towards the Southern Habsburg lands were witnessed prior to the first *Velika Seoba*, since mid-fifteenth century. The incoming Serbs settled in Buda, Saint Andrew, Komarno and Arad. Mitrović, 'Naseljavanje i kolonizacija Vojvodine', 197.

The peace between the two empires was short. The war started again in 1716 and a new peace treaty was signed in Passarowitz (i.e. modern-day Požarevac) in 1718. According to the treaty, the Ottomans surrendered the Banat, the entire Srem, Belgrade and most of Serbia proper, as far as Ćuprija. However, in the third war (1737–9), an overwhelming Ottoman counteroffensive pushed back the Habsburgs. In the final peace treaty, which was signed in Belgrade (1739), the Ottomans gained back Belgrade and Northern Serbia proper. The border between the two empires was settled along the Sava and Danube rivers. Once again, thousands of Serbs from Ottoman Serbia, this time led by Patriarch Arsenije IV Jovanović Sakabenta, preferred to migrate to the Habsburg lands than remain under Ottoman rule.[5] This reinforced the already existing Serbian population, even though no exact data regarding the size of the second *Velika Seoba* is available.[6]

The institutional framework for the Serbs (1690–early 18th century)

In the early eighteenth century, Habsburg policies towards the Serbs were dictated by the military needs of the Monarchy. Since mid-eighteenth century, though, the Serbian question was entangled in a bipolar antagonism of interests. On the one hand, there was Vienna's attempt to consolidate its control throughout the Monarchy and, on the other the determination of the Hungarians to resist it. On certain occasions, Vienna would satisfy Serbian demands just in order to countervail the aspirations of the Hungarians.

The collective status of the Habsburg Serbs was initially codified by the so-called 'Leopoldine Privileges', issued in the Latin language

---

[5] Đorđe S. Radojčić, 'Arsenije IV Jovanović Sakabenta', in *Enciklopedija Jugoslavije*, vol. 1 (Belgrade: SANU, 1955), 15–16.

[6] Apart from the Serbs, a certain number of Catholic Clementine as well as Orthodox Albanians moved from Ottoman Serbia towards the Southern Habsburg lands and settled in certain districts of Srem (Zemun, Mitrovica and Ilok). Outnumbered by their fellow-Catholics, the Croats, these Catholic Albanians were Croatized in the long term. Mitrović, 'Naseljavanje i kolonizacija Vojvodine', 206.

between 1690 and 1691.[7] According to the *Privilegium* issued on 21 August 1690, the Serbs were allowed to practise their religious rituals according to their religious calendar. The patriarch and the Orthodox clergy retained the same jurisdictions that they had under the Porte and only an Orthodox Serb elected by the *sabor* (ecclesiastical congress) could become patriarch. The patriarch had the right, as leader of the Orthodox Church within the Monarchy to appoint the metropolitans, bishops and other clerics. Moreover, the Serbs were granted the right to build monasteries and churches.

The *Privilegium* issued on 20 August 1691 enhanced the collective status of Serbs. This document recognized the Serbian patriarch as *caput nationis in spiritualibus et saecularibus*. The patriarch became the leader of all the Orthodox living within the confines of the Monarchy, in religious as well as in secular affairs. The patriarch, with his seat at Karlowitz, represented not only the Serbs but other ethnic groups as well, insofar as they were Orthodox (e.g. the Romanians). Later, on 4 March 1695, another *Privilegium* exempted Serbs from paying the imperial tithes. The swift confirmation of the Privileges by Leopold's successor Joseph I (1706) and later Charles III (1713) was also conditioned by the loyalty that the Serbs had demonstrated towards Vienna in the course of Count Rakoczi's rebellion (1703–11).[8] Consequently, the Habsburgs started considering the employment of Serbs as a barrier against detrimental Hungarian ambitions within the Monarchy as well.

Moreover, the Serbs who lived in designated zones along the Habsburg–Ottoman frontier (e.g. the Petrovaradin-Zemun defensive line along the Sava and Danube rivers in Srem) were exempted from feudal servitude as long as they provided the Aulic War Council with a quota of able-bodied men for military service. The *vojvode*

---

[7] Jovan Radonić and Mitja Kostić, eds., *Srpske privilegije od 1690 do 1792*, Special edition (Belgrade: SANU, 1954). Also, see Dušan J. Popović, *Srbi u Vojvodini*, vol. 2 (Novi Sad: Matica Srpska, 1959), 19–20.

[8] Mitrović, 'Naseljavanje i kolonizacija Vojvodine', 198.

elected by the Serbs would be under the direct control of the imperial government in Vienna.[9] Since the settlement of the Habsburg–Ottoman borderline in 1739, the *Vojina Krajina* (Military Frontier) stretched from Transylvania in the northeast, through the Banat, towards the southern parts of Srem and Slavonia.[10] The Military Frontier ended in the northeast Adriatic coast, through the highlands of Kordun, Lika and inner Dalmatia.

The Serbs enjoyed an exceptionally favourable status within the Habsburg Monarchy. No other group possessed such extensive guarantees of autonomy and exemption from the burdens of manorial land tenure. Nevertheless, one thing should be made clear. First, these privileges were not granted to a given number of individuals or social class but to an ethno-confessional collectivity, led by a patriarch who had negotiated with the emperor. Second, neither the imperial court in Vienna nor the patriarch had made any negotiations with representatives of the Hungarian kingdom, which now accommodated Serbs in compact masses. This particularly angered the Hungarian nobility. Later, in August 1747, Maria-Theresa established another representative institution for the Serbs: the Aulic Court for Transylvania, the Banat and Illyria. The establishment of this body was conditioned by geopolitical concerns which re-emphasized the vital role of the Serb border guards. The main concern was the danger of the reinvigorated Ottomans from the south. The role of the *graničari* was additionally stressed by the fact that at the same time the Habsburgs were waging the 'War of the Austrian Succession' over the possession of Silesia, against the Prussians (1740–8).

---

[9] Even though the Serbs formed the backbone of the Habsburg *graničari* (border guards), the territories along the Habsburg military frontier did not attract exclusively Serbs (Orthodox). As long as these territories were under Vienna's direct rule and not under the control of a regional aristocracy, Croatian (Catholic) peasants also came to escape the constraints of noble and ecclesiastical estates.

[10] Of all these parts of the Military Frontier, only the Transylvanian ones reverted to Hungarian rule earlier than the others in 1851. Also, between 1751 and 1785, Petrovaradin was a 'privileged military community' ('*Freie Militar Communitat*'). The inhabitants of this community were 'free' in that, even though they lived in the Frontier region, they were exempted from military duty paying a small fee instead.

Nevertheless, there existed some confusion over the administrative powers of the Illyrian Court and the exact basis and extent of Serbian autonomy. Whereas Transylvania and the Banat of Temeszvar were well-defined territorial entities, '*Illyrici*' was the collective term for the Serbian Orthodox subjects. Therefore, the Court was assigned with the task of governing two crown-lands and the Serbian ethno-religious group, irrespective of where its components resided. Furthermore, the Hungarian Chancellery always remained a vociferous bystander, assisted by the Roman Catholic hierarchy. The Hungarians regarded the privileges conceded to the Serbs as an intrusion upon the authority of their Diet[11] mainly because of the way that they perceived the term 'nation'. According to the Hungarians, the *natio Hungarica* was a feudal notion embracing the landowning nobility, living within the defined boundaries of the Hungarian kingdom, with the right to participate in the Hungarian Diet. This concept was not an ethno-linguistic one since it could include native speakers of Slovak, Romanian or other languages.

By contrast, for the Serbs, the *natio Illyrica* was defined by the Orthodox Church and was not territorially rooted to a historic homeland within the Monarchy. This Ottoman notion of an ethno-confessional group led by its religious leader seemed incomprehensible to the Hungarians who contested whether the legal status granted to the Serbs by Vienna should extent to all ethnic Serbs or only those who arrived in the 1690 migration. Keeping in mind that those Serbs who had entered the Hungarian kingdom before the *Seoba* had settled well to the north and the east of the then borders with the Ottoman Empire, the latter option would have been much more preferable to the Hungarians. As for the Habsburgs, they were content with the fact that the status granted to the *natio Illyrica* could be employed as a bulwark against the intensions of the occasionally rebellious Hungarians. The

---

[11] The Hungarian Diet was the focal legislative body within the jurisdiction of the Hungarian kingdom. Its members were responsible, among others, for legalizing the acts of the Habsburg Crown which were of significance to the Hungarian nation.

simultaneous colonization of Srem, Bačka, Baranja and the Banat with a variety of ethnic groups was another dimension of Vienna's strategy with the aim to put a check upon Hungarian ambitions.[12]

In the second half of the eighteenth century, changes would occur. By that time, the state was substituting the Church as an institution, which specified and enforced civil duties. Most important, the ideological and political developments throughout Europe (e.g. the Enlightenment) advocated the establishment of a novel political matrix based on the distinction between state and subject as well as the distinction between the public and the private spheres of society. Within this new matrix, Vienna started orientating towards the centralization of the empire, through the restriction of the jurisdiction enjoyed by the bodies that made up its mediated system of authority. A complementary goal was the secularization of the society. This novel orientation left negative connotations for the Hungarian nobility as well as the Serbian clergy. With regard to the latter, by 1777, Maria-Theresa dissolved the Illyrian Court and, two years later, stripped the Serbian patriarch of any secular rights. This negative situation for the Serbs was not reversed in the years to come, despite the *sabor*'s vocal protests.[13]

Throughout the eighteenth century, the Serbs were caught between monarchical centralism and the existing traditional structures. The latter comprised the Hungarian (also Croatian) Diet, the Roman Catholic Church and the bodies that made up the multilevel Habsburg administrative system (e.g. the Illyrian Court). The status of the Habsburg Serbs at that time can be described as that of a neither dominant nor subordinate group. Throughout that century, the Habsburgs provided the Serbs with institutions that offered the group the promise of self-government. This raised Serbian expectations which, when disappointed, heightened group consciousness and also

---

[12] By the late eighteenth century, a multitude of groups as diverse as Germans, Romanians, Slovaks, Ruthenes, Dalmatian Croats, Cincars (Vlachs), Catholic Bulgarians, Armenians, Italians, Spaniards (Basques and Catalans) and French speakers from Lorraine were attracted to the Southern Habsburg lands. Mitrović, 'Naseljavanje i kolonizacija Vojvodine', 199–206.

[13] Vucinich, 'The Serbs in Austria-Hungary', 36, 39.

led to conflicts with the Hungarians, thus again heightening group consciousness. The institutional predominance of the Orthodox clergy, though, kept this group consciousness to a rudimentary, non-secular and non-standardized level. In all of this, the question of the Habsburg Serbs' relation to their kindred below the Danube remained vague.

The rise of modern Serbian nationalism

Since the second half of the eighteenth century, the balance of power in various parts of Europe started to shift from the royal courts and the religious hierarchies towards the growing regional bourgeoisies. In relation to the Habsburg Serbs, the religious and cultural autonomy that they enjoyed within the Monarchy encouraged the economic development of certain Serbian communities and the gradual emergence of a Serb bourgeoisie. This was particularly true for the Serbs living in the Banat, Bačka and Srem – the regions where the centre of Serb religious and educational life was based.

Influenced by the Enlightenment and the French Revolution, the Serb bourgeoisie embarked upon an economic and then a political struggle against the claims of the Hungarian nobility. This middle class assumed an active role in the promotion of Serb interests. It was the Serb bourgeoisie who, for the first time, advocated the restoration of the mediaeval Serbian Empire.[14] Throughout the early nineteenth century, merchants and brokers from the Monarchy operated as a 'bridge' between the Habsburg and the Ottoman Serbs. When the Serbian insurrection against the Ottomans broke out in 1804, many Habsburg Serbs sent aid or actively joined the insurgents.[15] The contacts between the Serbs north and south of the

---

[14] This idea was promoted by the Serb nationalist intellectual Sava Tekelija, in the course of the early nineteenth century. Tekelija was largely inspired by the mediaeval Serbian kingdom. Nikola Radojčić, 'Sava Tekelija', *Istorijski Časopis* XII–XIII (1963): 9. See also Roger V. Paxton, 'Nationalism and Revolution: A Re-examination of the Origins of the First Serbian Insurrection 1804–1807', *East European Quarterly* VI, no. 3 (1972): 343.

[15] Paxton, 'Nationalism and Revolution', 340–3.

Danube intensified between 1804 and 1812 when many Habsburg Serb intellectuals were invited to organize the governmental institutions in Serbia proper.[16]

A landmark event, which shaped the history of the Habsburg Empire in the nineteenth century, was the Hungarian revolution of 1848. This event was triggered by the Hungarian nobility's resentment with Vienna's attempts to make German the official language throughout the Monarchy in the early and mid-nineteenth century. Meanwhile, the groups who were subordinate to them exerted simultaneous pressures on the Hungarians. Having been denied the right to separate nationhood by the Hungarians, the Serbs (also the Croatian *sabor*[17]) joined the imperial troops in the suppression of the insurrection. In the beginning, Emperor Franz Joseph rewarded the Serbs by granting them *Vojvodstvo Srpsko* (the Serbian Vojvodina) in a patent of 6 November 1849. Serbian Vojvodina, with its administrative centre in Temeszvar, comprised Baranja, Srem, part of Bačka and most of the Banat with the exception of the Military Frontier.

Nevertheless, Serb autonomy was restricted from an early stage.[18] Even worse, Vienna's declining strength (the military defeats of 1859 in Italy and 1866 in the Austro-Prussian war) prompted the Habsburgs to reach the *Ausgleich* ('Compromise') of 1867 with the Hungarians. As part of this process, on 29 December 1860, the emperor abolished *Vojvodstvo Srpsko* and gave its territory to Hungary. The Hungarian dominion now extended to Bačka and the Banat, while Srem was

---

[16] The most prominent example was the thinker and author Dositej Obradović. Obradović was the first minister of education appointed in Karageorge's government. Ivo J. Lederer, 'Nationalism and the Yugoslavs', in *Nationalism in Eastern Europe*, ed. P. Sugar and I. J. Lederer (Washington, DC: University of Washington Press, 1969), 413.
[17] The Croatian *sabor* (or Diet) was the focal legislative body within the Habsburg territory that corresponded to the old kingdom of Croatia-Slavonia. The status attributed to the *sabor* was indicative of the autonomy that the subkingdom of Croatia-Slavonia enjoyed within the Hungarian kingdom.
[18] First of all, the emperor himself was appointed the first Grand Serbian *vojvoda*, the government was placed in the hands of Austrian officials and German was made the language of the government. R. H. Kann, *The Multinational Empire: Nationalism and National Reform in the Habsburg Empire (1848–1918)*, vol. 2 (New York: Octagon, 1983), 430; Vucinich, 'The Serbs in Austria-Hungary', 5–6.

absorbed into the administrative system of Croatia-Slavonia. According to Seton-Watson, the history of the Habsburg Serbs after 1860 was 'one of slow decay'.[19] Nevertheless, a more pragmatic approach might prove this statement to be exaggerated. Despite all difficulties, the Serbs continued to build schools and cultural institutions. They set up their credit organizations and agricultural cooperatives. They also organized political meetings and demanded the recognition of their national rights from the imperial government, without much success though. Most important, it was at that time when the Serbian urban classes expressed more vehemently than ever the desire for the transition from the historico-confessional *Cultusgemeinschaft* to the secular nation.

Consequently, in 1869 the Serbian National Liberal Party was founded, with Svetozar Miletić, a Novi Sad lawyer-journalist, as its key spokesman.[20] The 'Bečkerek Programme' (adopted by the party in modern-day Zrenjanin in 1869) posited the rights of Serbs to national representation within the post-*Ausgleich* Hungary on secular foundations. No reference whatsoever was made to the *Privilegium*. Instead, full equality to all ethnic groups resident in the former Vojvodina and proportional representation of their interests, at all levels, were guaranteed. Miletić and his associates advocated neither separatism nor the dismemberment of Austria–Hungary in accordance with the ethnic principle. On the contrary, the National Liberals proposed the transformation of Hungary into an 'East European Switzerland'; in other words Hungary's cantonization in accordance with the demographic composition of each of its parts and the formation of territorial units with equal administrative competencies. Nevertheless, the National Liberals' project did not meet with much success. Even worse, in 1887 the party itself split into two new parties;

---

[19] R. Seton-Watson, *The Southern Slav Question and the Habsburg Monarchy* (London: Constable and Co., 1911), 51.
[20] Nikola Petrović, *Svetozar Miletić* (Belgrade: SANU, 1958), 112–15, 122–5, 169–80.

the Liberal (under the leadership of Mihajlo Polit-Desančić) and the National Radical Party (led by Jaša Tomić).

Special reference should be made to the more influential of these groupings, the National Radicals. A National Radical organization was already active in independent Serbia (1878) since 1880. The active cooperation between the Radical organizations above and below the Danube was a clear indication of independent Serbia's powerful appeal to the Habsburg Serbs. Both Serbian and Vojvodinian Radicals drew their support from the same strata (the peasantry and the lower middle classes) and had similar programmes. The Vojvodinian Radicals, in particular, maintained the essentials of the 'Bečkerek Programme' and advocated the solution of the Habsburg Serb question within the confines of the Monarchy via some sort of federal or confederal arrangement.

The relations between the Vojvodinian Radicals and the political establishment in independent Serbia were more complicated. Serbia's high appeal to the 'unredeemed' Serbs under Austria-Hungary had rendered the former increasingly unpopular in Vienna. Consequently, King Milan sought to prevent further friction with Serbia's more powerful neighbour by obstructing the contacts between the two Radical organizations. This was perceived by Vojvodinian Radicals as a gross expression of Belgrade's indifference towards their political struggle. Moreover, the Russophile inclination of both Serbian and Vojvodinian Radicals seriously clashed with the policy of compromise with Austria-Hungary, which was pursued by King Milan and his successor King Aleksandar. However, as soon as the more nationalistic and Russophile Petar I Karađorđević took over, and the Radical leader Nikola Pašić consolidated his status in Serbia (1903), the communication between the two Radical organizations was fully restored. From that point onwards, the Vojvodinian Radicals' platform started to shift from the Monarchy's constitutional reorganization towards unification with the Serbian state.

The same period saw the powerful emergence of 'proto-Yugoslavist' tendencies in Austria-Hungary. In December 1905, a Croatian-Serbian political coalition was formed and gained control of the *sabor* and the local executive in Croatia-Slavonia.[21] The Yugoslavism of this initiative was made possible through its emphasis on liberal–democratic political institutions and on the universal right of nations to self-determination. Its call for the separation of churches from politics removed a crucial obstacle to Croatian and Serbian cooperation. Until the end of the First World War, the influence of the coalition, at least within Austria-Hungary, on South Slav politics was greater than that of any other South Slav political party.

Vojvodina within the first Yugoslavia

This section examines Vojvodina as a constituent part of royal Yugoslavia. This concentrates on the political landscape of Vojvodina within the first Yugoslavia and the socio-economic conditions, as well as the climate of interethnic relations, prevailing in the region during that period. The clash between the political cultures of the Vojvodinian and the *Srbijanci* Serbs (those from Serbia proper), in light of the deteriorating economic situation, resulted in the transformation of the Vojvodinian Serb political attitudes from a pro-unitary orientation to the development of a certain regionalist movement.

Yugoslavia (1918–41)

The formation of Yugoslavia between 1918 and 1921 was received by South Slavs as the materialization of their aspirations for independent statehood. Nevertheless, the state's political landscape was soon to be marred by the polarization between Serbs and Croats over Yugoslavia's constitutional structure.

---

[21] This alliance comprised the Party of Croatian Rights, the Croatian Progressive Party, the Serbian People's Independent Party and the Serbian National Radical Party. Aleksa Djilas, *The Contested Country* (Cambridge, MA: Harvard University Press, 1991), 33–5.

The Yugoslav political map was structured along ethnic lines. The two parties that garnered most of the Serbian support were the National Radical Party (NRP) and the Democratic Party. Both parties favoured a unitary structure, though from a different angle. The Democrats had couched their pro-unitarism in the belief that federalism and regional autonomies were two options required in states consisting of different nations and not in the case of the Serbs, the Croats and the Slovenes who, in the party's view, constituted one and the same *narod* (people).[22] NRP worried that Yugoslavia's structuring along historic–national lines might endanger Serbia's status within the state.[23] At the opposite end of the spectrum, the Croatian Peasants' Party (CPP) enjoyed the support of the majority of Croats. The party leader, Stjepan Radić, opposed the Serbian proposals for the dissolution of historic–national regions and counter-proposed a confederal arrangement within which Croatia would be in a loose union with Serbia.[24] The only major party whose appeal transcended ethnic and regional cleavages was the Communist Party of Yugoslavia, formed in Belgrade in 1919.

The Yugoslav Constitution (1921) enhanced the prerogative of the King, established a single chamber legislature and formed a centralized state divided into thirty-three *oblasti* (districts) according to economic–functional and not historic criteria.[25] Centralism was the instrumental application of the principle 'one nation-one state' in the governing structures. The *oblasti* were granted some jurisdiction on social and economic matters (Article 95). Nevertheless, the state-appointed *župan* (prefect) possessed the highest authority in each district and was to closely cooperate with the Council of State (Articles 98–99). Also, the minister of Finance would decide over the percentage of each district's budget channelled towards its regional interests

---

[22] 'Govor Svetozara Pribičevića na kongresu jugoslovenskih profesora u Zagrebu', *Narodna Riječ*, 5 October 1921, 2.
[23] Nikola Pašić, 'Radikalima i radikalnim organizacijama', *Samouprava*, 9 September 1921, 1; 'Ko parčelira državu?', *Samouprava*, 5 June 1921, 1.
[24] Ivo Banać, *The National Question in Yugoslavia: Origins, History, Politics* (Ithaca, NY: Cornell University Press, 1984), 231–2.
[25] *Ustav Kraljevine Srba, Hrvata i Slovenaca* (Zagreb: Matica Hrvatska, 1923).

(Article 97). The state of tension between the CPP and the Serbian elites persisted throughout the 1920s, despite the occasional formation of political alliances motivated by short-term interests. It reached its peak in June 1928, when Radić was assassinated by a Radical deputy from Kosovo in the Yugoslav Assembly. This urged King Aleksandar to dissolve the Assembly, invalidate the Constitution and appoint an extra-parliamentary government under his control (6 January 1929).

Aleksandar restored some constitutional order in 1931. This was a decision prompted by the impact of the economic crisis on Yugoslavia as well as the rising Croatian discontent with the royal dictatorship. According to the new Constitution granted by the monarch on 3 September 1931, the state was re-designated into the 'Kingdom of Yugoslavia' from the 'Kingdom of the Serbs, the Croats and the Slovenes' which was its designation in the 1921 Constitution.[26] No other nationality except the 'Yugoslav' one was recognized; an indication of Aleksandar's insistence on imposing Yugoslavism from above. The King retained the highest authority and the state was reorganized into nine larger units (*banovine*). As in the previous Constitution, these units were drawn in accordance with instrumental instead of historic criteria and their jurisdiction was restricted (Articles 83, 92, 93, 95).

The inauguration of the new Constitution did not appease the radical anti-establishment trends. These culminated with the assassination of King Aleksandar in Marseilles (9 October 1934).[27] After 1935, the Yugoslav government started to tolerate political activity and the principle of single-nation Yugoslavism was no longer emphasized. Most important, Yugoslavia's centralized structure started to adjust into a novel matrix with the aim to accommodate a broad range of national and regional demands. This resulted in the asymmetric status granted to Croatia, following the *Sporazum* ('Agreement') of August

---

[26] 'Ustav Kraljevine Jugoslavije', *Službene Novine*, 3 September 1931.
[27] This assassination was carried out by the Croatian *Ustaše* ('Insurgent') movement. The *Ustaše* were largely influenced by Fascism and orientated towards Croatian independence by all means. The movement was launched by Ante Pavelić from abroad and sheltered by Hungary and Italy who used the *Ustaše* as a pressure force against the Yugoslav government.

1939 between the then Yugoslav Premier Dragiša Cvetković and the CPP leader Vladimir Maček.[28] However, the long-term viability of royal Yugoslavia's confederalization would never be assessed, since the Axis invasion of April 1941 put an end to the state as such.

Vojvodina (1918–41): The political context

The question of the Habsburg lands under Hungarian jurisdiction was settled after the First World War by the peace treaty between the Entente and Hungary, signed at Trianon on 4 June 1920. Yugoslavia acquired Croatia-Slavonia and a considerable portion of the former Habsburg Vojvodina. The annexed lands included Bačka and Baranja and two areas near the confluence of the Mur and Drava Rivers (i.e. Prekomurje and Međumurje). As for the Banat, it was divided between Romania and Yugoslavia.[29] The new borderline brought within the confines of Yugoslavia a large number of minorities, especially Hungarians and Germans (Table 1). Also, the division of the Banat brought within Yugoslavia a considerable number of Romanians (Ibid.). According to the 1921 Constitution, historic Vojvodina was divided into four administrative departments: Srem was represented almost in its entirety within the homonymous department; Western Bačka and Baranja formed one unit with Sombor as its capital; Eastern Bačka and Northern Banat were assigned to the department of Belgrade whereas Southern Bačka and Southern Banat to that of Smederevo.

In the beginning, the Vojvodinian Serb elites set as top priority their political unification with their southern kindred and demonstrated a positive disposition towards a unitary arrangement. This was particularly the case with the Vojvodinian branch of the National Radicals who demonstrated a more pronounced pan-Serbianism than

---

[28] Ljubomir Boban, *Sporazum Cvetković-Maček* (Belgrade: SANU, 1965), 403–4.
[29] C. A. Macartney, *Hungary and Her Successors: The Treaty of Trianon and Its Consequences* (London: Royal Institute of International Affairs, 1937).

Table 1 The ethnic structure of the population of Vojvodina in 1921

Ethnic groups	Figures
Serbs	526,134 [34.7%]
Hungarians	370,040 [24.4%]
Germans	333,272 [22.0%]
Croats	122,864 [8.1%]
Slovaks	58,273 [3.8%]
Romanians	65,197 [4.3%]
Ruthenes	13,644 [0.9%]
Others	25,182 [1.7%]
TOTAL	**1,514.426 [100.0%]**

Source: Vladimir Đurić, Slobodan Čurčić and Saša Kicošev, 'The Ethnic Structure of the Population of Vojvodina', in *The Serbian Question in the Balkans*, University of Belgrade-Faculty of Geography (Belgrade, 1995).

their *Srbijanci* kindred.[30] This reflected the Vojvodinian Serbs' anxious desire to transit from the status of a subordinate group to that of a dominant one. Vojvodinian Serbs also feared that any model other than the unitary might imperil their status in Srem, Bačka and the Banat where they constituted only a relative majority (37.7 per cent of the total population). Indeed, the NRP triumphed in Vojvodina at the first Yugoslav elections.[31] The Vojvodinian branch of the Democrats equally adhered to the central party's Yugoslavist and pro-unitary platform.

Soon, a swing of mood occurred in the Vojvodinian political map. The dominant *Srbijanci* bureaucracy was accused of inadequate qualifications, a drive towards clientelistic attitudes and the maintenance of semi-feudal mentalities.[32] The Vojvodinian bourgeoisie started

---

[30] According to the Vojvodinian Radical leader, Jaša Tomić, even if the Serbo-Croat disagreements rendered the establishment of a South Slav state unworkable, 'Serbia, comprising the predominantly Serbian parts of the Western Balkans, could still exist on its own'. Jaša Tomić, *Krajnje je vreme da se razumemo* (Novi Sad: Matica Srpska, 1919), 8–15.

[31] Banać, *The National Question in Yugoslavia*, 388.

[32] B. Hrabak, 'Borba demokrata za samosvojnost Vojvodine (1919–1928)', *Zbornik Istorijskog Instituta Slavonski Brod*, broj 1 (1982): 82–3.

to contend that their more 'up to date' and 'European' qualifications would be of a better use for the state's administration, especially in their native region. Economic grievances were voiced too. It is estimated that by 1924–5 Vojvodina was paying approximately twenty-two different kinds of taxes, including the particularly heavy *dohodarina*.[33] To this should be added the dissatisfaction with the failure of the agrarian reform in the region.

The emergence of a Vojvodinian regionalist alternative was accelerated by the royal dictatorship of 1929. The first attempt to summarize Vojvodinian grievances was concretized in the 'Sombor Resolution' of July 1932, which was drafted by local Radicals, Democrats and Agrarians on a multiparty basis. This document deplored the territorial alteration of Vojvodina by the 1921 and 1931 constitutions[34] and called for the staffing of regional administration with local cadres as well as the revision of the taxation system.[35] Later, in December 1932, the 'Novi Sad Resolution' (also drafted on a multiparty basis) placed the Vojvodinian question within the project for constitutional reform endorsed by the anti-dictatorship opposition. This document, actually an expansion of the 'Zagreb Declaration'[36] on Vojvodina, went a step further than the 'Sombor Resolution' and demanded that Yugoslavia is reorganized as a federation and Vojvodina is granted the status of a federal unit.

The 'Novi Sad Resolution' polarized the Serbian political landscape. The Radicals, as well as the Democrats of Serbia proper, insisted on

---

[33] Ibid., 37–8.
[34] According to the 1931 Constitution, most of Vojvodina together with Srem and some north-central districts of Serbia proper became part of the Danube *banovina* with its seat in Novi Sad.
[35] Ranko Končar, *Opozicione partije i autonomija Vojvodine 1929-1941* (Novi Sad: Matica Srpska, 1995), 88–92.
[36] According to the 'Zagreb Declaration', issued between 5 and 7 November 1932, by the Independent Democrats (a secession from the Democratic Party) and the Croatian Peasants, Yugoslavia was to be divided into seven regions, on the basis of their 'past experience of sovereign statehood' (Serbia, Croatia and Montenegro) as well as their 'cultural-historic particularities' (Vojvodina, Macedonia, Bosnia-Herzegovina and Slovenia). Each unit was to enjoy extensive budgetary, legislative and cultural autonomy. Ibid., 93–7.

the 'common political struggle of all Serbs for democratization' and castigated 'parochial' initiatives which divided Serbs into *prečani*[37] and *Srbijanci*. This, however, did not discourage the regionalists in Vojvodina. The formation of the 'Vojvodinian Front' in July 1935 signalled the standardization of the regionalist initiative. As recommended by the Vojvodinian Radicals, the Front was not launched as a separate political grouping but as a think tank where Vojvodinian regionalists retained their party identities and formulated proposals on Vojvodina's status within Yugoslavia. The Vojvodinian Radicals possibly assessed that the launching of a separate Vojvodinian party might restrict regionalist initiatives to a parochial extent and raise undesirable parallels, among the *Srbijanci* elites, with 'quasi-secessionist' groups such as the CPP. By contrast, the organization of the Vojvodinian Front as a multiparty forum might prove a more effective move, since this would enable the Vojvodinian regionalists to promote the Front's resolutions to the influential circles in Belgrade.

The Front underlined that Vojvodina, encompassing Bačka, Baranja, Srem and the Banat, should gain the status of a unit in a federally restructured Yugoslavia.[38] All units would be equal, enjoy legislative as well as budgetary autonomy and their assemblies have some main areas under their jurisdiction (e.g. internal administration, education, the regional judiciary).[39] The Vojvodinian Front found support among the bourgeois strata who were particularly affected by regional mismanagement and the failure of the agrarian reform: landowners, bankers and traders. The Front vocally expressed Vojvodinian grievances between 1935 and 1938. Still, its endeavours were in vain since Yugoslavia's restructuring, in the minds of the Serbian elites, remained a synonym of the need to reach a *modus vivendi* with the Croats. The 1939 *Sporazum* legitimized the prevalence of the ethnic over the regional criterion. This had a

---

[37] This is a term used to denote the Serbs resident above the Sava, Drava and Danube rivers, within the old Habsburg realm.
[38] The other units proposed were pre-war Serbia (including Vardar Macedonia), Croatia, Montenegro with Dalmatia, Bosnia-Herzegovina and Slovenia.
[39] The fields reserved for the central government were citizenship, state security and the military, foreign policy and macroeconomic issues.

particularly negative impact on Vojvodina, since Baranja and parts of Western Srem were conceded to the enlarged Croatian *banovina* on grounds of their demographic structure.

However, the regionalist endeavours of the interwar Vojvodinian bourgeoisie possess particular significance. On that occasion, some Vojvodinian Serbs appealed for autonomy not to an alien power but to their fellow-nationals in Belgrade. This was the first time that demands for autonomy were expressed by the Vojvodinian bourgeoisie on a regional and not a national basis, as was the case prior to the establishment of Yugoslavia. The Front's platform is recalled up to date by Vojvodina's *autonomaši* (pro-autonomy) groupings. Nevertheless, this does not imply any sort of linear continuity in regard to Vojvodinian regionalism. The demands for autonomy, expressed in Vojvodina in different periods, were and still are predominantly conditioned by the prevailing political and socio-economic circumstances.

Socio-economic conditions

A socio-economic development of primary importance, which was undertaken after the formation of Yugoslavia, was the expropriation of the formerly Ottoman and Habsburg land estates. Promises of land reform had already been made by the pre-war Serbian government as well as the Zagreb National Council during the war. The Yugoslav government immediately established a special Ministry for the Agrarian Reform and set out the instructions for the process in an interim decree. In short, large estates were to be broken down and redistributed. Landowners would receive compensation in state bonds and all those who obtained land were to repay the state after a period of thirty years. Sharecropper land was to be handed over to tenants.[40]

---

[40] Stevan K. Pavlowitch, *Serbia: The History behind the Name* (London: Hurst & Company, 2002), 119.

The objectives of the reform were to calm the revolutionary potential of the landless peasants, eliminate the foreign landowning class linked to the empires and reward war veterans. With regard to the latter aim, the period after the end of the war saw the planned settlement of landless peasants from the Dinaric parts of Yugoslavia (Montenegro, Bosnia-Herzegovina, Lika) in Vojvodina. Many of the settlers had fought during the war in the Serbian and Montenegrin armies or legions (the so-called *dobrovoljici*/volunteers). Their presence in Vojvodina was necessary for the establishment of a northern frontier consisting of 'reliable national elements'.[41] The colonists were given 8.5 yokes apiece. The *dobrovoljici* took their land for free and were exempted from repaying the state over a thirty years period. By the end of 1928, 12,625 families of war veterans had received 100,689 yokes; 4,730 families of other colonists had received 30,088 yokes and 58,193 families of local applicants 171,950 yokes.[42] Much of the land granted to the colonists previously belonged to Hungarian or German large landowners.[43]

According to Pavlowitch, 'politically unavoidable, socially desirable, the reform in the northern regions turned out to be economically doubtful'.[44] In contrast to Dalmatia or Bosnia-Herzegovina, in Vojvodina we did not have to do with remains of feudal relationships but with large private estates. The liquidation of all agricultural estates above 100 hectares, as provided by the law, led to the formation of very small holdings while the new owners lacked both capital and experience of modern agricultural techniques. The break-up of the estates caused a decrease in labour demand in exactly these areas where labour supply was more than sufficient, since there was not much expropriated land to go around. Meanwhile, the departure of quite a few *dobrovoljici* from

[41] Most volunteers settled in Bačka and the Banat where Hungarian and German presence was particularly compact. By 1939, Bačka accommodated 3,268 volunteer and 1,195 other colonist families. Also, by 1941, 6,238 volunteer and 2,146 other colonist families lived in the Banat. Mitrović, 'Naseljavanje i kolonizacija Vojvodine', 216–17.

[42] Macartney, *Hungary and Her Successors*, 401.

[43] It is estimated that some 40,000 hectares were lost by German large landowners in the 1920s, as a result of the land expropriation. A. T. Komjathy and P. Stockwell, *German Minorities and the Third Reich* (New York: Holmes and Meier, 1980), 129.

[44] Stevan K. Pavlowitch, *Yugoslavia* (London: Ernest Benn, 1971), 55–6.

Vojvodina shed doubt about the success of the colonization as well. The crisis facing the agricultural producers in Vojvodina was somehow alleviated through their transactions with Hungary and later Germany.[45]

The state of interethnic relations

The Trianon Treaty included certain clauses for the protection of national minorities. According to Article 9 of the Yugoslav minority protection treaty, in these areas where a significant percentage of their inhabitants belonged to a minority, the government had to provide elementary education for their children in their mother tongue. The state and local authorities were also obliged to allocate from their budgets proportionate subsidies to the minorities for educational and religious purposes. Even though the Trianon Treaty had established basic principles, it was up to the Yugoslav state to fill in the details of its minority legislation. The applicability of Article 9 was restricted to these areas acquired by the Yugoslav kingdom after 1 January 1913.[46]

A major political concern of the Yugoslav government, in regard to its minority policies in Vojvodina, was the necessity to dissolve the Hungarian-German bond. According to the state's officials, this could be achieved through the assumption of a lenient stance towards Vojvodinian Germans and the ensuing cultivation of loyalty to the Yugoslav kingdom. Consequently, quite a few formerly Hungarian schools were converted into schools with parallel German classes in the 1920s. Moreover, by 1927, the number of ethnic German teachers employed at all levels of education in Vojvodina was satisfactory.[47]

---

[45] Yugoslavia exported to Hungary wood and agricultural products whereas Hungary exported to Yugoslavia industrial products. Since 1934, Germany became a steady purchaser of Vojvodinian wheat, maize and livestock. Vuk Vinaver, 'O Jugoslovensko-Madarskoj Trgovini (1933–1941)', *Zbornik Matice Srpske za Istoriju*, broj 1 (1970): 37–78.

[46] Jozsef Galantai, *Trianon and the Protection of Minorities* (New York: Atlantic Studies on Society and Change No.70, 1992), 73–7.

[47] By that year, 259 Vojvodinian German teachers were employed in Bačka and 60 more in Podunavlje. By 1927, the number of German students in Bačka was 13,022 and in Podunavlje 2,504. Goran Nikolić, *Društvena obeležja nemačke nacionalne manjine u periodu 1918–1929 godine* (magistrarski rad), Matica Srpska archives (Novi Sad: Matica Srpska, 1992), 220.

The Yugoslav government demonstrated a relatively lenient attitude towards more institutionalized forms of German representation as well. On 20 June 1920, the *Schwabisch-Deutscher Kulturbund* was founded in Novi Sad by local *Völksdeutsche* (ethnic Germans). The *Bund* was set up with the aim to safeguard the cultural–linguistic identity and promote the economic activities of the German minority in Yugoslavia.[48] At the same time, it pledged its loyalty to Yugoslavia and worked for the abandonment of any pro-Magyar sympathies among the *Völksdeutsche*. In the long term, the emergence of pro-Nazi sympathies among the *Völksdeutsche* backfired against the 'state-sponsored' reinforcement of ethnic German identity.[49] The radicalization of the *Völksdeutsche* alarmed many Serbs who interpreted it as one more indication that the *Srbijanci* bureaucrats did not know how to handle Vojvodina's particularities properly.

By contrast, the Yugoslav officials remained suspicious of Hungarian irredentism and this had a negative impact on their policies towards the Hungarian minority. By 1934, the Hungarians possessed 132 parallel sections at elementary schools. This figure suggests a steady decline in comparison to the 645 Hungarian elementary schools that operated in Vojvodina before the war.[50] As for higher education in the Hungarian language, this was practically non-existent. The discrimination against Hungarians in education fuelled anti-Yugoslav tendencies within that group. As far as the Vojvodinian Romanians were concerned, a reciprocal Romanian-Yugoslav agreement, signed in the summer of 1933, allowed them to open at their own expense their private elementary schools under state's supervision but with the examinations conducted and the certificates issued by Romanian teachers. Relations between Serbs and Romanians remained positive on the grassroots level and to this helped the religious affiliation as well as the similar social status of the two

---

[48] Ibid., 195–6.
[49] By mid-1940 the balance of power within the *Bund* had decisively shifted towards the pro-Nazi faction. Sepp Janko, the then *Bund* leader, was no doubt a Nazi sympathiser whereas similar tendencies were witnessed among other high-rank *Völksdeutsche*. Komjathy and Stockwell, *German Minorities and the Third Reich*, 130–40.
[50] Macartney, *Hungary and Her Successors*, 419.

groups. The state's policies towards Vojvodina's minor Slavic groups (e.g. Slovaks, Ruthenes) were equally positive.[51]

Vojvodina under Axis occupation

In this section, the focus shifts to the situation in Vojvodina during the years of Axis occupation. Particular attention is paid to the administrative system and the state of interethnic relations in the region over that period. Certain 'particularities' of the occupation in Vojvodina facilitated the long-term healing of the war wounds, despite the state of interethnic strife that prevailed between 1941 and 1945.

Yugoslavia 1941–5

Yugoslavia capitulated to the Axis on 17 April 1941. The country was partitioned among the Axis partners and their regional allies (Hungary and Bulgaria). Meanwhile, Pavelić's *Ustaše* were allowed to proclaim their *Nezavisna Država Hrvatske* ('Independent State of Croatia') extending over 40 per cent of the former kingdom of Yugoslavia; ranging from inner Croatia, across Bosnia-Herzegovina, to the gates of Belgrade.

Resistance to the occupation forces was coordinated by two political and military organizations. One of them was the Communist Partisans under the leadership of the Croat Josip Broz 'Tito'. In November 1942, the Communists set up the 'Anti-Fascist Council for the National Liberation of Yugoslavia-AVNOJ' in Bihać, Northern Bosnia. The Bihać manifesto envisaged the establishment of a broad democratic

---

[51] Throughout the interwar era, the educational and cultural life of Slovaks in Vojvodina flourished. With regard to the Ruthenes, since 1921 this group was enabled to write in their standardized Ruthene language with its own alphabet. Some information on this issue was disclosed to the author in the course of his field research in Vojvodina (Interview with Ruthene journalist at RTS Novi Sad; 22 April 2002); On the Slovaks, see Jan Siracki, 'Slovaci u Vojvodini kao Istorijsko-Etnografski Fenomen', *Zbornik za Istoriju*, broj 102–103 (1997): 115.

government that would recognize the rights of all national groups in Yugoslavia. At its second meeting (29 November 1943; Jajce), the AVNOJ declared itself the supreme legislative and executive institution in Yugoslavia – a provisional government.[52] The other resistance movement was the Chetniks, whose leader was the former minister of War, Dragoljub 'Draža' Mihailović. The Chetniks drew predominantly Serbian support and until 1943 had the backing of Britain. Mihailović was convinced that the Axis was bound to lose the war. So the Chetniks' main aim would be to fight the internal competitors for the post-war leadership of Yugoslavia, the Communists, until the Western allies would be there to assist the general uprising against the Axis.

Nevertheless, by mid-1943, the course of the war had changed in favour of the Partisans since the Allies had found out that the latter were doing more damage to Wehrmacht than the Chetniks. Moreover, the Partisans had managed to recast Yugoslavism in a new fashion and use it as a unifying and defensive ideological tool during the war. Consequently, people from all ethnic groups were attracted to their ranks. In line with these developments, on 24 May 1944, Churchill announced to the House of Commons that the supply of arms to Mihailović had ceased and the largest possible supplies would be sent to Tito. Later, on 20 October 1944, the Soviet Red Army marched triumphant in Belgrade and forced the Chetniks of *uža Srbija* (Serbia proper) to capitulate. This was the final act that paved the way to Tito's victory and the establishment of the Socialist Federal Republic of Yugoslavia.

Vojvodina 1941–5: The administrative system

In April 1941, the Banat was placed under German administration. This decision was taken after a Romanian refusal to claim the Yugoslav Banat or let Hungary have it. By 14 June, an agreement was reached

---

[52] 'Državnopravno konstituisanje Nove Jugoslavije', in *Istorija Socijalističke Jugoslavije*, knjiga prva, ed. Branko Petranović and Cedomir Štrbac (Belgrade: Radnička Štampa, 1977), 23–6.

between the Banat *Völksdeutsche* leadership and the Serbian quisling government: the Banat was formally included to the administrative-legal system of occupied Serbia. At the same time, the Banat Germans were conceded extensive rights in local administration.[53]

The *Vizebanus*, a Nazi official, was to become the bearer of the highest civil authority in the Banat and supervise the function of the autonomous administration. Sepp Janko became the leader of the German *Völksgruppe* in Serbia and the Banat. The major governing body of the Banat's *Völksdeutsche* was the local administration (*Landesleitung*) based in Petrovgrad (modern-day Zrenjanin). Through this institution the *Völksdeutsche* enjoyed administrative autonomy in a variety of fields (fiscal management, legal affairs, education).[54] Soon tensions arose between the Nazi authorities and the *Völksdeutsche* over the military duties of the latter. Many *Völksdeutsche* refused to serve in the local police force, especially after the latter started to be deployed against Serbian civilians.[55] These tensions heightened when the local police force was transformed into the SS Division *Prinz Eugen* in spring 1942. The atrocities committed by *Prinz Eugen* against Serbian civilians, in combination with the fact that the *Völksdeutsche* never felt compelled to actively protest at the exploitation that they suffered at Nazi hands, rendered Banat Serbs extremely hostile towards the German community.

The official incorporation of Bačka and Baranja to Hungary was accomplished on 14 August 1941. Leo Deak, an intellectual from Sombor, was appointed major governor of Bačka-Baranja with his seat at Sombor. Soon agrarian and economic reforms were initiated, which had a particularly negative effect on Serbs and Jews. As a result of the land reform, which took place between mid-1941 and early 1942, land was

---

[53] On this issue, see the 'Verordungsblatt der Völksgruppenführung' (number 3) of August 1941, as cited in Petar Kačavenda, *Nemci u Jugoslaviji* (Belgrade: Institut za Savremenu Istoriju, 1991), 32.
[54] The broad autonomy enjoyed by the *Völksdeutsche* leadership can be summarized in this official statement: 'All instructions for legal administration, education and the appointment of local officers are issued by us, and only us, in concordance with the occupation forces.' Ibid., 34.
[55] Komjathy and Stockwell, *German Minorities and the Third Reich*, 144.

given to 13,158 Hungarian families, 770 Croatian families, 34 German families, 4 Slovene families and only 6 Serb families.⁵⁶ The group that profited the most from the reform was the newly arrived Hungarian settlers; mainly Szekely Hungarians from Bukovina and elsewhere.⁵⁷ The agrarian reform and the colonization process were part of the broader plan to alter the ethnic structure of Bačka-Baranja and Magyarize the county.

Srem was a region with a Serb majority. When Italy annexed Dalmatia, Srem, with its rich Central Danube basin, became a bone of contention between *Volksdeutsche* and *Ustaše*. Hitler found a *modus vivendi*: Srem would formally pass under Croat control but *Ustaše* administration would function in coordination with the *Volksdeutsche* leadership. In April 1941, a series of laws were enacted in the NDH, all of which were directed against Serbs, Jews and their properties. Even though the *Ustaše* and the *Volksdeutsche* agreed on these laws, tensions began to surface over the distribution of the properties confiscated by Serbs and Jews. At the same time, Milovan Zanić, a member of Pavelić's apparatus, had provoked Srem's *Volksdeutsche* by saying that 'Srem is Croatian and villages will be filled with *Ustaše*'.⁵⁸ When *Ustaše* atrocities became horrendous this provoked a wave of revolt among Nazis themselves. Consequently, in September 1942, the *Ustaše-Volksdeutsche* condominium ended and the Germans assumed full control of the region. They kept the Special Courts and all existing legislation but without further harassing the Serbs.

Interethnic strife

In the years of occupation, certain events occurred that either alienated one ethnic group from the other(s) or fomented an atmosphere of explicit hatred. On the one hand, the occupation forces implemented a series

---

[56] Josip Mirnić, *Denacionalizorska politika mađarskog okupatora u jugoslovenske zemlje-1941* (Novi Sad: Matica Srpska, 1967), 145.
[57] P. Lorinc, *Hacban a Foldert* (Budapest: Akademia Kiado, 1981), 181.
[58] *Novi List*, 3 June 1941.

of repressive measures, directed against Serbs and Jews in particular, which ranged from population deportations to mass executions. On the other hand, reprisals against Germans and Hungarians took place after liberation. War crimes in Axis-occupied Yugoslavia have been a field of major disagreement among historians. Different historians, often originating from different groups, have produced highly controversial and disparate accounts of the atrocities committed in the Second World War. Also, much evidence has been concealed or destroyed. Nevertheless, it is not the aim of this work to assess the credibility of the sources available. The primary aim is to estimate the degree to which the memory of these atrocities has affected group identity and interethnic relations in present-day Vojvodina. The sources regarding the war crimes are mainly Yugoslav state reports.

In the Banat, the first mass executions were carried out as early as April 1941.[59] At the same time, the confiscation of the properties of the Serbian interwar colonists was initiated. Later, on 22 June 1941, a series of concentration camps were built.[60] By the time of liberation, approximately 56,000 Banat civilians had lost their lives in the concentration camps based in the Banat and abroad.[61]

In Bačka and Baranja, rapid Magyarization became the priority of the Hungarian administration. As early as 25 April 1941, an order for the deportation of the Serbian and Montenegrin interwar colonists was issued and a series of prison camps were set up. The transfer of Hungarian colonists to Bačka was planned in due time. By 18 June 1941, 2,921 Szekely families consisting of 13,200 members had settled in the county.[62] The Szekely families took over the houses and the

---

[59] On these executions, see the relevant report of the Yugoslav state's committee for the investigation of the crimes committed during occupation as cited in *Istorijski arhiv PK SK Vojvodine, Novi Sad, br. A.K. 7992, 3-21*. Also, see *IA PK SK Inv. Br. A.K. Reg. Br. 7388, 7913*.

[60] The central concentration camp, which soon became the major symbol of Nazi terror in the Banat, was opened in Petrovgrad, on 20 July 1942. On this issue, see *IA PK SK Vojvodine, Fond A.K. br. 7550*.

[61] Sandor Veg, 'Sistem nemačke okupacione vlasti u Banatu', *Zbornik Matice Srpske za Društvene Nauke*, broj 35 (1963): 92.

[62] Aleksandar Kasas, *Mađari u Vojvodini (1941–1946)* (Novi Sad: Matica Srpska, 1996), 40.

land previously owned by Serbian settlers. The favourable conditions offered to the Szekely caused the discontent of local Hungarians and Germans alike.[63] By 1942, the Hungarian officials needed to create Reich authorities the impression that the 'Southern Hungarian lands' were threatened by a joint 'Communist-Zionist' uprising, so that Hitler would cease his pressures for more Hungarian soldiers to be dispatched to the Eastern front. This caused the radicalization of Hungarian policies towards Serbs and Jews. The worst came in January 1942, when the Great *Racija* (Persecution) commenced in Novi Sad. When it ended, on 30 January 1942, the *Racija* had claimed the lives of 4,000 civilians, mostly Serbs (2,578) and Jews (1,068).[64]

Things were even worse in Srem. All Serbs and Jews from 15 to 50 years of age were forced to perform labour from 6 a.m. to 8 a.m. In his speech, delivered in Vukovar on 14 August 1941, Pavelić threatened that 'Srem is now part of the NDH and must be permanently cleansed of Serbs and Jews'.[65] By the time that the *Ustaše-Völksdeutsche* condominium in Srem ended, around 15,000 Serbs and Jews had been executed through summary procedures.[66]

By 7 November 1944, the *Völksdeutsche* leadership, in conjunction with the German Ministry of Interior, had completed the evacuation process of Yugoslavia's German community to Germany. The Germans who did not manage to flee Yugoslav territory were taken to concentration camps by the Partisans. There exists evidence that the treatment of the inmates was not always proper.[67] On 1 December, though, the release of

---

[63] Ibid., 65.
[64] Ibid., 91. For a thorough account of the *Racija* and other wartime atrocities in Bačka see the full report of the Yugoslav Committee for the Investigation of War Crimes: *Zločini okupatora u Bačkoj 1941–44* (Novi Sad, 1948), 121–33, 166–79, 240–7.
[65] Edmond Paris, *Genocide in Satellite Croatia (1941–1945)* (Chicago: The American Institute for Balkan Affairs, 1961), 184.
[66] For a thorough account of the *Ustaše* atrocities in Srem, see the full report of the Yugoslav Committee for the Investigation of War Crimes: *Zločini okupatora u Sremu (1941–44)* (Novi Sad, 1948), 40–9, 112–19, 128–33, 204–13, 299.
[67] On this issue see the relevant Yugoslav report: *AJ, F 153, k.25, III-3/138*. Also, the Military Administration order, issued on 1 December 1944, admitted that in certain places the treatment of the incarcerated Germans and Hungarians was improper. On this issue see *AVII, VO, k. 1661, f. 1, d. 1*.

Hungarians from concentration camps was decreed. There exists some speculation that a certain number of Germans were killed in reprisals, between October and November 1944. However, there does not exist any reliable evidence in the official state's archives.[68] Some indications exist that a certain number of Hungarians were killed in reprisal attacks.[69]

In all of this, one thing must be born in mind: most of the wartime atrocities in Vojvodina were perpetrated by outsiders. In Bačka, *honved* (militias) from Hungary proper played a leading part in the *Racija* and other atrocities.[70] Quite similar was the case in Srem, where many leading *Ustaše* were not locals, whereas many reprisal attacks were carried out by Partisans who came from other parts of Yugoslavia. This clearly contrasts with what was the case in Bosnia-Herzegovina where the atrocities were largely committed among locals and negative memories persisted for the years to come, even though restricted to the family level. Consequently, the healing of the war wounds in Vojvodina would be quicker and more effective in comparison to the other parts of Yugoslavia.[71]

---

[68] One source which comprises a brief account of such events is Zoran Janjetović's book: *Between Hitler and Stalin: The Disappearance of the Ethnic Germans from Vojvodina* (Belgrade: Institut za Savremenu Istoriju, 2000). For more details, see Janjetović, ibid., 213–19.

[69] Some Hungarian sources suggest an exaggerated number of around 40,000 Vojvodinian Hungarians who died in acts of reprisal between October and early December 1944. On this issue, see Robert Aspalagh, 'Trianon Dissolved: The Status of Vojvodina Reconsidered?', *Yearbook of European Studies* 5 (1992): 127. Tibor Cseres gives a slightly lower number: 39,941. For this figure, see Janjetović, *Between Hitler and Stalin*, 220.

[70] Some information over this issue was disclosed to the author in the course of his field research in Vojvodina (Interview with sociologist at the University of Novi Sad; 13 March 2001).

[71] A similar observation was made by Judy Batt in the course of her fieldwork in another multiethnic East European region, Transcarpathia in Ukraine. Most of the Nazi-occupation atrocities, as well as the Soviet reprisals, were committed in that region by outsiders. Consequently, the healing of the wounds inflicted by interethnic strife was more effective in that Ukrainian region as well. Judy Batt, 'Transcarpathia – A Peripheral Region at the "Centre of Europe"', *Regional & Federal Studies* 12, no. 2 (2002): 155–77.

Vojvodina within the Socialist Federal Republic of Yugoslavia

In autumn 1944, the Communist Partisans emerged as the victors of the internal power-contest in Yugoslavia. This development saw the establishment of a new order in what was the Kingdom of Yugoslavia: the Socialist Federal Republic of Yugoslavia. This section highlights the system of regional administration, the socio-economic aspects and the management of interethnic relations. Even though the establishment of Vojvodina as an autonomous province was dictated from above, in the long term, Vojvodina's successful economic performance stimulated a powerful popular commitment to Vojvodinian regional identity and its system of autonomous administration among Serbs and 'others' alike.

The ideological content of Socialist Yugoslavism and the constitutional framework of the Socialist Federal Republic of Yugoslavia

According to Article 2 of the Constitution of the Socialist Federal Republic of Yugoslavia[72] (31 January 1946), the new federation was to comprise the socialist republics of Serbia, Croatia, Slovenia, Bosnia-Herzegovina, Macedonia and Montenegro. Five Yugoslav *narodi* (peoples) with an equal status were recognized: the Serbs, the Croats, the Macedonians, the Montenegrins and the Slovenes. Serbia was to comprise the autonomous *pokrajina* (province) of Vojvodina and the autonomous *oblast* (district) of Kosovo and Metohija. The Constitution stated that 'Yugoslavia is a community of nations equal in rights who, on the basis of the right of self-determination, including

---

[72] The initial designation of the new federation in the 1946 Constitution was *Federativna Narodna Republika Jugoslavije* ('Federal People's Republic of Yugoslavia'). The state was officially renamed into the Socialist Federal Republic of Yugoslavia in the text of the 1963 Constitution. Throughout this text, the 'second' Yugoslav federation will be referred to as the Socialist Federal Republic of Yugoslavia.

the right of secession, have expressed the will to live together in a federative state'.[73]

Despite its federal structure, the Yugoslav state was, in its concentration of real power, a unitary mechanism. The Presidium of the Federal Assembly combined the functions of a parliamentary coordinating and standing committee and those of a corporate Head of State. Supreme in theory, the role of the Assembly was limited to the approval of the bills submitted to it by the executive. Even though the Constitution made no formal mention of the Communist Party, yet all power emanated from the Party at the head of which was its Secretary-General Tito, assisted by Edvard Kardelj, Milovan Djilas and Aleksandar Ranković. Tito was head of the government, minister of Defence, commander-in-chief, member of the Presidium and head of the Popular Front. At that early stage, federalization of the state did not equal federalization of the party apparatus. The CPY was organized according to the Stalinist model, leaving little room for regional loyalties. Centralization of authority was prompted by the need for Yugoslavia's rapid reconstruction after the war and the necessity for the new regime to consolidate its status first against the remaining pockets of anti-Communist resistance and, following the Stalin-Tito rift in 1948, the possible machinations of pro-Moscow circles within the CPY.

The brand of Yugoslavism, which was promoted by the CPY after the war, was characterized by: anti-nationalism (opposition to particularistic nationalisms within Yugoslavia); patriotism (adherence to the principles of the Partisan movement); internationalism (primacy of ideology over nationality in the universal struggle for a social revolution). The CPY favoured an integral version of Yugoslavism, according to which a Yugoslav nation was in the process of making and all particularistic affiliations would wither away. The federal system was interpreted as a temporary measure dictated by national heterogeneity.

---

[73] 'Ustav Federativne Narodne Republike Jugoslavije', in Petranović and Štrbac 1977, Dokumenti I, knjiga druga, 116ff.

Soon, innovations were introduced on the structural level. Following the successful break with Moscow, the Yugoslav leadership aimed at the formulation of an ideological anti-model to the Soviet one. Consequently, the new Constitutional Law of 1953 introduced a multilevel pattern of political and economic administration, that consisted of the People's Committees of Municipalities and Districts, the workers' and the producers' councils. Self-management (*samoupravljanje*) was seen as an efficient alternative to the Soviet 'bureaucratic' model and the instrument through which old sectional, regional and ethnic interests would be absorbed and the state itself would wither away when the process of the establishment of a classless society was complete. In line with these developments, the Party's designation was changed to League of Communists of Yugoslavia in an attempt to demonstrate that members were to fulfil their responsibilities as Communists, not through the Party as an organization, but as volunteering individuals within the institution where they were employed. Similarly, the Popular Front was renamed into the Socialist Alliance of the Working People of Yugoslavia.

The new Yugoslav Constitution promulgated in April 1963 introduced the framework for one of the most complicated political systems in existence at that time.[74] The focal constituent part of the Federal Assembly would be the Chamber of Representatives (120 deputies). The Assembly comprised the Chamber of Nations (10 delegates from each republic and 5 from each autonomous province). The latter provision codified the practice of a balanced republican representation within the Federal Executive Council. Certain concessions were made to the component republics. The Constitutional Court of Yugoslavia was introduced with its counterparts in the republics. This body would be responsible to examine republican appeals against federal laws that infringed on the republics' jurisdiction as well as federal appeals against their legislation. Later, in 1967, a series of constitutional amendments were introduced. The competencies of the Chamber of Nations were extended to comprise

---

[74] Union of Jurists' Association of Yugoslavia, *The Constitution of the Socialist Federal Republic of Yugoslavia (A Preliminary Draft)*, English-language edition (Belgrade, 1962).

all issues affecting the interests of the republics, rendering the body in question a largely independent agent within the Assembly. Some further amendments, added in 1971, introduced the institution of collective presidency which would comprise three delegates from each republic and two from each autonomous province (Amendment 35).

The federalization of the Party and government was prompted by certain factors. The federal officials might have assessed that the Chamber of Nations could function as a forum where the clashes between the regional leaderships or conflicts with nationality implications would be resolved more effectively than it was the case until then in the central party leadership.[75] The expansion of the competencies enjoyed by the Chamber of Nations, as well as the increase of republican/provincial control over its decisions, left a clear implication that the need for the government to achieve inter-republican consensus on federal policy prior to its submission to the Assembly had increased. Therefore, Socialist Yugoslavism, since the mid-1960s, embraced the following principles: full endorsement of the particularities of all nations and nationalities and their right to cultural self-determination; affirmation of dual consciousness – that is, national consciousness combined with Yugoslav consciousness; rejection of both unitarism and separatism as perilous deviations.

The relaxation of federal control was accompanied by an emphatic display of discontent with the status quo. The opposition to the established order also acquired quasi-nationalist overtones, the most notable example of this kind being the Croatian crisis of 1967–72. Throughout that period, the Croats had become increasingly insecure over the cultural, economic and demographic future of their *narod* and republic. When the crisis aggravated in autumn 1971, Tito handled it by means of expulsion of thousands of members from the Croatian LC and the imposition of long prison terms to others.[76]

---

[75] Steven L. Burg, *Conflict and Cohesion in Socialist Yugoslavia: Political Decision Making since 1966* (Princeton, NJ: Princeton University Press, 1983), 66.

[76] Pedro Ramet, *Nationalism and Federalism in Yugoslavia (1963–1983)* (Bloomington: Indiana University Press, 1984), 138–40.

As became obvious in the new Yugoslav Constitution inaugurated in 1974, the Croatian crisis did not affect the drive towards Yugoslavia's 'confederalization'. The new Constitution set up as the imperative an electoral system to the various legislative assemblies based on delegations drawn from occupational and interest groups. The Federal Assembly consisted of a 220-strong Federal Chamber (comprising 30 members from each of the 6 republics and 20 from each of the autonomous provinces) and an 88-member Chamber of Republics and Provinces (comprising 12 members elected by the republican and 8 by the provincial assemblies). The strict order of rotation was not applied in Tito's case, who was elected president of Yugoslavia for an unlimited term of office. The new Constitution enhanced the role of the military in that it increased the number of army officers in the governing bodies of the LCY. In this way, the LCY and the Yugoslav People's Army, both agents of federal rather than republican authority, were mutually reinforced.

The Yugoslav Constitution of 1974 outlined the rights, obligations and interactions of a multitude of organizations. The proper function of this system, however, was to rely on the civic consciousness and political idealism of all individuals involved in it, from the top-level Party officials down to ordinary citizens.[77] On 4 May 1980, Tito passed away in Ljubljana. Tito's absence as a decisive single man factor, who could exert vast informal power and impose order when necessary, became manifest in the 1980s. Throughout the 1980s, the deteriorating economic situation was accompanied by the virulent awakening of particularistic nationalisms all over the federation.

Vojvodina as a socialist autonomous province: The administrative system

The carving out of the autonomous provinces in Serbia was justified on grounds of their ethno-cultural heterogeneity. Vojvodina and Kosmet

---

[77] Union of Jurists' Association of Yugoslavia, *The Constitution of the Socialist Federal Republic of Yugoslavia*, English-language edition (Belgrade, 1974).

were two regions inhabited by a multitude of ethnic groups. Therefore, the most effective way, the Party officials contended, to safeguard the collective rights of all groups resident in those regions was to promulgate the administrative autonomy of Vojvodina and Kosmet.[78]

However, this decision should be better viewed in line with the establishment of SR Macedonia and SR Montenegro as republics: Both policies aimed to weaken the political status of Serbs within Yugoslavia and allay fears of 'renewed Serbian predominance' in the other republics and among other ethnic groups. At the same time, the demands by some Dalmatian Communists for the concession of autonomy to their region within Croatia, as well as the appeals by Moša Pijade and other Serbian Communists for the establishment of a Serb autonomous area in inner Dalmatia (the areas around Knin) were rejected by the CPY.[79] The motives behind this decision are not difficult to discern, considering that towards the end of the war the CPY urgently needed to gain the support of the Croatian masses.

The prevalence of the Communists over their domestic rivals saw the marginalization of the national–liberal current among Vojvodinian Serbs. A certain percentage of Vojvodinian national–liberals fled abroad following the victory of the Partisans. There can also be made speculations that a strain within the pre-war national–liberal generation modified their previous positions, joined the Communist structures and continued to exert some political influence in the province, even though subordinated to the Party line. Still, little information about the post-war purges and the fate of the pre-war national–liberal elites in Communist Vojvodina is available.

According to Article 4 of the 'Law on the Constituent Assembly' (August 1945), the citizens of Vojvodina could elect fifteen

---

[78] 'Zaključak plenuma GNOO Vojvodine o priključenju Vojvodine Federalnoj Srbiji', as cited in Jelena Popov, 'Glavni narodnooslobodilački odbor Vojvodine 1943–1945', *Istraživanje*, broj 4 (1974), 411. The CPY decided to give Baranja to Croatia on grounds of its demographic composition. Vojvodina within the Socialist Federal Republic of Yugoslavia comprised most of historic Srem, Bačka and the Banat.

[79] Vladimir Dedijer, *Novi prilozi za biografiju Josipa Broza Tita*, vol. 3 (Mladost: Rijeka, 1981–1984), 172; Djilas, *The Contested Country*, 172.

representatives to the Chamber of Nations and those of Kosmet ten. Vojvodina was endowed with its Supreme Court and Assembly but Kosmet was not. These early policies on Kosmet aimed at keeping a check upon the unreliable elements among the ethnic Albanians. In the 1950s, both provinces were little more than administrative divisions of Serbia. Their status was further marginalized when the Constitutional Law of 1953 relegated the Chamber of Nations to a component part of the Federal Chamber, with little legislative competence. With regard to Vojvodina, in the period between 1947 and 1963, a few acts apart from the provincial statute were passed by its assembly. In most cases, these were sub-legal acts of Serbian laws that focused on matters of minor significance.[80] The status of the provinces in the 1950s may be partially interpreted as consequence of the drive towards the integral version of Socialist Yugoslavism. It was also a necessity dictated by external factors, namely the rift with the Soviets. In Vojvodina, the local Party committee had gathered evidence that some ethnic Hungarians were influenced by Cominform's anti-Yugoslav propaganda.[81]

The status of the autonomous provinces was upgraded with the transition from integral to 'organic' Socialist Yugoslavism in the 1960s. The 1963 Constitution did not introduce any changes in regards with Vojvodina's status.[82] Nevertheless, by the second half of the 1960s, Kosmet and Vojvodina were urging for a more equal treatment within the federation. Some of these desiderata were granted by the amendments that were passed between 1967 and 1968. Amendment 7 formally recognized Vojvodina and Kosmet as constitutional elements of the federation. Moreover, Amendment 18 (Paragraph 3) guaranteed that the boundaries of the provinces could not change without the assent of their assemblies. This guarantee was incorporated into the Serbian Constitution in 1968. The same amendment (Paragraph 2) upgraded

[80] Milivoj Kovačević, 'Normativna Funkcija Autonomne Pokrajine Vojvodine u Razdoblju 1945–1968. Godine', *Zbornik za Društvene Nauke*, broj 58 (1973): 114–16.
[81] Paul Shoup, *Communism and the National Yugoslav Question* (New York: Columbia University Press, 1968), 137.
[82] In the case of Kosmet, the province was now officially designated as *autonomna pokrajina* just as Vojvodina, and granted its Assembly and Supreme Court.

the statutes of Vojvodina and Kosovo to constitutions. This enabled the establishment of constitutional–judicial branches of the Supreme Courts of Vojvodina and Kosovo that could perform the same duties as the republican constitutional courts.[83] Amendment 18 (Paragraph 4) also upgraded the legislative power of the provincial assemblies and specified that any changes to the provincial legislation should have had the assent of both the provincial and the republican supreme courts.

Finally, in late 1967, Vojvodina and Kosovo had gained the right to independent representation in the Chamber of Nations, after a change permitted each republic to send twelve delegates to this body and each autonomous province eight, while leaving the procedural law intact. By the late 1960s, the secretary general of the Vojvodinian LC was Mirko Čanadanović. Alongside Marko Nikezić and Latinka Perović at the Serbian LC, Čanadanović and his team were anti-centralist liberals and proponents of structural decentralization. The constitutional amendments of 1967–71 were largely introduced, with respect to the provinces, with the intention to reach a compromise at least with the legitimate demands of the Albanians in Kosovo.[84] The 1971 amendments granted additional legislative and judicial powers to the provinces, which now enjoyed almost the same degree of autonomy as the republics. The Vojvodinian and Kosovan assemblies were enabled to introduce amendments to their constitutions without consultation with SR Serbia.

This is not to say that no restraints were placed on the Vojvodinian organs. In 1972, the LCY accused the Vojvodinian LC of promoting its younger and better-educated cadres to positions of responsibility up to then monopolized by older representatives of the Partisan generation. Consequently, in December 1972, certain provincial cadres (including Čanadanović) were removed from their posts. These changes were largely prompted by the Croatian crisis.[85] At that time, the LCY

---

[83] The official establishment in the autonomous provinces of the constitutional courts did not take place before 1972.

[84] John R. Lampe, *Yugoslavia as History: Twice There Was a Country* (Cambridge: Cambridge University Press, 2000), 302–4.

[85] Savka Dabcević-Kućar, the then dissident leader of the Croatian LC, maintained particularly positive relations with Čanadanović and his team.

adopted the medium of the so-called democratic centralism. This tactic consisted in the maintenance of the decentralized system but, at the same time, the appointment of trusted individuals to key posts. Apart from Vojvodina, an effective check was placed upon vocal liberals in the Serbian Committee. The concession of extensive competencies to Vojvodina and Kosovo was codified in the 1974 Yugoslav Constitution. Article 244 specified that the common interests within the state would be served: through federal agencies, with participation on the basis of *equality* and *responsibility* of the republics and autonomous provinces in these agencies and in the formulation and execution of foreign policy; through federal agencies and organizations on the basis of decisions or *agreement* by the republics and autonomous provinces; through *direct cooperation and agreement* among the republics, the autonomous provinces, communes and other socio-political communities.

In its Constitution, Vojvodina was designated as 'part of SR Serbia and constitutional element of the Yugoslav socialist federation'. It was clarified that 'SAP Vojvodina participates in decision-making in the federation, on the principles of consensus among the republics and autonomous provinces ... in the organs of the federation *on a basis of equality*'. The Supreme Court of Vojvodina was the highest judicial organ in the province. According to Article 292, Vojvodina was empowered to make contacts and enter into agreements with 'organs and organizations' of foreign states.[86] The broad autonomy enjoyed by the two provinces was rendered a target of criticism by the Serbian LC in the early 1980s, especially following the Kosovan riots in 1981. Progressively, a dispute arose between Vojvodina and SR Serbia over provincial autonomy, especially in the realms of national and civil defence, the economy and foreign trade. In the beginning, Vojvodina succeeded in defending its political gains. Nevertheless, the aggravation of interethnic tensions in Kosovo soon took its toll on Vojvodinian autonomy.

---

[86] SAP Vojvodina, *Ustav Socijalističke Autonomne Pokrajine Vojvodine* (Belgrade: Savremena Administracija, 1974).

Socio-economic aspects

The end of the Second World War found Vojvodina in a state of devastation. Around 800,000 hectares of land had been abandoned, while 10,138 buildings had been destroyed or severely damaged.[87] Most of the damage was inflicted on Srem, the centre of the Partisan movement in the province.[88] There was also an extreme shortage in petrol and other primary resources.

On the very early days after liberation, the Vojvodinian Party Committee, in conjunction with the Central Committee, had started planning the reconstruction of Vojvodina. Urgent attention was paid to the reconstruction of the system of agricultural production. By June 1945, the agricultural campaign had been completed. Approximately 2,200.000 hectares of land (i.e. 95 per cent of the total arable land in Vojvodina by then) had been cultivated. This was the first major step towards Vojvodina's economic integration to the new federation. Even though ravaged itself, Vojvodina contributed considerable support to the other parts of Yugoslavia after liberation.[89] This assistance was soon repaid in a different kind. After the war, Vojvodina suffered from a shortage in labour force, qualified and unqualified one alike. Apart from the volunteers from the other parts of Yugoslavia, some temporary solution to that problem was offered, between late 1944 and early 1945, through forced labour performed by *Völksdeutsche* and Hungarian prisoners in labour camps.[90]

The situation called for more drastic measures. At that time, many peasant families associated with the Partisan movement had been left landless in Western Yugoslavia (e.g. in Banija, Sinjsko

---

[87] Jelena Popov, 'Prilog proučavanja pomoći Vojvodine ratom opustošenim krajevima Jugoslavije (novembar 1944–novembar 1945)', *Zbornik za Društvene Nauke*, broj 48 (1967): 55; 'Jedno svedočanstvo o problemima Vojvođanske poljoprivrede neposredno posle oslobođenja 1945', *Zbornik za Društvene Nauke*, broj 47 (1967): 176.

[88] Arhiv APV Sremski Karlovci f.GNOOV-a – Odeljenje građevinsko-tehniko, *Pregled ostecenih zgrada u Vojvodini*, 4 October 1944.

[89] Popov, 'Prilog proučavanja pomoći Vojvodine ...', 64–6.

[90] Aleksandar Kasas, 'Ekonomske mere vojne uprave za Banat Bačku i Baranju (17 oktobar–15 februar 1945)', *Zbornik za Društvene Nauke*, broj 47 (1967): 178.

Polje, Montenegro, Lika, Kordun, Bosnia-Herzegovina). The CPY, in conjunction with the Vojvodinian Committee, made arrangements for their transfer to Vojvodina (spring–summer 1945). The restoration of the landless families to the province was aimed at two directions: the manning of the deserted German estates with qualified and unqualified staff; the reward of the Partisan families from Western Yugoslavia for their contribution to the war effort.[91] According to the Land Reform Act of 23 August 1945, 400,000 hectares were given to the families from Western Yugoslavia.

The majority of the post-war colonists in Vojvodina were Serbs and Montenegrins. Nevertheless, there also existed some Croatian families associated with the Partisan movement (mainly from Lika, Kordun and Sinjsko Polje) who moved to Vojvodina. It is estimated that 60,000 Croats settled in Vojvodina.[92] In total, by 1948, 36,430 families consisting of 216,306 members had moved to Vojvodina from other parts of Yugoslavia. It is estimated that 62.9 per cent of all colonists (8.3 per cent of Vojvodina's population at that time) originated from the Bosnian and Croatian hinterlands. Overall, in 1948, 13.2 per cent of Vojvodina's 1,640,757 inhabitants were *novodošeljenici* ('new newcomers').[93] Their majority settled in Bačka where most deserted estates existed.[94] Like the post–First World War settlers, those colonists were characterized by a deep sense of loyalty towards the state and the new Yugoslavism.

During the early post-war period, priority in Vojvodina was given to the reorganization of agricultural production and the development and expansion of the basic industries. No major industrial plants

---

[91] As Moša Pijade put it, 'The restoration of the families and the orphans of the fighters fallen in combat was bestowed as a great national duty on their comrades in the Yugoslav army and the various Partisan units, after the completion of the national-liberation struggle.' Moša Pijade, *Agrarna reforma* (Zagreb: Školska Knjiga, 1948), 17.

[92] Fred Singleton, *Yugoslavia in the Twentieth Century* (New York: Columbia University Press, 1976), 232.

[93] The term *novodošeljenici* is used in contrast to the *došeljenici*/newcomers of the 1920s. For statistical information see Vojvođanski Arhiv, *Fond 184* (Sremski Karlovci, 1953).

[94] It is estimated that in 1948, 125,769 colonists had settled in Bačka, 74,465 in the Banat and 11,162 in Srem. Ibid.

were built. Even by 1966, a rough majority of Vojvodina's labour force was engaged in agriculture, largely owing to the province's farming resources.[95] However, as a result of the development of light industry, the percentage among Vojvodina's workforce engaged in agriculture declined by 1977.[96] The gradual development of agricultural and industrial production corresponded to an improvement in Vojvodina's living standards. By 1970, Vojvodina was at third place in Yugoslavia, in regard with per capita income, while the illiteracy rate was low.[97] Also, between 1971 and 1977, an increased investment in industry took place.[98] However, the problem of demographic stagnation persisted.[99]

Vojvodina's stance on federal economic policies was characterized by a more liberal orientation. The Vojvodinian officials favoured decentralization of the economic mechanism, lower federal taxation of republican–provincial enterprises and a more positive attitude towards laissez-faire economics. At the same time, the Vojvodinian officials were cautious so as not to transgress certain prerogatives regarding Yugoslavia's economic administration. Indeed, at the escalation of the Croatian crisis in the early 1970s, the Vojvodinian representatives rejected the Croatian arguments over that republic's alleged economic exploitation. In the late 1970s and throughout the 1980s, Vojvodina made active use of Article 292 of its Constitution. Large quantities of agricultural products were exported to other East European states (e.g. Hungary, Romania and Czechoslovakia). The relegation of Vojvodina's Constitution to a statute, in line with the 1990 Serbian Constitution, had a definitive impact on its independent economic policies.

[95] Savezni Zavod za Statistiku, *Statistički godišnjak (1947–66)* (Belgrade, 1968).
[96] Momir Čečez, 'O efikasnosti društvenih sredstava u privredno nedovoljno razvijenim područjima', *Pregled* 70, no. 1 (January 1980): 34–5; Savezni Zavod za Statistiku, *Statistički Godišnjak Jugoslavije* (Belgrade, 1981), 438.
[97] Savezni Zavod za Statistiku, *Statistički Godišnjak Jugoslavije* (Belgrade, 1972).
[98] Stevan Bek, 'Vojvodina's Economy Today', *Review of International Affairs* 29, no. 666 (5 January 1978): 35.
[99] Nicholas R. Lang, 'The Dialectics of Decentralization', *World Politics* 27, no. 3 (April 1975): 332; Slobodan Stanković, 'Yugoslavia's Census-Final Results', *Radio Free Europe Research Report*, 10 March 1982, 2.

The spectrum of interethnic relations: Institutional provisions

According to Article 13 of the 1946 Constitution, 'national minorities in the Federal People's Republic of Yugoslavia shall enjoy all rights and all kinds of protection over their cultural development, and they shall be able to use their languages freely'. Even though established on grounds of national heterogeneity, the autonomous provinces were not regarded as areas where the national minorities could enjoy a homeland analogous to that available to the Yugoslav *narodi*.[100] They were thought of as areas of ethno-cultural diversity that required special status in the light of the problem of adjusting relations among different national groups. The Party officials expected that the new arrangement would, at a first phase, encourage an atmosphere of interethnic understanding and cooperation and then lead to the progressive disintegration of particularistic national affiliations in line with Marxist historicism.

During that early period, the Vojvodinian Party Committee was dominated by Serbs (Table 2). The disproportionate under-representation of ethnic Hungarians in the 1950s partially reflected a mistrustful attitude on behalf of the CPY apparatchiks towards unreliable tendencies within the Hungarian community. In contrast, the favourable attitude towards South Slav groups, such as the Montenegrins, can be explained on grounds of their high commitment to the new Yugoslavism and as a reward for their contribution to the resistance movement. The Serbian preponderance in the Vojvodinian Committee, in the 1950s, was also subject to an internal specificity. The majority of the urban population in Vojvodina was Serbs. The majority of Montenegrins and other colonists had also settled in the province's urban centres where new complexes had been built in order to house them. Party membership was always higher in the urban parts of Vojvodina and Yugoslavia in general. By contrast, the majority of

---

[100] Officially, the recognized *narodi* were based in Yugoslavia whereas *nacionalne manjine*/national minorities (later *narodnosti*/nationalities) were overspills from *narodi* based in other, mostly neighbouring, states.

Table 2 Membership of the League of Communists of Vojvodina, 1953–8

Nationality	1953	1958	Percentage of nationality in Vojvodina's population, 1953
Serbs	74.6	73.5	51.1
Croats	5.6	5.9	7.5
Macedonians	1.4	1.2	0.7
Hungarians	7.4	8.4	25.4
Montenegrins	6.1	6.4	1.8

Source: Paul Shoup, *Communism and the National Yugoslav Question* (New York: Columbia University Press, 1968), 72.

ethnic Hungarians, at that time, resided in rural areas where Party membership was considerably lower.

More favourable conditions to Vojvodina's minorities were offered from the mid-1960s onward, as consequence of the decentralization process. A formal indication of this trend was the reformulation of national minorities to 'nationalities' in the 1963 Constitution. In line with the relaxation of tension in the Soviet-Yugoslav relations, the LCY, at its 8th Congress (1964), referred to Vojvodina and Kosmet as 'bridges and not barriers with the neighbouring states', whereas Yugoslavia as a whole was defined as a 'multinational community'.[101] Later, in 1972, Vojvodina over-represented its Hungarian minority vis-à-vis the Serbian majority in the Yugoslav Presidency.[102]

The strategy of the Yugoslav government in regard with the management of interethnic relations, at that time, can be summarized as follows: the new representative structure was expected to isolate the radical nationalists in the republics and autonomous provinces by making it clear that a genuine attempt was being made to equally represent the components of the federal state in its administrative apparatus. The new directive referred to the republics and the autonomous provinces and

---

[101] Dušan Bilandžić, *Istorija SFRJ* (Zagreb: Školska Knjiga, 1979), 301.
[102] In 1972, the one of the two Vojvodinian representatives in the collective presidency was Hungarian (21.7 per cent of Vojvodina's population at that time was Hungarian).

not to nationality as such. Nevertheless, the federal policies introduced in the 1970s had a definitive impact on the representation of the nationalities in the provincial and federal bodies of authority and the improvement of their collective status in all fields of socio-political activity. Yugoslavia was no longer the 'land of the South Slavs' exclusively; it was transforming into that of fifteen or so nations and nationalities.

The Vojvodinian Constitution of 1974 codified a series of provisions to the nationalities (Articles 4 and 194). The same document recognized the equal status of five languages and six alphabets: the Serbo-Croatian and Croato-Serbian languages and alphabets and the Hungarian, Slovak, Romanian and Ruthenian languages and alphabets. In line with these provisions, provincial laws, resolutions, declarations, the social plan, recommendations and other texts were published in all recognized languages. Minority-language education was provided from the elementary to the high, or technical, school level.[103] Each nationality had its own publishing house and a state-subsidised newspaper (e.g. the Hungarian *Magyar Szo*, the Slovak *Hlas Ludu* and the Romanian *Libertatea*). The extent of the concessions made to Vojvodina's minorities can be comprehended by reference to this example: There existed minority-language elementary schools for the 30,000 Ruthenes resident in Vojvodina but not for the 50,000 Serbs (members of a Yugoslav *narod*) who lived in SR Macedonia.[104]

The grassroots dimension

The Soviet-Yugoslav rift took its toll on interethnic relations in Vojvodina on the early days of the Socialist Federal Republic of Yugoslavia. The ethnic Hungarians, for instance, were associated by Serbs, on the one hand, with the Axis occupation and, on the other, with the pro-Soviet

---

[103] Hugh Poulton, 'The Hungarians, Slovaks, Romanians and Rysyns/Ukrainians of the Vojvodina', in *Minorities in Central and Eastern Europe* (London: Minority Rights Group International, 1993), 27.
[104] Pavlowitch, *Yugoslavia*, 357–8.

regime in Budapest. The collective vindication of an ethnic group was a deviation from the proclaimed principles of Socialist Yugoslavism and prohibited. However, a state of segregation was tangible.

The arrival of the colonists impacted on interethnic relations. The adaptation of the colonists to the new environment was initially hindered by tensions between them and the old settlers. These became subject to the competition for jobs between the two groups, as well as the fact that quite a few colonists proved incompetent to perform the work that they had been assigned.[105] Consequently, both groups remained introvert and little indication of interaction between them was observed in the early 1950s.[106] This was reminiscent of the old settler-colonist segregation during the interwar period.[107] The integration of the colonists to the new environment accelerated since the mid-1950s. Through their mutual participation in agricultural cooperatives and socio-political groupings, the old settlers and the colonists would get to cooperate with each other in a variety of activities and get to know and understand each other better.

The industrialization and urbanization process also served as a long-term leveller of the group divide between old settlers and colonists, especially those who were resident in rural communities. The bridging of the gap between the two groups became manifest in the conclusion of mixed marriages.[108] It might well be argued that in the course of the interaction between the old settlers and the colonists, it was the ways of the former that exerted a powerful influence on the latter and not so much the other way around. The extended households broke down and transformed into nuclear family units, while some local rituals were

---

[105] Borislav J. Dimković, 'Neki aspekti sociološkog proučavanja starosedelaca i kolonista u Rumi posle Drugog Svetskog Rata', *Zbornik za Društvene Nauke*, broj 48 (1967): 135–9.

[106] Sava N. Živkov, 'Oblici socijalne integracije u dva kolonistička sela u Banatu: Stajićevo i Lukićevo', in various authors, *Priloži za poznavanje naselja i naseljavanja Vojvodine* (Novi Sad: Matica Srpska, 1974), 128–9.

[107] M. Erić, *Agrarna reforma u Jugoslaviji (1918–1941)* (Sarajevo: Akademija Nauke i Umjetnosti Bosne i Herčegovine, 1958), 411.

[108] Vladimir Đurić, *Najnovije naseljavanje Bačke kolonistama iz Hrvatske* (Novi Sad: Matica Srpska, 1960), 17–18, 33–4, 77, 90; Živkov, 'Oblici socijalne integracije u dva kolonistička sela u Banatu', 152–4.

adopted by colonists. In a way, 'the Pannonian plain slowly devoured many of the newcomers'.[109] This is not to say that the colonists' emotional links to the old territory were in any way severed.[110]

One notable dimension of the colonists' group solidarity was their almost unconditional support to the CPY. This attitude did not have solely ideological undertones. It was also a pragmatic speculation since in this way those colonists hoped that their group interests would be served more effectively. Indeed, quite a few Party officials, as well as individuals employed in the police and other institutions in Communist-era Vojvodina, came from a colonist background. However, it remains true that the chasm between old settlers and colonists was drastically levelled during the Communist era. This was particularly true in the urban areas (e.g. Novi Sad) where the frequency of intermarriage between the two groups was high.[111] Consequently, the second generation of colonists started to perceive themselves as 'locals'. Especially when it comes down to self-definition, the question 'who is *precisely* an old settler/colonist?' cannot be offered a genuine and thoroughly accepted answer in Vojvodina since the mid- to late 1970s.

By the late 1960s, Vojvodina was the Yugoslav region where inter-group relations were more positive than in any other ethnically diverse part of the country (Table 3).[112] The positive interethnic climate in Vojvodina over that period was highly subject to the following intersection: the constitutional concessions to the national minorities; the grass-roots interaction between Serbs and 'others' in the self-management organizations; Vojvodina's successful economic performance. The prevalence of positive inter-group relations in Vojvodina became additionally manifest through the high frequency of ethnically mixed marriages. The offspring of mixed marriages would

[109] Milivoje Milosavljević, 'Kolonizacija Banatskog Aranđelova, Malog Sigeta i Podlokanja (1921–1941)', in *Priloži za poznavanje naselja i naseljavanja Vojvodine*, 105–6.
[110] Đurić, *Najnovije naseljavanje Bačke kolonistama iz Hrvatske*, 15–16.
[111] Pokrajinski Zavod za Statistiku, *PSDS 1981.godine* (Novi Sad: Knjiga III, 1983), 320; Dragoljub Bugarski and Saša Kicošev, *Stanovništvo Srema* (Novi Sad: GIS Institute, 1999), 46.
[112] Singleton, *Yugoslavia in the Twentieth Century*, 234.

Table 3 Opinions concerning relations among nations and nationalities in Yugoslavia, in per cent

Opinions	Total	BiH	Mont.	Cro.	Mac.	Slo.	Ser.	Kos.	Voj.
Good	**73.0**	78.7	72.1	73.8	87.0	56.6	67.3	74.4	75.9
Satisfactory	**8.0**	8.0	6.0	8.8	1.8	18.7	9.5	3.6	6.9
Poor	**5.3**	4.1	3.8	6.7	2.6	12.6	3.7	1.8	8.0
Unknown	**13.7**	9.2	18.1	10.7	8.6	12.3	19.5	20.2	9.2

Source: Savezni Zavod za Statistiku, *Jugoslovensko javno mnenje*, A-3 (Belgrade, 1964), 66 (Sample size: 2,527 respondents).

often declare themselves 'Yugoslavs'. But even in these cases that they would grow up to attain a Serbian national consciousness (e.g. in Novi Sad and other urban centres) still the personal consciousness of the mixed parentage would function as a catalyst for the development of a more tolerant outlook on other groups.

Vojvodina's prosperity led many Serbs and 'others' to believe more firmly that their province must have its own say over its administration, especially in regard to the management of economic facilities and resources. This strengthened popular commitment to Vojvodinian regional identity. This was reinforced by the high frequency of mixed marriages as well as the long-standing tradition of grassroots cohabitation among populations with different origins. To these should be added the emphasis given on Vojvodina's cultural plurality and different historic experience, in relation to the rest of Serbia, in the provincial schooling curriculum.[113] This, however, in no way did ever correspond to the encouragement of crypto-secessionist trends. In short, Vojvodina was one part of Yugoslavia where the Titoist slogan '*bratstvo i jedinstvo*' ('brotherhood and unity') found its practical implementation to a very large extent.

---

[113] Some information on this issue was disclosed to the author in the course of his field research in Vojvodina (Interview with historian at the University of Novi Sad; 13 March 2001).

3

Vojvodina in the 1990s: From the Termination of Autonomy to the Fall of Slobodan Milošević

In the beginning, this chapter positions Vojvodina inside the context of Slobodan Milošević's 'anti-bureaucratic revolution' and the new wave of Serbian nationalism. Major attention is paid to the recall of provincial autonomy for Vojvodina within the frame of the constitutional reforms. Then, the focus shifts towards the deterioration of the socio-economic situation in Vojvodina with the emphasis on the impact of Serbia's economic crisis and the influx of refugees from Croatia and Bosnia. This chapter underlines the politicization of Vojvodina's regional identity, since the second half of the 1990s, and its operation as a catalyst which provided a common ground for a variety of opposition forces in the province.

The termination of Vojvodina's autonomy

This section centres on the suspension of Vojvodina's autonomy as part of the constitutional reforms implemented within the frame of Slobodan Milošević's 'anti-bureaucratic revolution'. By the late 1980s and early 1990s, the ideological vacuum caused by the dissolution of the Socialist Federal Republic of Yugoslavia, in combination with the failure of the self-management system, generated much collective insecurity among Vojvodinians. At a first instance, this manifested in the support that Vojvodinian voters expressed towards the nationalist and re-centralizing agenda endorsed by the new Serbian elites.

The rise of Slobodan Milošević and Serbia's new multiparty landscape

Under the leadership of Ivan Stambolić, the Serbian LC had become highly vocal over the state of interethnic relations in Kosovo and the increasing political sovereignty of its Albanian population. Serbian fears intensified after the troubles of 1981 and the ethnic harassment of Kosovo's Serbs and Montenegrins. Moreover, the high birth rate of the Kosovan Albanians boosted anxieties over the prospects of the Kosovan Serbs' 'demographic extinction'. Quite a few Serbian grievances did bear legitimacy. The problem of resurgent Albanian nationalism in Kosovo was a living reality. So was the plight of the province's Serbs and Montenegrins, many of whom emigrated from Kosovo not solely on grounds of the deteriorating economic situation but also under harassment.

The crucial problem was that, even well into the mid-1980s, there was little indication that the LCY apparatus would make any compromise with regard to the reorganization of the self-management system, let alone a constitutional revision. This irritated many in Serbia, encouraging the cultivation of nationalist tendencies. Even Serbia's dissent was channelled through the structures of the Serbian Party bureaucracy. Therefore, there always remained a possibility that the Serbian Party elites might take advantage of their self-assigned role as 'defenders of the Serbian national interests' in order to gain popular legitimacy and cement their status in the transitional phase to come. Public grievances were soon voiced more concretely on the governmental level. Slobodan Milošević, an Ivan Stambolić protégé, was the then chairman of the Serbian LC. Until that time, Milošević fit into the category of the conformist bureaucrat and was no prone at all to nationalistic deviations.[1] Nevertheless, he soon discovered the benefits of the tactical employment of nationalist rhetoric as a means of mass mobilization and legitimization of authority.

---

[1] Tim Judah, *The Serbs: History, Myth and the Destruction of Yugoslavia* (New Haven, CT and London: Yale University Press, 2000), 160.

On 22 September 1987, at the 8th Session of the Serbian LC, Milošević called a no-confidence vote and deposed his former mentor, Stambolić. Popular support to Milošević's programme largely sprang from the dissatisfaction with the 1974 system of provincial autonomies (mainly on Kosovo) among many in Serbia. This interceded with the discontent of many Serbs over the fact that several politicians and senior administrators had been able to enrich themselves and evade accountability by means of short-term service. In mass rallies held throughout Serbia (*događaji naroda*/'happenings of the people'), Milošević castigated the Party *fotelјaši* ('sitters in armchairs') who were so distanced from the problems of the ordinary people and so self-centred in their ambition to maximize political profit.[2] The rise of the Milošević phenomenon heightened the tension between Serbia and the other republics. This culminated at the 14th Congress of the LCY (January 1990), when the Slovene delegates left the session, followed by the Croats. The ensuing development, following the end of the LCY, was the official affirmation of political pluralism across the country. Nevertheless, having to choose between *ethnos* and *demos* as a source of legitimization of their authority, the emerging elites throughout Yugoslavia opted for the former.[3]

On 16/17 July 1990, the Serbian LC merged with the Socialist Alliance of Working People of Serbia into the *Socijalistička Partija Srbije* (Socialist Party of Serbia, SPS). The congress affirmed Slobodan Milošević's role as the president of the new party. SPS declared that Serbia must be a united (*jedinstvena*) republic within Yugoslavia. It was added that 'the autonomous provinces cannot have the attributes of states; only some form of territorial autonomy' and that 'those

---

[2] The peak-point was Milošević's speech to an estimated crowd of 1 million Serbs on 28 June 1989, at Gazimestan, Kosovo (the Vidovdan celebration and the 600th anniversary of the Battle of Kosovo). This speech was an amalgamation between older strands of national myth and legend and socialist-style slogans about socio-economic prosperity. Robert Thomas, *Serbia under Milosevic: Politics in the 1990s* (London: Hurst and Company, 2000), 50.

[3] Lenard Cohen, *Broken Bonds: The Disintegration of Yugoslavia* (Colorado: Westview Press, 1993), 88–107; R Lampe John, *Yugoslavia as History: Twice There Was a Country*, Cambridge: Cambridge University Press (2000), 357–64.

competencies typical of a state must be exercised by the republican organs throughout the entire territory of Serbia'. SPS stressed that it was its obligation to secure the return and safety of the evicted Serbs and Montenegrins to Kosovo, whereas Vojvodina's experience of peaceful multiethnic cohabitation was proposed as an example to be used in the case of Kosovo.[4]

Later, in 1992, the party designated Vojvodina as 'an indivisible part of Serbia, with all its historical and other specificities'.[5] Regarding the province's national minorities, SPS specified the following rights: the right to education and public information in their mother tongues; the right to preserve their cultural heritage and develop their cultural identity; and the right to equal participation in political life. SPS underlined that they would fight against all political forces that opted for the division of Vojvodina or its separation of Serbia (without naming them). The party stated that it would respect the economic particularities of Vojvodina but underlined that 'these particularities must always be viewed in relation to the wider spectrum of the republic's economic policies'.

The formation of parties with little or non-existent affiliation to the Communist legacy became manifest in 1990. The most notable of them was the *Srpski Pokret Obnove* (Serbian Renewal Movement, SPO), founded in August 1990 by Vuk Drašković, a Banat-born dissident writer and journalist. The party's programme reflected an idiosyncratic amalgamation between selected elements from Western European Christian Democracy and Serbian neo-traditionalism. It combined features of classical liberalism, neo-traditionalism (e.g. SPO's allusions to the monarchy and the Chetnik movement) and moderate nationalism.[6] Further to the right stood *Srpska Radikalna Stranka*

---

[4] *Programske osnove Socijalističke Partije Srbije*, Prvi Kongres (16 jula 1990. godine, Beograd).
[5] *Osnove programa Socijalističke Partije Srbije* (Drugi kongres, 23/24 oktobra 1992.godine, Beograd).
[6] SPO condemned the atrocities committed by all sides in the interethnic conflicts and demonstrated a flexible attitude over the resolution of the Yugoslav crisis, during the first half of the 1990s. *Program Srpskog Pokreta Obnove* (http://www.spo.org.yu).

(Serbian Radical Party, SRS), formed on 23 February 1991, under the leadership of Vojislav Šešelj.[7] The Radicals promoted an overarching notion of Serbian national identity which was to overshadow any societal/ideological cleavages and prioritized the unification of all Serb-inhabited territories in the former Yugoslavia.[8]

A different initiative, in comparison to SPO and SRS, was undertaken by the *Demokratska Stranka* (Democratic Party, DS), formed on 12 December 1989. The party leadership designated the DS as 'a civic party of liberal orientation' and, programmatically, espoused new norms of political engagement such as individualism and secularism, consensus politics, respect to private ownership and social egalitarianism.[9] The *Demokratska Stranka Srbije* (Democratic Party of Serbia, DSS) was a conservative right-wing party that sprang from the bosom of the DS in July 1992. The party leader, Vojislav Koštunica, is a constitutional theorist and publisher of certain works with a critical attitude towards the structures and operation of the old Yugoslavia. Koštunica and his team had departed from DS on grounds of tactical disagreements.[10]

The first multiparty elections in Serbia, in December 1990, were won by the Socialists and Milošević amid charges of media manipulation by the opposition. The international recognition of Bosnia-Herzegovina in April 1992 brought about groundbreaking developments. On 27 April 1992, the allied leaderships of Serbia and Montenegro agreed on the formation of a joint state under the designation the 'Federal Republic of Yugoslavia'. The hurried way that the first federal elections were scheduled caused the main opposition parties to boycott the poll in an act of protest. SPS gained an easy victory, followed by the Radicals. The dissolution of the old federation was accompanied by the imposition of

---

[7] The Serbian Radical Party was formed by the merger of the smaller Serbian Chetnik Movement and the equally small National Radical Party. Vojislav Šešelj is a Sarajevo-born lawyer who, during the 1980s, had been repeatedly sentenced to prison on accusations of nationalist activities.

[8] *Program Srpske Radikalne Stranke* (http://www.srs.org.yu).

[9] *Politički Program Demokratske Stranke* (http://www.ds.org.yu).

[10] 'Kad jaganci utihnu', Vojislav Koštunica interviewed by Bogdan Ivanišević, in *NIN*, 3 April 1992.

sanctions on the 'third' Yugoslavia by the UN Security Council (30 May 1992)[11] which took a devastating toll on the economy.

The 'anti-bureaucratic revolution' in Vojvodina: Actors and developments

Although the situation in Kosovo possessed a focal locus in the rhetoric of the 'anti-bureaucratic revolution', it was the other autonomous province, Vojvodina, which felt the impact of this political phenomenon first. Slobodan Milošević had called for a revision of the autonomies system, as early as in the mid-1980s.[12] Soon words matched with deeds. Between July and September 1988, groups of Kosovan Serb protesters travelled to Novi Sad in order to voice their plight under ethnic harassment to the Vojvodinian public.[13] In the course of the demonstrations, the Vojvodinian LC were castigated as '*lopovi i izdajnici*' ('thieves and traitors') and the imposition of urgent measures for the protection of the Serbian population in Kosovo was demanded. The protesters were welcomed by the local clergy and the workers in certain Novi Sad firms (e.g. *Jugoalat*).

By that time, the Vojvodinian Central Committee comprised figures such as Boško Krunić, former general Petar Matić, Đorđe Stojšić and Milovan Šogorov. The Vojvodinian leadership's initial reaction to the impending developments was to condemn the organization of mass rallies and the accusations directed against it by the Serbian leadership as 'the escalation of the Serbian nationalist and bureaucratic struggle for the unscrupulous violation of the Constitution'.[14] Đorđe Stojšić went a step further and accused Milošević of preparing the soil for a civil war

---

[11] Jovan Teokarević, 'Neither War nor Peace: Serbia and Montenegro in the First Half of the 1990s', in *Yugoslavia and After: A Study in Fragmentation, Despair and Rebirth*, ed. D. A. Dyker and I. Vejvoda (London and New York: Longman, 1996), 185–6.
[12] Boarov Dimitrije, *Politička Istorija Vojvodine* (Novi Sad: Matica Srpska, 2001), 213–14.
[13] The first major '*narodni događaj*' was organized on 9 July, the second on 25 September.
[14] Statement by Živan Berisavljević (a member of the Vojvodinian Central Committee) in *NIN*, on 5 July 1988. Boarov, *Politička Istorija Vojvodine*, 214.

in Yugoslavia. Nevertheless, the Vojvodinian LC was powerless and its popularity in the province was remarkably low. This had resulted from the countrywide disappointment with the deficiency of the administrative mechanism, the malfunction of the self-management system and the ensuing deterioration of the economy and the living standards. Consequently, a declining percentage among the Vojvodinian population, especially the youth, wished to join the LCY by the late 1980s.[15]

On the top level, the Vojvodinian leadership could not seek support from the other federal units (let alone Kosovo's predominantly Albanian leadership) in its antagonism with the Serbian Party apparatus, since this would not have positive repercussions for the leadership on Vojvodina's Serbian majority. The powerlessness of the provincial LC, in combination with Vojvodina's Serbian national majority, was the major factor that made the 'anti-bureaucratic' experimentation most likely to commence from the Serbian north. The peak point of the 'anti-bureaucratic' happenings was the *narodni miting* organized in Novi Sad on 5 October. The leading part was played by Mihalj Kertes, an ethnic Hungarian and secretary of the Party Committee in Bačka Topola. Kertes was joined by Radovan Pavkov and Nedeljko Sipovac. In the course of the so-called 'yogurt revolution',[16] an approximately 100,000 strong crowd marched through the streets of the Vojvodinian capital. As a result of the mounting pressure, the Vojvodinian Party Committee resigned on the following day. The first battle of Milošević's 'anti-bureaucratic revolution' had been won.

At this point, it might be interesting to make a reference to the Yugoslav leadership's stance vis-à-vis the Vojvodinian crisis. On 30 July, the Federal Presidium issued a statement according to which 'illegal *narodni mitinzi* such as those organized in Novi Sad should be prevented as far as possible'.[17] The Presidium, however, equally

---

[15] Srečko Mihajlović, 'Od dobrih podanika ka pluralizmu', in *Pregled Rezultat Istraživanja*, ed. Nadezda Bogdanović (Belgrade: Savez Socijalističke Omladine Srbije, 1990), 21.

[16] This '*narodni događaj*' was nicknamed 'the yogurt revolution' because the protesters repeatedly pelted with yogurt the headquarters of the Vojvodinian LC.

[17] *Politika*, 31 July 1988.

criticized the Vojvodinian LC for not having received a delegation from the demonstrators and not having engaged in 'a broad discussion with them'. Even further, the Presidium recommended that certain 'constitutional reforms' should be initiated within Serbia. In other words, the Presidium's statement gave Milošević the green light he needed in order to carry on with his objectives.

First of all, one might argue that the LCY's position was conditioned by ideological catalysts. At that time, the head of the Federal Central Committee was Stipe Šuvar, a Croat and a committed Communist. By the late 1980s, Šuvar and other high-rank federal officials had started getting increasingly worried with the way that the authority of the federal organs and the cohesion of the federation as such had deteriorated in the process of Yugoslavia's 'confederalization'. In the Vojvodinian case, Stipe Šuvar and his associates possibly saw the extended jurisdiction enjoyed by Serbia's autonomous provinces as detrimental to the function of the federal mechanism. This assumption is reinforced through reference to the criticism levied towards the Kosovan leadership in the same statement for 'not having cooperated adequately with the Serbian Central Committee over the Kosovan question, as specified by the Federal Central Committee'. Therefore, one might contend that a common ground was found by default between the worries of federal officials over the lack of cohesion within Yugoslavia and Milošević's direct objectives within Serbia.

According to a complementary assumption, one might argue that the LCY's stance was prompted by tactical considerations. The emergence of the Milošević phenomenon and the fashion that the Serb grievances were forthrightly voiced might have warned the federal officials of the wider dynamics of the Serb resentment within Yugoslavia. Despite the fact that Vojvodina was constitutionally granted its independent representation at the federal presidency, the federal officials might have preferred to treat the issue of the autonomous provinces as an 'intra-Serbian' matter so as to appease the virulent new leadership in Serbia. In the case of Vojvodina, the adoption of this approach might have been facilitated by the fact that the Vojvodinian Central Committee consisted predominantly of Serbs as well as by the fact that the province's national majority was Serbian. Therefore, the clash between the republican and the Vojvodinian elites might appear as an 'internal' clash between two essentially Serbian bureaucracies. This argument is reinforced by the fact that the federal leadership held almost the same stance in regard with the developments that took place a little bit later in Serbia's 'sister-republic', Montenegro.[18] Finally, the absence of a 'single-man factor' (e.g. Tito) who could handle the situation in a more drastic manner might have additionally urged the federal leadership towards the adoption of a more compromising stance on Vojvodina.

Popular bases of support and the impact of the 'anti-bureaucratic revolution' in Vojvodina

The 'anti-bureaucratic revolution' in Vojvodina found broad support among pro-Milošević functionaries such as Mihalj Kertes. These individuals, regardless of whether they were old settlers, colonists or even belonged to one of the province's ethnic minorities, saw the emergence of the new order in Serbia as a fine opportunity for their social and political advancement. The 'anti-bureaucratic' movement was regarded from a positive angle, as was the case all over Serbia, by a younger generation of functionaries who saw themselves marginalized within the provincial Party structures by the representatives of the Partisan generation.[19] Following the resignation of the Vojvodinian LC in October 1988, Milošević took advantage of the internal cleavage between the younger and the older generations and recruited his loyalists within the 'reformed' Vojvodinian LC mainly from the former segment.

---

[18] The installation of Momir Bulatović as Party chief in Montenegro, in December 1988, was not compatible to the established procedures, according to which such appointments were to be made locally and not in Belgrade.

[19] By early 1988, younger people made up a mere 14 per cent of the participants in the Vojvodinian LC. Dubravka Stankov, 'Kretanja ka socijalno-klasnoj i nacionalnoj strukturi SKJ', *Komunist*, 1 January 1990, 14–15.

When it comes to the popular bases of support of the 'anti-bureaucratic' revolution in Vojvodina, the question becomes more complicated. One thing that is for sure is that the province's minorities did not see from a positive angle the curtailment of Vojvodinian autonomy since this would imperil the constitutional rights, which they had enjoyed so far. As far as the Serbian national majority was concerned, it is quite difficult to assess whether their either positive or negative disposition towards the 'yogurt revolution' was decisively conditioned by the old settlers/colonists fragmentation. Sociological surveys conducted in Vojvodina over the late 1980s had observed the emergence of pro-authoritarian and 'messianic' trends among the populace. Largely prompted by the malfunction of the administrative system, a notable percentage of Vojvodinians longed for the advent of an 'honest and powerful leader' who could impose the law and reform the system's ills with no hesitations.[20] There was also felt a necessity for essential changes in the political landscape.[21] Under these circumstances, there was always a possibility that the emergence of a movement such as the 'anti-bureaucratic revolution', claiming to heal all aforementioned ills, would gain some popular support in Vojvodina, at least at an initial stage.

Nevertheless, other surveys conducted in Vojvodina over the same period hint towards a high percentage of colonists in the 1988 *narodni mitinzi*.[22] It is not difficult to assess why the 'anti bureaucratic revolution' might appeal to quite a few colonists. As previously mentioned, the colonists had generally enjoyed political and social benefits in Vojvodina, as a result of theirs, or their families', participation in the Partisan movement. Therefore, in the face of the

---

[20] Molnar Aleksandar, *Osnovna Prava Čoveka i Raspad Jugoslavije* (Novi Sad: Visio Mundi Academic Press, 1994), 101.
[21] Interview with sociologist at the University of Novi Sad; 13 March 2001.
[22] According to a joint research carried out by the political analysts Sava Kerčov, Jovo Radoš and Aleksandar Raić, only two out of the twenty-eight *narodni mitinzi* in total were held in Vojvodinian localities with a majority old settler population. By contrast, most of these events were organized in urban or rural communities where a significant percentage of colonists resided. Sava Kerčov, Jovo Radoš and Aleksandar Raić, *Mitinzi u Vojvodini 1988. godine-rađanje političkog pluralizma* (Novi Sad: Matica Srpska, 1990).

deterioration of the administrative structures and the slow dissolution of the federation, it is certain that a considerable portion among the colonists felt that all their benefits would evaporate in case a radical change in the political status quo took place. Consequently, the 'anti-bureaucratic' revolution's programmatic adherence to the values of the Partisan movement would appear to quite a few colonists as an, if only formal, guarantee that their erstwhile gains would not be lost in the uncertain transitional era.

In regard to the old settlers, there can be made some assumptions that this segment might be more sensitive towards the prospect of their province being stripped of its competencies. First, the pre-'yogurt revolution' elites in Vojvodina consisted predominantly of Serbian old settlers. Moreover, Vojvodina had taken advantage of quite a few post-1974 constitutional guarantees, especially economic, and the province's population enjoyed living standards higher than the Serbian average. Consequently, any possible harmonization of the province's economic planning with that of the rest of Serbia would be potentially detrimental to the living standards enjoyed by Vojvodinians so far.

However, there is evidence that the nationalist upheaval of the late 1980s and the early 1990s also had repercussions among Vojvodina's old settlers. Quite a few old settlers started taking pride again in the fact that Vojvodina was the cradle of the modern Serbian national movement. This attitude manifested on a popular as well as on an elite level (e.g. political circles, academics) during that period. The Novi Sad sociologist Lazar Vrkatić offers a specific explanation regarding the emergence of that trend among Vojvodina's old settlers. Vrkatić claims that the ideological touchstones of 'brotherhood and unity' and self-management were replaced in Serbia by an adherence to some equally collectivist but peculiarly Serbian ethno-cultural concepts which find their full manifestation in the spirit of the nineteenth-century *Načertanje*. With regard to Vojvodina's old settlers, Vrkatić contends that 'they were soon entangled in a renewed obsession with traditionalist beliefs (e.g. Eastern Orthodoxy) as well as a feeling of nostalgia for the 19th century romantic ethno-cultural ideals'.[23]

In accordance with this trend, the post-1974 system of autonomies was not viewed from a positive angle. It might be argued that, just like Ljuba Jovanović did in 1918, quite a few old settlers came to see autonomy for a predominantly Serbian-populated region within Serbia as unnecessary.[24] Consequently, regardless of their stance towards the rising Serbian apparatus, these old settlers did not see from a negative perspective the termination of Vojvodina's autonomy. The following excerpts from a work published in 1991 by the historian Čedomir Popov (an old settler himself) summarize the earlier described trend among Vojvodina's old settlers. According to Popov, 'there does not exist any historical evidence for the affirmation of a distinct "Vojvodinian identity" as contrasted to the Serbian one ... this was a fairly recent endeavor by Kardelj and the Comintern in their attempt to weaken the status of Serbs and Serbia within Yugoslavia.'[25] The author adds that it was in Vojvodina where 'the Serbian *narod* acquired for the first time a modern national consciousness and flourished culturally through the establishment of its schools, cultural institutions and the development of its literature and arts ... this is where the contribution of Vojvodina to the entire Serbian nation lies'.[26]

The 'anti-bureaucratic revolution' resulted in the swift removal of key employees from their posts.[27] No structural changes in the system of the administrative bureaucracy were introduced. Milošević kept the existing system almost intact and appointed a more loyal staff at the various posts. As was the case all over Serbia, the changes came from within the

---

[23] Lazar Vrkatić, 'Srbi u Vojvodini i njihov državno-pravni osnov', *Sociološki Pregled* XXXIV, no. 3–4 (2000): 129.

[24] Ljuba Jovanović, a Vojvodinian National-Radical, had stated in 1918 that 'the Serbian idea in Vojvodina did not imply its independence in relation to its south but it meant independence from Budapest and the Magyars only'. Boarov, *Politička Istorija Vojvodine*, 247.

[25] Čedomir and Jelena Popov, *Autonomija Vojvodine-Srpsko Pitanje* (Novi Sad: Matica Srpska, 1991), 66–70.

[26] Ibid.

[27] Boarov, *Politička Istorija Vojvodine*, 217–18.

former Communist bureaucracy and the newly appointed staff normally originated from the younger strata within that bureaucracy. Even more crucial was the external significance of Milošević's 'revolutionary' experimentation in Vojvodina. Following the purge of the Vojvodinian elites, the rising apparatus could focus on the next target, namely Montenegro. Although a constituent republic and not an autonomous province, just as in Vojvodina the national majority was Serbian, in Montenegro it was Montenegrin, a *narod* akin to the Serbs. Therefore, the rhetoric of the 'anti-bureaucratic revolution' in regard to the plight of the Kosovan Serbs and Montenegrins could gain a mass appeal, also bearing in mind that Montenegro possessed its own, still unreliable, Albanian minority. As soon as 7 October 1988, crowds as large as those in Novi Sad gathered in Titograd in order to demand the resignation of the Montenegrin leadership. By the end of 1988, the Montenegrin LC was staffed by figures loyal to the Belgrade apparatus (including the future chief engineer of Montenegrin independence, Milo Đukanović).

Vojvodina and Kosovo: A comparison

Having dealt with the Vojvodinian and the Montenegrin cases successfully, Milošević could aim at the 'heart of the matter', Kosovo. A specificity that would not render the mass mobilization tactic fruitful in Kosovo was the demographic preponderance of its Albanian population (90 per cent by 1991). In this case, the provincial leadership was replaced by means of pressures from behind the scene and the reinforcement of the policing mechanism. As an initial indication of this strategy, in May 1988, the vocal Azem Vllasi was replaced in the leadership of the Kosovan LC by the less vocal, though no Milošević protégé, Kaqusha Jashari. More crucial developments occurred in November 1988, when the entire Kosovan leadership was forced to resign, due to its opposition to Belgrade's proposals for a revision of the status of the autonomous provinces, and Rahman Morina was appointed the new chairman. At the same time, an additional 400 police was brought in from outside the province.

Soon after the replacement of the Kosovan leadership, a notable difference between the Vojvodinian and the Kosovan cases became manifest. Whereas in the former case, mass mobilization was employed as a means to depose the provincial leadership, in the latter case the deposed elites made use of the same tactic in order to reclaim their lost status. In late 1988, Kosovan Albanians were mobilized through happenings such as the student rallies in Priština and the miners' hunger strike in Trepća. On 27 February 1988, Morina and his team were forced to resign as a result of public pressures. Nevertheless, following the Federal Presidium's announcement for the imposition of special measures in Kosovo, the policing of the province intensified. On 2 March, Vllasi was arrested on charges of 'counterrevolutionary activity' and the provincial assembly accepted the proposed amendments (24 March). A Serb, Tomislav Sekulić, became the new Kosovan Party chief. Since then, Kosovo was marked by the imposition of a chronic state of alert in the province by Belgrade, the gradual reduction of Albanian cultural and educational activities, as well as the organization of ethnic Albanians within 'parallel' structures.

Another crucial qualitative difference between Kosovo and Vojvodina was the historic–cultural dynamics of the former. The renewed emphasis attached on Kosovo as the symbolic capital of Serbdom resulted in the gradual elevation of the province to the status of a 'sacred territory' and a master symbol of the new wave of Serbian nationalism.[28] This process was facilitated by the intelligentsia and the re-elaboration of highly romantic interpretations of the history of the Serbian *narod*, in terms of martyr-images often emanating from the symbolism of the medieval battle at Kosovo Polje (e.g. the 'Serbian Golgotha'). The latter touched a sensitive chord among Vojvodina's old settlers as well, many of who would collectively view the first Serb settlers in Vojvodina as the glorious continuation of the, evicted from the 'sacred territory', *Velika Seoba* generation.

[28] Kosovo was the cultural heartland of the medieval Serbian Empire and home to cultural and religious monuments of primary significance to the Serbs (e.g. the Patriarchy of Peć, the monasteries of Dečan and Gracanica).

The major qualitative difference between the two cases was that in Kosovo ethnicity was rendered the main determinant in the contested claims between Belgrade and Priština. The Albanian LC elites defended Kosovo's autonomy by reference to the constitutional right granted to the Albanian *narodnost* to self-determine within the province. Following the developments in 1989, Albanian demands were forthrightly voiced by reference to the 'historic right' of the Albanian population to self-determine within Kosovo where it constituted the local majority. In turn, Belgrade responded with accusations of separatism and its formal adherence to a civic interpretation of the right to self-determination whereby Albanians constituted the local majority in Kosovo but a minority within Serbia and FR Yugoslavia. Furthermore, the right to self-determination was vested to the entirety of the 'people' (the citizens) of Serbia and FR Yugoslavia and not to national minorities on ethno-territorial grounds.[29]

In Vojvodina, the dispute between Belgrade and Novi Sad could in no way be couched in an ethnic phraseology. Contrary to Kosovo where the Albanian community was compact and demographically preponderant, in Vojvodina not only was the regional majority Serb (Table 4) but the 43 per cent of the population that was not Serb belonged to a multitude of ethnic affiliations, with an uneven territorial distribution, that had no common ground with regard to their aspirations. The antagonism between Novi Sad and Belgrade was of an essentially ideological character, focusing on the structural organization of Yugoslavia. In short, it was a case of 'reformists versus neo-integralists'. Although at the various sessions of the LCY, over the 1980s, the viewpoints of the Serbian and Vojvodinian apparatuses had clashed, it seems very unlikely that a predominantly Serb provincial committee would ever engineer the separation of a predominantly Serbian province from the rest of the republic. The intercultural substratum that manifested as 'Vojvodinian identity' over the Communist era served, among others, as a catalyst that facilitated the development of positive inter-communal relations on the

---

[29] *The Constitution of the Socialist Federal Republic of Yugoslavia*, 1974, Articles 1–3.

Table 4 The ethnic structure of the autonomous province of Vojvodina according to the 1991 national census

Ethnic groups	Figures	Percentages
Serbs	1,143.723	56.79
Hungarians	339,491	16.86
Croats	74,808	3.71
Slovaks	63,545	3.16
Romanians	38,809	1.93
Montenegrins	44,838	2.23
Ruthenes	17,889	0.9
Albanians	2,556	0.13
Yugoslavs	174,295	8.65
Roma	24,336	1.21
Muslims	5,851	0.29
Others	83,718	4.14
TOTAL	**2,013.889**	**100.00**

Source: Savezni Zavod za Statistiku, *Popis stanovništva 1991*, knjiga 3 (Belgrade, 1993).

grassroots level. It never evolved to a trans-ethnic notion of identification that could challenge the established Serbian identity and generate fears of potential secession, as was the case with Kosovo and its Albanian elites' aspirations that were entrenched in the core notion of their *ethnos*.

There also exist qualitative differences in the way that Belgrade managed ethnopolitics in Kosovo and Vojvodina. In the former case, the method employed by the Serbian authorities in order to handle the issue of ethnic Albanian nationalism fits within the scope of 'hegemonic control'. This can be defined as coercive and/or co-optive rule with the aim to prevent an ethnic challenge to the state's order.[30] The means for preventing such a challenge are the monopolization of certain institutions (e.g. the police, the judicial system) and the

---

[30] J. McGarry and B. O'Leary, *The Politics of Ethnic Conflict Regulation: Cases of Protracted Ethnic Conflicts* (London: Routledge, 1993), 35–7.

practice of discrimination in employment allocation, public housing and education against the ethnic minority by the dominant group.³¹ In Kosovo, Belgrade pursued a policy of positive discrimination towards Serbs and Montenegrins in the police, the educational sector and the health services. Moreover, a tangible reduction of public information in the Albanian language was observed.

In Vojvodina, no such direct action was taken. No minority publications were banned or closed down and the RTS Novi Sad broadcasts in Vojvodina's minority languages were not seriously obstructed. The ruling apparatus remained cautious so as not to create the impression of generalizing when denouncing the 'separatist tendencies' among Vojvodina's national minorities. Such accusations were normally brought forward in a 'personalized' manner, directed against specific Hungarian or Croat interest groups. Also, the SPS officials stressed the participation of non-Serb nationals in the party's Vojvodinian branches, as a means to fight back on domestic and international accusations of nationalism.

There is a variety of explanations that can be offered with respect to SPS's policies on Vojvodina's national minorities. The one of them is that the apparatus's policies were largely conditioned by the absence of an imminent irredentist threat to the state's order, deriving from any of the province's national minorities. The other is that the generally satisfactory interethnic relations prevailing in Vojvodina might serve the regime in the propaganda field, domestically as well as internationally. On the domestic level this could serve in two ways. First, it could be used in order to convince Serbia's citizens that the regime knew how to manage interethnic relations. Even further, this would enable the regime to juxtapose those minorities and their political elites that pursued their aspirations through participation in the mainstream political arena (e.g. Vojvodina's Hungarians) to others that abstained or tried to sabotage the operation of mainstream political structures (namely,

---

³¹ One typical example of hegemonic control was the British policies in Northern Ireland between 1970 and 1972 in favour of the Unionist majority against the Republican minority – i.e. 'majoritarian' version of hegemonic control.

the Kosovan Albanians). In regard to the international dimension, this would enable the governing apparatus to capitalize on Vojvodina's multiethnic example in order to countervail international criticism on the situation in Kosovo and the rise of Serbian nationalism. In addition, this would enable the regime to contrast the situation of non-Serb ethnic groups in Vojvodina to the maltreatment of the ethnic Serbs resident elsewhere in the former Yugoslavia (most notably, Croatia).

Vojvodina in the early 1990s: Other sociopolitical aspects

Opinion polls witnessed particularly strong pro-federal tendencies among Vojvodinians.[32] On the one hand, this may serve as indication of worries that the strengthening of Belgrade's jurisdiction in Vojvodina might have a negative impact on the use of economic resources and the management of interethnic relations in the province. A somewhat complementary explanation might be given with regard to Vojvodina's Serb majority. In other words, many Vojvodinian Serbs presumably saw the enforcing power of the federal organs as the main guarantee that the collective rights of Serbs outside Serbia (e.g. Bosnia-Herzegovina and Croatia) would not be transgressed by the rising nationalist elites in the other republics. This explanation is highly valid in the case of the colonists, many of who had a 'personalized' interest in the fate of kin and friends in the old territory as well as a traumatic and easily manipulated collective memory of the *Ustaše* terror. The equation of powerful federal institutions with the protection of the collective rights of those Serbs outside Serbia seems to have been the case with the public opinion in *uža Srbija* and Montenegro as well.

[32] Stefica Bahtijarević and Goran Milaš, 'Reakcija javnost na mere i politiku SIV-a', in *Jugoslavija na kriznoj prekretnici*, ed. Liljana Bačević (Belgrade: Institut Društvenih Nauka, 1991), 97–8; Savezno Izvršno Veće, *Šta Misli Jugoslavija* (Belgrade: Federal Executive Committee, 1990), 31.

Finally, the late 1980s and early 1990s saw the reversion of Yugoslavia's citizens towards their ethno-cultural affiliations and Vojvodina was no exception to that trend.³³ Nevertheless, as becomes obvious in certain surveys, the frequently mixed ethnic background of quite a few Vojvodinians, as well as their residence in ethnically mixed localities functioned as catalysts for the development of a more flexible outlook towards 'others' and their cultural idiosyncrasies.³⁴ This factor, among others, facilitated maintaining positive intercultural relations in Vojvodina, always in comparison to what was the case elsewhere in the former Yugoslavia over the 1990s.

Vojvodina inside the new constitutional order of Serbia and the 'third' Yugoslavia

The new Serbian Constitution was passed by the Serbian Assembly on 28 September 1990.³⁵ In regard to the autonomous provinces, Article 6 clarified that 'the Republic of Serbia includes the Autonomous Province of Vojvodina and the Autonomous Province of Kosovo and Metohija, these being the forms of territorial autonomy'. Article 108 specified that 'the autonomous provinces have been formed in accordance with the particular national, historical, cultural and other characteristics of their areas'. It added that 'the territory of an autonomous province shall be determined by republican law'. This latter clause clearly contravened Article 5 of the 1974 Constitution.

The provisions of the 1990 Constitution stripped the autonomous provinces of their legislative and judicial competencies. From that point

---

³³ Molnar 1994, 91.
³⁴ According to an opinion poll carried out by the 'Belgrade Institute for Political Studies', a mere 5.4 per cent of the Vojvodinian respondents stated that they regarded their national group as 'sacred'. Marija Obradović, 'Vladajuća stranka: Ideologija i tehnologija dominacije', in Various authors, *Srpska strana rata* (Budapest: CEU Press, 1999), 494. Also, by 1991, 8.4 per cent of Vojvodina's inhabitants identified themselves as 'Yugoslavs', still the highest percentage throughout the crumbling federation. Especially in eight of Vojvodina's municipalities, individuals declaring that identity made up 10 per cent or more of the local population. Savezni Zavod za Statistiku, *Nacionalni sastav stanovništva po opštinama* (Belgrade: Federal Agency for Statistics, 1992).
³⁵ 'Ustav Republike Srbije', *Službeni Glasnik Republike Srbije*, broj 1/90.

onward, the main competencies of the provincial assemblies would be to appoint executives to the local government and enact sub-legal acts of a provincial jurisdiction, always in accordance with republican legislation. The relegation of their constitutions to statutes clearly signified that the autonomous provinces would no longer be constitutional parts of the crumbling federation in any sense. The 1990 Constitution defied the 1974 arrangements and amounted to a 'sovereignty declaration' for Serbia. As defined in Article 135, 'The republican authorities are empowered to adopt acts seeking to defend the interests of the republic, should Serbia faces threats to its rights and duties from either the Socialist Yugoslav federation or other republics.' The removal of the legislative and judicial competencies from the autonomous provinces was the first and major step towards this direction. As Miodrag Jovičić put it, 'Serbia's new constitution is not conceptualized as the constitution of a federal unit, but as the constitution of an independent state.'[36]

The Constitution of the Federal Republic of Yugoslavia was promulgated shortly after the state's formation on 27 April 1992.[37] The new Constitution no longer made any formal reference to the status of Serbia's autonomous provinces within the federation. Article 6 specified that 'a member republic shall be a state in which power is vested to its citizens ... a member republic shall be sovereign in matters which under the present Constitution are not reserved to the jurisdiction of FR Yugoslavia'. This clause placed, if only subtly, the administrative statuses of Vojvodina and Kosovo firmly inside the new arrangement stipulated in the 1990 Serbian Constitution. The Constitution of FR Yugoslavia established a loose union between Serbia and Montenegro. Political power remained within the component republics and into the hands of their presidents. Throughout the 1990s, this arrangement suited the objectives of the then allied Serbian-Montenegrin elites but, later, it evolved into a boomerang for Belgrade as a result of the centrifugal tendencies in Montenegro.

[36] Miodrag Jovičić, 'Konfederacija vodi u haos', *Stav*, 2 November 1990, 20–3.
[37] 'Ustav Savezne Republike Jugoslavije', *Službeni List Savezne Republike Jugoslavije*, 27 April 1992.

Serbia's 'lost decade' and its impact on Vojvodina

The early and mid-1990s were particularly turbulent times for Serbia and the 'third' Yugoslavia. This section critically outlines the political landscape, as well as the socio-economic realities, in Vojvodina during that period. Then, it assesses the state of interethnic relations. The economic sanctions, in combination with domestic mismanagement, resulted in the decline of living standards and the relative deterioration of inter-group relations in Vojvodina.

Serbia in turmoil: The SPS–SRS condominium and the political ramifications of the UN sanctions

The informal partnership between the Socialists and the Radicals marked Serbia's political landscape throughout the early 1990s. This manifested in their joint no-confidence vote against the Yugoslav PM Milan Panić and the Yugoslav President Dobrica Ćosić in winter 1992 and spring 1993. These individuals were deposed on the accusation of pursuing policies 'detrimental to the Serbian national interests'. Both parties had adopted the same strategy in regard to the developments in the former Yugoslavia. SRS, as well as SPS, favoured the territorial division of Bosnia-Herzegovina and Croatia along ethnic lines and the secession of *Republika Srpska* and the 'Serbian Republic of Krajina' from each republic, as internationally recognized by then. The two parties derived their support from similar social layers. These were the urban working class, the *lumpen* proletariat, pensioners and the residents in certain rural communities.[38] The economic programmes of SPS and SRS lured these target-groups to the two parties.[39] Both adhered to the principle of solidarity to pensioners and other 'endangered' groups. These standpoints exerted much influence on the lower strata that

---

[38] Vladimir Goati, *Izbori u SRJ od 1990 do 1998.-Volja građana ili izborna manipulacija* (Belgrade: CESID, 2001), 95.
[39] *Ekonomski i socijalni program SRS (1992)*, (http://www.srs.org.yu).

saw their status imperilled in the event of application of the liberal programme espoused by the opposition.[40]

During the December 1992 campaign for the Yugoslav and Serbian elections, the regime exerted much informal influence through media manipulation and voting irregularities.[41] Under these circumstances, the SPS won 1,478,918 votes and 73 seats at the Federal Assembly's Chamber of Citizens. The Radicals garnered 1,024,980 votes and 47 seats, whereas the DEPOS coalition finished third (809,731 votes/20 seats) and DS fourth (280,183 votes/5 seats). As for the Serbian parliamentary elections, SPS garnered 28.8 per cent of the votes and 40.4 per cent of the seats, SRS won 22.6 per cent of the votes and 29.2 per cent of the mandates, whereas DEPOS occupied the third place with 16.9 per cent of the votes and 20 per cent of the seats. Even though Milan Panić had managed to secure 1,516.693 votes (32.1 per cent), Slobodan Milošević was the winner of the presidential race with 2,515,047 votes (53.2 per cent).

Soon changes were triggered by the reinforced sanctions and their impact on the economy. Popular discontent with the socio-economic crisis was the key factor that made SPS emphasize its Socialist side instead of the nationalist one. Slogans of social egalitarianism and interethnic tolerance dominated the party's rhetoric. As for the opposition coalition (DEPOS),[42] its slogans were once again characterized by calls for strengthening the democratic institutions in Serbia as well as the necessity to reach an internationally acceptable solution over the conflicts in Croatia and Bosnia-Herzegovina. DSS was the only party, together with SRS, that maintained a hard line on the 'national question' as a result of their discontent with the allegedly unfavourable terms offered to the Bosnian Serbs by the Vance-Owen Peace Plan.

[40] Goati, *Izbori u SRJ od 1990 do 1998*, 88.
[41] Borislav Džuverović et al., *Izborna upotreba medija* (Belgrade: Institut društvenih nauka, 1994), 3. On the electoral irregularities, see the relevant report by the OSCE in *Borba*, 18 January 1993.
[42] DEPOS consisted of SPO and the smaller parties of the Citizens Alliance of Serbia (GSS) and the New Democracy (ND).

In the 1993 urgent Serbian elections, the Socialists won 36.7 per cent of the vote and 123 seats (49.2 per cent). Nevertheless, they were three seats short of commanding an absolute parliamentary majority. As for SRS, they suffered an utter defeat, garnering only 13.8 per cent of the votes and thirty-nine seats in the parliament (15.6 per cent). DEPOS secured 16.6 per cent of the votes and forty-five seats (18 per cent), DS 11.6 per cent of the votes and twenty-nine seats (11.6 per cent) and DSS 5.1 per cent of the vote and seven seats at the Serbian parliament (2.8 per cent). SPS managed to form a government with the support of the New Democracy's six representatives who decided to depart from DEPOS. The results of the 1993 elections signalled the gradual 'de-radicalization' of the electorate. This was prompted by the dominant belief within the society that the deteriorating socio-economic situation was primarily a by-product of the embargo.[43] Therefore, the adoption of a more flexible policy vis-à-vis the international community on the Yugoslav crisis came to be seen as the most viable option for the improvement of the situation. Serbia's electorate had shifted from ideological voting to 'issue voting'. The latter term regards the prevailing socio-economic situation as the definitive criterion for the choice of a party or candidate. In this light, voters opt for the parties that come closest to their micro-level interests and personal priorities.

Political participation in times of crisis: Elections in Vojvodina

The results of the Yugoslav/Serbian elections held in December 1992 and the urgent Serbian elections in December 1993 demonstrated the marginal preference of the Vojvodinian electorate, first, towards the Socialists and, to a secondary extent, the Radicals. These two parties were followed by DEPOS, DS, DSS and regionalist and minority parties

---

[43] According to a public survey, conducted by the Belgrade Centre for Politics and the Media and involving 1,000 respondents throughout Serbia, a rough majority of 35.7 per cent stated that Serbia's deteriorating socio-economic situation had resulted from the 'unjust UN sanctions regime'. *Politika*, 7 December 1993.

(Tables 5, 6 and 7). These results were, on the one hand, subject to 'objective' variables relevant throughout the whole of Serbia. One of them was the collective insecurity caused by the collapse of the old order within the former Yugoslavia, as well as certain policies by the international community towards the 'third' Yugoslavia (namely, the UN sanctions). Vojvodina's proximity to the war zone of Eastern Slavonia and the arrival of the first Serb refugees from Croatia intensified the anxieties of the province's Serb majority.

This insecurity generated a renewed emphasis on the importance of national solidarity as a means to overcome the crisis. This trend was communicated on the political level through support to parties with a

Table 5 The results of the Serbian parliamentary elections in Vojvodina, December 1992

SPS	284,685 votes	22.86 %	17 mandates	30.35% of the mandates
SRS	281,688 votes	22.62 %	17 mandates	30.35% of the mandates
VMDK	140,825 votes	11.3 %	9 mandates	16.07% of the mandates
DEPOS	191,603 votes	15.38 %	11 mandates	19.64% of the mandates
DS and RDSV	71,865 votes	5.77 %	2 mandates	3.57% of the mandates

Source: Savezni Zavod za Statistiku, *Statistički Godišnjak Savezne Republike Jugoslavije* (Belgrade, 1993).

Table 6 The results of the Yugoslav parliamentary elections in Vojvodina, December 1992

SPS	305,117 votes	24.45%	8 mandates	33.33% of the mandates
SRS	243,021 votes	19.47%	6 mandates	25% of the mandates
DEPOS	179,302 votes	14.37%	4 mandates	16.66% of the mandates
LSDV and NPP	35,943 votes	3.2%		
DS, RDSV and GSS	159,379 votes	12.8%	3 mandates	12.5% of the mandates
VMDK	106,036 votes	8.4%	3 mandates	12.5% of the mandates

Source: Savezni Zavod za Statistiku, *Izbori '92* (Belgrade, 1992).

Table 7 The results of the early Serbian parliamentary elections in Vojvodina, December 1993

SPS	340,227 votes	31.02%	23 mandates	41.07% of the mandates
DEPOS	134,230 votes	12.24%	9 mandates	16.07% of the mandates
SRS	168,937 votes	15.40%	11 mandates	19.64% of the mandates
DS	129,109 votes	11.77%	8 mandates	14.92% of the mandates
DSS	34,891 votes	3.18%		
VMDK	112,456 votes	10.25%	5 mandates	8.93% of the mandates
Democratic Coalition for Vojvodina	41,097 votes	3.75%		

Source: Republički Zavod za Statistiku, *Prevremeni izbori za narodne poslanike u Narodnoj Skupštini Republike Srbije* (Belgrade, 1994).

more vocal 'national' agenda, namely SPS and SRS. The success of the Socialists was facilitated by the favourable disposition of the provincial media towards SPS during the pre-electoral period.[44] It is needless to add that, just as it was the case elsewhere in Serbia, the Socialists had inherited almost intact the organizational structure of the Vojvodinian LC while the managers of the provincial firms (e.g. *Jugoalat* and the petrochemical industry in Novi Sad and Pančevo) were overtly sympathetic to SPS.

As far as the opposition parties are concerned, the objective variable that proved detrimental for the Serbian 'democratic opposition' in Vojvodina was its high degree of fragmentation. In December 1992, the opposition parties and coalitions (e.g. DEPOS, the LSDV–National Peasants' Party alliance and the DS–Reformist Party of Vojvodina [RDSV] coalition) secured altogether 30.37 per cent of the provincial vote. One year later, in December 1993, DS, the DSS, DEPOS and *Koalicija Vojvodina* (the latter comprising LSDV, RDSV and the National Peasants' Party) garnered altogether 30.94 per cent of the vote. Nevertheless, it was the lack of a common ground that prevented these

---

[44] D. Valić and B. Kostić, 'Samo budala veruje', *Nezavisni*, broj 40, 1993.

parties from forming a compact block against the Socialists in Vojvodina and taking advantage of the proportional electoral system. Another objective catalyst that affected the electoral landscape in Vojvodina was the remarkable degree of the electorate's abstention from voting. Approximately 21 per cent of the province's voters abstained from the republican and the federal elections held in December 1992. This percentage jumped to 31 per cent in December 1993. In regard to SRS, the Serbian electorate's swing towards less nationalist options, also took its toll on the Radicals' performance in the 1993 elections in Vojvodina.

Apart from these objective variables, the persistence of regional particularities played a pivotal part; most importantly the cleavage over the question of Vojvodina's autonomy. This brought about a clash of prerogatives between the *autonomaši* circles and the representatives of the larger, Belgrade-based, opposition parties in Vojvodina. Throughout the early and mid-1990s, SPO ruled out any prospects for regional cooperation with either LSDV or RDSV on the grounds that the need to bring an end to the Socialists' rule in Serbia, as a whole, and resolve the interethnic conflicts in the former Yugoslavia must take precedence over the *autonomaši*'s allegedly 'parochial' insistence on Vojvodina's status.

This is not to say that no common ground was found between the regionalist elites and the representatives of the Belgrade-based parties in Vojvodina. A suitable example was the conclusion of a regional alliance between DS and the Reformists in the December 1992 Serbian elections. On that occasion, the DS's provincial representatives turned out to be flexible and underlined the necessity for regionalization in Serbia, thus securing the backing of Vojvodina's second largest pro-autonomy party. However, the participation of a rival pro-autonomy coalition in the same elections, comprising the National Peasants' Party and LSDV, demonstrated that programmatic affinity cannot always provide common ground among political actors. By contrast, what became transparent was that the micro-level interests of party leaderships can often take precedence over any sort of programmatic or ideological affinities.

The formation of a solid opposition block to SPS in Vojvodina was equally hampered by the 'ethnic' factor; namely the Democratic Community of Vojvodina's Hungarians (*Vajdasagi Magyarok Demokratikus Kozossege*, VMDK) and their aspirations. Even though this party had delivered a decent performance in the early and mid-1990s, its insistence on the concept of ethno-territorial autonomy for Vojvodina's Hungarians stood as a primary obstacle in forging any alliance with the opposition parties. DS, DSS and DEPOS rejected VMDK's concept, on the basis that it would generate ethnic segregation and interethnic tensions in Vojvodina. The *autonomaši* criticized the party's ethno-territorial concept on the grounds that it contravened their civic orientation towards an 'autonomous Vojvodina for all'.

Political preferences in Vojvodina: The grassroots and socio-psychological dimensions

In both the December 1992 and December 1993 elections, the Socialists and the Radicals secured several votes among the urban proletariat resident in Vojvodina's industrial centres such as Novi Sad, Zrenjanin, Pančevo and Kikinda (Table 8). Empirical research demonstrates that the support of the lower strata towards these two parties interweaved with symptoms of ethno-cultural introversion. According to a survey conducted in Vojvodina during the early 1990s, by the sociologists Vladimir Ilić and Slobodan Cvejić, the ongoing developments across the former Yugoslavia somewhat reinforced the ethnic cleavages between Serb workers and their colleagues belonging to other nationalities, especially Croats and Hungarians.[45]

---

[45] Vladimir Ilić and Slobodan Cvejić, 'Vojvođani i nacionalizam', *Sociologija* XXXV, broj 4 (1993): 545.

Table 8 Electoral results by number of votes at selected municipalities in Vojvodina (including break-up by occupational, social and ethnic structure)

Novi Sad

Parties	Yugoslav Presidential 1992	Serbian 1992	Yugoslav 1992	Serbian 1993
SPS	76,315	32,543	40,451	38,643
SRS		43,009	32,222	27,524
DEPOS		31,608	30,590	17,898
DSS				5,793
DS				21,210
DS-RDSV		19,454		
DS-RDSV-GSS			24,445	
NPP		1,253		
VMDK		5,676	5,950	4,139
DEPOS-Milan Panić	71,995			
Others	15,594	26,112	26,159	25,721

Occupational structure

Social sector	Industry and mining	Trade	Education and culture	Private entrepreneurs
99,855 employees	25,880 employees	12,428 employees	12,920 employees	14,367 employees

Total population: 265,464 residents

Pančevo

Parties	Yugoslav Presidential 1992	Serbian 1992	Yugoslav 1992	Serbian 1993
SPS	36,796	19,737	17,390	22,131
SRS		16,621	18,216	9,199
DEPOS		19,778	17,352	14,763
DSS				3,715
DS				12,098

Parties	Yugoslav Presidential 1992	Serbian 1992	Yugoslav 1992	Serbian 1993
DS-RDSV		3,143	6,323	
DS-RDSV-GSS				
NPP		762		
VMDK		1,319	874	726
DEPOS-Milan Panić	30,800			
Others	6,336	9,772	11,599	5,000

Occupational structure

Social sector	Industry and mining	Trade	Education and culture	Private entrepreneurs
36,591 employees	18,568 employees	2,720 employees	1,878 employees	2,655 employees

Total population: 125,261 residents

Zrenjanin

Parties	Yugoslav Presidential 1992	Serbian 1992	Yugoslav 1992	Serbian 1993
SPS	40,580	20,190	18,211	23,862
SRS		20,706	21,744	12,694
DEPOS		13,596	9,176	8,471
DSS				2,990
DS				12,147
DS-RDSV		5,483	15,923	
DS-RDSV-GSS				
NPP		1,033		
VMDK		4,783	1,716	3,374
DEPOS-Milan Panić	31,771			
Others	7,552	11,015	10,066	7,143

Occupational structure

Social sector	Industry and mining	Trade	Education and culture	Private entrepreneurs
38,958 employees	16,326 employees	3,984 employees	2,631 employees	2,871 employees

Total population: 136,778 residents

Sremska Mitrovica

Parties	Yugoslav Presidential 1992	Serbian 1992	Yugoslav 1992	Serbian 1993
SPS	33,226	14,293	17,738	16,493
SRS		17,323	12,351	10,559
DEPOS		8,294	8,778	6,226
DSS				1,260
DS				5,262
DS–RDSV		2,276		
DS–RDSV–GSS			3,229	
NPP		1,176		
VMDK		309	348	109
DEPOS-Milan Panić	14,153			
Others	5,168	6,357	7,409	5,453

Stara Pazova

Parties	Yugoslav Presidential 1992	Serbian 1992	Yugoslav 1992	Serbian 1993
SPS	18,449	7,182	9,228	9,229
SRS		10,326	7,104	6,944
DEPOS		6,020	6,074	5,053
DSS				1,293
DS				3,153
DS–RDSV		1,397		

Parties	Yugoslav Presidential 1992	Serbian 1992	Yugoslav 1992	Serbian 1993
DS-RDSV-GSS			2,126	
NPP		563		
VMDK		248	271	81
DEPOS-Milan Panić	11,151			
Others	2,702	4,925	5,798	3,026

Sombor

Parties	Yugoslav Presidential 1992	Serbian 1992	Yugoslav 1992	Serbian 1993
SPS	30,107	14,448	17,714	17,618
SRS		14,904	10,826	8,328
DEPOS		7,064	7,741	4,812
DSS				2,407
DS				5,899
DS-RDSV				
DS-RDSV-GSS		3,871	5,305	
NPP		685		
VMDK		5,778	5,796	4,476
DEPOS-Milan Panić	22,761			
Others	4,561	8,643	8,212	5,598

Municipalities	Sremska Mitrovica	Stara Pazova	Sombor
Number of refugees out of the total population	12,485 out of 85,238 residents	16,177 out of 57,291 residents	25,311 out of 96,105 residents

Percentage of colonists in the total population (as in the 1981 census):

Sombor: 19.4 per cent Sremska Mitrovica: 27.4 per cent Stara Pazova: 32.6 per cent

Temerin

Parties	Yugoslav Presidential 1992	Serbian 1992	Yugoslav 1992	Serbian 1993
SPS	7,570	2,883	2,464	3,229
SRS		4,515	4,804	3,483
DEPOS		1,720	1,295	1,065
DSS				322
DS				790
DS-RDSV		445	2,000	
DS-RDSV-GSS				
NPP		57		
VMDK		4,833	3,837	4,451
DEPOS-Milan Panić	7,666			
Others	755	999	1,062	717

Ratio of Serbs/Montenegrins and Hungarians in the local population	Serbs and Montenegrins	Hungarians
%	52.99	38.68

Total population: 24,939 residents

Subotica

Parties	Yugoslav Presidential 1992	Serbian 1992	Yugoslav 1992	Serbian 1993
SPS	17,618	9,928	8,959	12,586
SRS		8,421	8,943	4,938
DEPOS		12,484	8,329	5,696
DSS				1,248
DS				5,482
DS-RDSV		5,435	23,118	
DS-RDSV-GSS				
NPP		699		

Parties	Yugoslav Presidential 1992	Serbian 1992	Yugoslav 1992	Serbian 1993
VMDK		29,113	19,089	25,098
DEPOS-Milan Panić	64,725			
Others	4,752	17,256	15,236	14,203

Ratio of Serbs/Montenegrins and Hungarians in the local population	Serbs and Montenegrins	Hungarians
%	16.00	42.70

Total population: 150,534 residents

Čoka

Parties	Yugoslav Presidential 1992	Serbian 1992	Yugoslav 1992	Serbian 1993
SPS	2,988	1,299	1,178	1,963
SRS		1,659	1,761	808
DEPOS		848	572	610
DSS				125
DS				488
DS–RDSV		213	2,531	
DS–RDSV–GSS				
NPP		107		
VMDK		4,332	2,756	3,508
DEPOS-Milan Panić	6,357			
Others	678	1,077	763	887

Ratio of Serbs/Montenegrins and Hungarians in the local population	Serbs and Montenegrins	Hungarians
%	33.12	56.47

Total population: 15,271 residents

Ada

Parties	Yugoslav Presidential 1992	Serbian 1992	Yugoslav 1992	Serbian 1993
SPS	1,353	591	545	814
SRS		885	910	502
DEPOS		1,079	746	724
DSS				116
DS				400
DS–RDSV		491	3,691	
DS–RDSV–GSS				
NPP		72		
VMDK		8,792	6,493	7,286
DEPOS-Milan Panić	11,418			
Others	547	1,093	605	1,380

Ratio of Serbs/Montenegrins and Hungarians in the local population	Serbs and Montenegrins	Hungarians
%	15.45	77.30

Total population: 21,506 residents

Kovin*

Parties	Yugoslav Presidential 1992	Serbian 1992	Yugoslav 1992	Serbian 1993
SPS	11,004	6,492	6,115	7,200
SRS		4,035	4,371	2,097
DEPOS		5,094	4,887	4,631
DSS				650
DS				2,852
DS–RDSV		749	1,900	
DS–RDSV–GSS				
NPP		708		

Parties	Yugoslav Presidential 1992	Serbian 1992	Yugoslav 1992	Serbian 1993
VMDK		932	646	525
DEPOS-Milan Panić	9,141			
Others	1,529	2,468	2,643	1,760

*Approximately 86 per cent old settler populated.

Total population: 38,263 residents.

Alibunar**

Parties	Yugoslav Presidential 1992	Serbian 1992	Yugoslav 1992	Serbian 1993
SPS	6,858	3,707	3,301	4,355
SRS		2,922	3,236	1,503
DEPOS		3,083	3,273	4,671
DSS				665
DS				1,357
DS-RDSV				
DS-RDSV-GSS		469	1,145	
NPP		575		
VMDK		172	153	40
DEPOS-Milan Panić	7,451			
Others	1,204	3,803	3,667	1,305

**Approximately 90 per cent old settler populated.

Total population: 26,535 residents.
Source: http://www.cesid.org.

Qualified labourers appeared keener on a nationalist orientation than unqualified ones.[46] In regard to qualified labourers of Serb nationality, they generally displayed a tendency to interlink national solidarity and their dominant status in the province with the desire

---

[46] Ibid., 542.

to secure their posts. The latter observation gains higher significance, taking into account the unemployment crisis and the harsh economic realities for Serbia. Especially as far as the Socialists were concerned, the promotion of the party's standpoints at the workplace, by the managers of the companies and the leaders of the trade unions, assisted the SPS in securing more votes there.[47]

Vladimir Ilić's research demonstrates that the assumption that Vojvodina's colonists might be keener on a nationalist orientation than the old settlers is rather unsubstantiated. The former segment did not seem to be less inclined towards mixed marriages or the ethnically mixed composition of the workplace than the latter.[48] Nevertheless, quantitative data demonstrates that, especially in the December 1992 elections, the Radicals had managed to establish a stronghold in Srem's municipalities where a notable presence of colonists is resident (e.g. Sremska Mitrovica, Stara Pazova; Table 8), whereas the same party performed quite well in colonist settlements in Bačka (e.g. Sombor; Ibid.). To this should be added that, during the military mobilization throughout the early 1990s, quite a few colonists joined the regular as well as irregular Serbian units operating in Bosnia-Herzegovina and Croatia.[49] In regard to SRS, this party's activity in *Republika Srpska* and the 'Serbian Republic of Krajina' might have attracted additional votes for the Radicals from the colonist segment in Vojvodina.[50]

Lazar Vrkatić mentions that 'a notable percentage of colonists are receptive to nationalist ideas as demonstrated by their "disciplined" voting for nationalist options'. In the author's own words, 'Throughout the whole of Serbia one cannot find such a newly-established emphasis on pseudo-patriarchal customs as it is the case with Vojvodina's colonists.'[51] In all of this, however, it should be taken into account that

---

[47] Ibid.
[48] Ibid., 538–9, 540.
[49] Misha Glenny, *The Fall of Yugoslavia: The Third Balkan War* (London: Penguin, 1992), 122.
[50] Some information on this issue was disclosed to the author in the course of his field research in Vojvodina (Interview with SRS functionary, Novi Sad; 1 April 2002).
[51] Vrkatić 'Srbi u Vojvodini i njihov državno-pravni osnov', 129.

there were some predominantly colonist-populated localities where the Radicals never managed to elect a single candidate throughout the 1990s.[52] Such instances suffice in order to show that, in spite of the positive disposition among a certain percentage of colonists towards the Radicals, the strict categorization of colonists as a group with a nationalist orientation would be imprecise.

As far as DEPOS, DS and DSS are concerned, they became quite popular among the younger generation of students, the academics and the entrepreneurs of various kinds resident in Vojvodina's urban centres (Table 8). These parties and the regionalists augmented their popularity in some predominantly old settler municipalities (e.g. Alibunar, Bački Petrovac, Vršac, Kovačica, Kula and Novi Bečej; Table 8). Although a certain sub-group among the old settlers did not see from a negative angle the curtailment of Vojvodina's autonomy, they still did not harbour positive sentiments towards SPS which they viewed as continuers of the Communist legacy (e.g. the employment of Partisan symbolism and Socialist slogans). Meanwhile, the Radicals' informal partnership with SPS did not render this party a credible option to the eyes of these old settlers either.

On the other hand, the successful performance of the DS–RDSV coalition at certain old settler municipalities in December 1992 may serve as an indication that a strain among the old settlers had started becoming more conscious over Vojvodina's administrative status (e.g. Kovin, Alibunar, Vršac; Table 8). The popularity of the same coalition in municipalities with an ethnically mixed population is an indication that its non-nationalist agenda appealed to the inhabitants of these communities, many of whom came from a mixed family background (e.g. Subotica, Kovačica and Bački Petrovac; Table 8). The successful performance of the DS–RDSV alliance in predominantly Hungarian districts may serve as evidence that a certain percentage of ethnic Hungarians preferred a pro-autonomy option focusing on a 'Vojvodina for all' to the ethnically minded agenda of the VMDK (e.g. Subotica, Ada,

---

[52] Interview with SRS representative; Novi Sad, 1 April 2002.

Bečej, Čoka, Kanjiza and Senta; Ibid.). It is an interesting coincidence that the DS–RDSV alliance was rather powerful, in the same elections, in two districts with a dense Slovak population (Bački Petrovac and Kovačica).

Vojvodina's political landscape during the early and mid-1990s was characterized by the paradox of a population largely voting for a multitude of opposition groupings and a ruling party (SPS) maintaining its position, thanks to the fragmentation in the opposition ranks. Therefore, more than two-thirds of the representatives at the Vojvodinian assembly were elected from the SPS's ranks. Meanwhile, the representatives of the 'democratic opposition' in Vojvodina did not add any particularly regional dimension to their agenda. The only exceptions were the cases of the Reformists and LSDV and the tactical move by DS in the December 1992 federal elections. As far as DEPOS and the larger opposition parties are concerned, their Vojvodinian representatives did not adopt a distinctly different agenda from that of their counterparts elsewhere in Serbia.

Vojvodina's society and economy in crisis

Vojvodina immediately sensed the impact of the UN embargo. With the imposition of the economic blockade, the export of the province's agricultural produce to the neighbouring and other East European states reached its nadir. Only some limited trading activity with Hungary was maintained, thanks to the absence of a visa barrier between Hungary and FR Yugoslavia. Nevertheless, it was basically Hungary that profited from all this, since the import–export ratio between Serbia and Hungary remained unfavourable to the Vojvodinian/Serbian side.[53]

The prohibition of cargo transport through FR Yugoslavia had an additionally negative impact on Vojvodina. Owing primarily to its location, at the meeting point between Southern and Central-east

---

[53] Even in 2001, Serbian exports to Hungary amounted to $65 million whereas Hungarian imports into Serbia to $194 million.

Europe, the province was one of the main links in the transportation of cargo from Northern and Central Europe towards Greece and Turkey. The transit of cargo and the passage of tourists from Northern Europe through the province was an additional source of exchange currency. With the imposition of the sanctions and the outbreak of the conflict in adjacent Croatia all this changed. Some Vojvodinians sought a way out of the crisis through the formation of informal trading networks with foreign partners along the borderline. Such networks were often set up according to the black market principle and involved the smuggling of petrol and other primary goods (e.g. medical items) into Serbia, from Hungary and Romania. Soon, quite a few rural communities in the Romanian Banat, in the proximity of Timisoara, became rich 'overnight' through sanctions-busting activities.

Grey economy accounted for the remarkable influx of German marks into Vojvodina and the greater Belgrade area. This caused the dinar to devalue and inflation to soar in the poorer southern areas such as Leškovac and Vranje. This differential inflation further underlined Serbia's north–south divide since the poorer southerners expressed their grievances in regard to non-transparent economic activities in the Serbian north. Moreover, the accumulation of considerable amounts of wealth in the hands of a few sanction-busters (also war-profiteers) generated cleavages and boosted corruption within the society. Meanwhile, the unemployment crisis worsened and Vojvodina's regional income decreased.[54]

The gradual shift from industrial to agricultural production had some positive repercussions for Vojvodina.[55] Its agricultural wealth and developed food industry helped the province have a less traumatic experience, in comparison to the other parts of the country, during the

---

[54] Savezni Zavod za Statistiku, *Statistički Godišnjak 1996.godine* (Belgrade, 1996), 92, 96, 128 and 156.
[55] Michael Palairet, 'Economic Retardation, Peasant Farming and the Nation State in the Balkans: Serbia 1830–1914 and 1990–1998', in *Economic Change and the Building of the Nation State in History*, ed. A. Teichova and H. Matis (Cambridge: Cambridge University Press, 2000).

embargo.⁵⁶ Nevertheless, this was the one side of the coin. The drive towards agriculture was not generally met with success. Vojvodinian farmers soon started to retreat from the market and consume their produce on a household basis. This was the outcome of two combined factors. The first was the fact that much of the cash income from output marketed by private farmers was devoted to the payment of high agricultural taxes and the purchase of indispensable material inputs (e.g. diesel oil, seed and fertilizer). The second, and perhaps the major, cause of farmers' hardships was the unrealistically low prices paid by the state for their output. This contributed to the inflation crisis, since the bankrupt government, lacking the funds to pay the farmers, constantly asked the central bank to print new money in order to finance them.⁵⁷

Agricultural and other production in Vojvodina were equally hampered by infrastructural deficiencies. Agriculture was damaged by under-investment in water management. The state-owned drainage systems in the province remained neglected for a long period of time and by 2000 their maintenance spending had fallen to approximately 5 per cent of the customary standard. This rendered Vojvodina's crop production highly vulnerable in the, not so rare, event of floods.⁵⁸ Vojvodina's metal and petrochemical industries were heavily affected by the UN sanctions. The technical equipment in many factories remained out of date since the import of new machinery was not possible. Petrochemical industry, in particular, was affected by the shortage in natural gas supply and other primary resources.⁵⁹

---

[56] According to 1994 figures, Vojvodina enjoyed an average per capita income of 2,519 dinars (Serbian average: 1,621 dinars) and had an average number of 282 employed citizens in every 1,000 citizens in total (Serbian average: 229 out of 1,000). Republički Zavod za Statistiku, *Opštine u Republici Srbiji* (Belgrade, 1996).

[57] Palairet, 'Economic Retardation, Peasant Farming and the Nation State in the Balkans'.

[58] This reached its peak in spring 2000, when massive floods caused DEM 230 million of damage in Vojvodina.

[59] Pavle Tomić and Jovan Romelić, 'Industry in the Yugoslav Part of the Banat', in *Geographic Monographs of European Regions: Banat*, ed. University of Novi Sad, West University of Timisoara and Jozsef Attila University Szeged (Novi Sad: GIS Institute, 1997), 169–81.

The influx of refugees: Legal definition and demographic aspects

According to the definition issued by the UNHCR in 1967, a refugee is a person who, under serious fear of persecution because of his/her race, religion, national/social affiliation, or political convictions, resides outside the state of which he/she is a citizen; a person who does not hold citizenship of the state where he/she previously resided and which he/she fled under fear of persecution and cannot or, because of the aforementioned fear, does not want to return to his/her native place of origin.[60] The legal framework of FR Yugoslavia, however, provided a case-specific distinction.

First, there were those refugees in the international legal sense. These were persons who had fled the war zones of Croatia and Bosnia-Herzegovina after those two states' official recognition by the UN and did not possess any valid documents regarding their citizenship. On the other hand, there were the displaced persons or *'prognanena/raseljena lica'* according to the Serbian terminology. These were people who had fled to FR Yugoslavia before those two states' international recognition. Those persons held documents that made them eligible for Serbian/Yugoslav citizenship, so they could not be regarded as refugees in the international legal sense.[61] The first wave of refugees consisted of ethnic Serbs fleeing Baranja and Eastern Slavonia in early 1991. More ethnic Serbs from the other parts of Slavonia, Baranja, Kordun, Lika and Croatian urban centres (e.g. Zagreb) arrived in the province by the end of the same year.[62] The influx of refugees from Croatia and Bosnia-Herzegovina continued over the next couple of years. In mid-

---

[60] United Nations High Commission for Refugees, *Census of Refugees and Other War-Affected Persons in the Federal Republic of Yugoslavia*, UNHCR High Commissioner for Refugees in the Republic of Serbia (Belgrade: UNHCR High Commissioner for Displaced Persons in the Republic of Montenegro, 1996), 113.

[61] According to the 1996 UNHCR data, 29,908 out of the 259,719 refugees stationed in Vojvodina by that time fit into the category of displaced persons.

[62] According to the Serbian Bureau for Statistics, approximately 151,512 persons of Serb ethnicity fled Croatia towards Serbia throughout 1991.

Table 9 War-displaced persons accommodated in the territory of FR Yugoslavia

Area	Refugees	%	Evicted persons	%	Total	Total population (%)
Serbia	537,937	95.0	79,791	100	617,728	6.3
Central Serbia	282,022	51.0	48,801	61.2	337,830	5.8
Vojvodina	229,811	40.6	29,908	37.5	259,719	12.9
Kosovo	19,097	3.4	1,082	1.3	20,179	1.0
Montenegro	28,338	5.0	0	0	28,338	4.5
FR Yugoslavia	566,275	100.0	79,791	100.0	646,006	6.2

Source: United Nations High Commission for Refugees, *Census of Refugees and Other War-affected Persons in the Federal Republic of Yugoslavia*, UNHCR High Commissioner for Refugees in the Republic of Serbia (Belgrade: UNHCR High Commissioner for Displaced Persons in the Republic of Montenegro, 1996).

1993, 497,000 refugees were based in FR Yugoslavia, most of them in Vojvodina (Table 9).[63]

The turning point was the operations *Bljesak* ('Dazzle') and *Oluja* ('Storm') conducted by the Croatian military in Western Slavonia (May 1995) and Krajina (August 1995).[64] More ethnic Serbs came from Bosnian districts around Sarajevo after the signing of the Dayton Agreement.[65] According to the estimation, by the Humanitarian Centre for Integration and Tolerance, a Novi Sad-based NGO, 293,823 refugees were stationed in Vojvodina by mid-August 2000. This means that approximately 50 per cent of the total number of refugees stationed in Serbia at that time was accommodated in the province.

---

[63] *International Migration Bulletin*, No. 3 (1993): 27–8.
[64] It is estimated that over 200,000 ethnic Serbs from those two territories sought refuge to Serbia. Branislav Đurđev, *Problem izbeglistva u Jugoslaviji* (monografska publikacija) (Novi Sad: Matica Srpska, 1997), 307.
[65] 134,125 Serbian refugees from Croatia (58.36 per cent) and 91,129 more from Bosnia-Herzegovina (36.69 per cent) were stationed in Vojvodina by mid-1996. UNHCR, *Census of Refugees and Other War-Affected Persons in the Federal Republic of Yugoslavia*, 9.

The majority of refugees settled in Bačka and Srem. Two basic factors affected the refugees' choice of their places of resettlement. The first was the frequency of colonists, among whom they had friends and relatives, in the Vojvodinian municipalities (Table 10).[66] By contrast, refugees, just like the colonists, made up a low percentage of the population in those communities that are predominantly inhabited by national minorities (Table 11). The second factor was the economic infrastructure of the places of resettlement and their proximity to the major urban centres (Novi Sad and Belgrade). Consequently, a dense concentration of refugees was encountered in the industrially and economically more developed areas of Southern Bačka and the Southern and central Banat. The same thing may be argued for Srem, an area rich in farming resources and with a developed agricultural industry. A third factor, related to refugees from Croatia, is the proximity of the refugees' places of resettlement to their former hearths. Therefore, a dense concentration of Croatian Serb refugees along the Croatian border was encountered in Srem and Western Bačka.[67] In the case of those refugees from Eastern Slavonia and Baranja, their resettlement along the border might facilitate their contacts with the kin and friends left behind and future repatriation plans.

The social integration process

The migration of the displaced Bosnian and Croatian Serbs towards Vojvodina fit under the category of forced migration. Forced migrations cause a variety of psychological traumas to the migrants, which hinder their adaptation to the new environment. In Vojvodina, this was particularly the case with the older refugees from the mountainous parts of Bosnia-Herzegovina and Croatia. The non-regulated refugee

---

[66] In Srem the majority of refugees originated, just like the colonists, from the Croatian Krajina. Also, in the municipality of Bačka Palanka (western Bačka) most refugees, as well as colonists, are Bosnian Serbs.
[67] By 2000, 62.6 per cent of the refugees accommodated in Srem originated from Croatia.

Table 10 Colonists and refugees in Vojvodina (1948–96)

Area	Colonists (1948)	Total population (1948)	% of colonists in total population (1948)	Total population (1991)	Refugees (1996)	% of refugees in total population (1991)
Bačka	125,684	802,235	15.7	1,032,915	127,214	12.3
N.Bačka	9,032	262,449	3.4	286,354	15,942	5.6
W.Bačka	72,100	200,465	36.0	215,916	33,200	15.4
S.Bačka	44,552	339,321	13.1	530,645	78,072	14.7
Banat	79,465	599,120	13.3	648,611	45,720	7.0
N.Banat	15,818	100,864	15.7	98,830	8,404	8.5
C.Banat	31,126	219,164	14.2	221,353	15,324	6.9
S.Banat	35,251	279,092	11.7	328,428	21,992	6.7
Srem	11,162	224,752	5.0	332,363	84,805	25.5

Source: http://www.cesid.org.

Table 11 Number of refugees in municipalities with a dense or a majority Hungarian and other ethnic minority population (1996)

Ada	438 out of 21,506 residents
Bačka Topola	3,816 out of 40,473 residents
Bečej	3,541 out of 42,685 residents
Kanjiza	905 out of 30,668 residents
Mali Idoš	194 out of 14,394 residents
Senta	620 out of 28,779 residents
Subotica	4,091 out of 150,534 residents
Temerin	1,732 out of 24,939 residents
Čoka	493 out of 15,271 residents

Source: http://www.cesid.org.

status of many refugees emerged as an additional factor that aggravated their psychological tension. As a result of their collective insecurity, the majority of refugees developed a powerful attachment to Serbia. On some occasions, the psychological frustration involved in the loss of the homeland encouraged the adoption of nationalist and militant political options by some refugees. For instance, the results of the first round of the 2002 Serbian elections demonstrated that Vojislav Šešelj had established a power base in those municipalities of Srem and Western Bačka where a dense concentration of refugees and colonists is encountered.[68] Moreover, a notable participation of young refugees in the Vojvodinian SRS youth committee plus certain groupings with a militant nationalist orientation (e.g. *Obraz*) had been witnessed. Nevertheless, it is not an easy task to assess precisely the voting patterns of the refugee population, since many refugees were yet not entitled to vote. In addition to political options, psychological frustration took its toll on other group aspects

---

[68] This was the case with the municipalities of Apatin, Odžaci and Bačka Palanka in Western Bačka, plus the seven municipalities of Srem. 'Predsednički Izbori 2002' (http://www.cesid.org).

of the refugees. A survey conducted in Srem demonstrated that the low birth rate of the refugee population in that part of Vojvodina, between 1991 and 1996, was highly subject to psychological factors.[69]

The second major obstacle in the path of the refugees' social integration was legal complications. The displaced persons of the early 1990s usually possessed passports of the Socialist Federal Republic of Yugoslavia and were duly granted citizenship of FR Yugoslavia, a state regarded as the continuation of the crumbling federation. As for those refugees originating from *Republika Srpska*, their recognized citizenship by the Serbian/Yugoslav authorities was that which they were earlier granted by the Bosnian Serb authorities. However, the Croatian Serb refugees who arrived in the mid-1990s made up another category. The official norm for the solution of the refugee issue, adopted by the Serbian/Yugoslav government by then, became the repatriation of the refugees to their native places of origin. The most notable consequence of this policy on the Croatian Serb refugees was a prolonged lack of citizenship, which corresponded to the restriction, even deprivation, of basic civil rights (e.g. the right to vote, the right to social security).[70] Meanwhile, the Croatian authorities rendered the acquisition of Croatian citizenship, by the evicted Serbs, a complicated and long legal procedure. Consequently, many Croatian Serb refugees remained stateless for a long period of time.

Furthermore, the social integration of the newcomers was hindered by the socio-economic circumstances. During the mid-1990s, only small-scale humanitarian support could be provided by the Vojvodinian NGOs and the Serbian emigration centre.[71] Instances of friction between refugees and locals for the allocation of scarce job opportunities were soon witnessed.[72] Unemployment obstructed the utilization of a well-qualified labour potential among refugees for

---

[69] D. Madžić, S. Petaković, D. Malobabić and V. Solarević, 'Utičaj izbegličke populacije na kretanje nataliteta u Sremu', *Zbornik za Društvene Nauke*, broj 91 (1997): 201–3.
[70] According to UNHCR data, by December 1999, a mere 40,000 out of the total 340,000 Serb refugees from Croatia stationed in Serbia possessed Serbian/Yugoslav citizenship.
[71] Đurđev, *Problem izbeglistva u Jugoslaviji*, 312–13.
[72] According to UNHCR 1996 data, 74.1 per cent of the refugees stationed in the territory of FR Yugoslavia were unemployed.

the benefit of the Vojvodinian society. These were usually refugees originating from the economically developed, with a greater experience in laissez-faire economics regions of Baranja and Slavonia.[73]

Finally, the successful integration of refugees to the regional environment was obstructed by cultural factors. The drive towards ethnocentrism, as it became manifest in the Serbian and Croatian societies during the 1990s, took its toll on the social integration of refugees. This ethnocentric drive frequently resulted in the identification of the western Serbo-Croat variant spoken by the newcomers (*ijekavica* – also their more frequent use of the Latin alphabet) with Croatia and the Croats. Therefore a certain social pressure was exerted on many refugees from Croatia and Bosnia-Herzegovina to switch to the eastern variant (*ekavica*) as much as possible. On the other hand, parochial patterns of group identification emerged among refugees, largely resulting from their relative social marginalization. For example, quite a few refugees from Lika tended to identify themselves primarily and almost exclusively as '*Ličani*' (i.e. natives of Lika), others from Herzegovina as '*Hercegovci*' (Herzegovinians). As a result of these combined catalysts, one might argue that, throughout the 1990s, the refugees formed a distinct segment within the Vojvodinian society.

The spectrum of interethnic relations: Institutional provisions

The rights of the national minorities in the Republic of Serbia and FR Yugoslavia were to be regulated by a variety of documents. Certain provisions were included in the Yugoslav as well as the Serbian Constitution. Nevertheless, as long as neither FR Yugoslavia nor its component republics had a specific law on national minorities, the constitutional rights of national minorities were also codified in republican legal statutes.

---

[73] Nikolić Vera, 'Progon i Prihvatanje Srba iz Hrvatske 1991. Godine', *Zbornik za Društvene Nauke*, broj 88, 1994: 189–204, 193; Milka Bubalo, *Najnovije demografske promene u Novom Slankamenu* (Diplomski rad) (Novi Sad: GIS Institute Library [University of Novi Sad], 1994), 11.

From a theoretical perspective, these provisions were compatible with the international standards on minority rights. In this text, particular reference is made to the guidelines of the *Framework Convention for the Protection of National Minorities*, issued by the Council of Europe.[74] Articles 46 and 32 of the Yugoslav and the Serbian Constitution respectively, as well as the provisions of the Serbian statutes on education the media and radio-television,[75] are fully consistent with Articles 12, 14 and 9 (Paragraph 3) of the convention. Moreover, Article 48 of the Yugoslav Constitution is compatible with Article 17 (Paragraph 1) of the convention. This is also the case with Articles 15 and 8 of the Yugoslav and the Serbian Constitution respectively, as well as with the Law on Official Languages and Alphabets,[76] which are consistent with the convention's Article 11 (Paragraphs 2 and 3). Article 77 of the Yugoslav Constitution went a step beyond the convention itself. Article 13 (Paragraph 2) of the convention does not oblige the state's agencies to finance projects undertaken by national minorities. To all these might be added that Articles 55 and 44 of the Yugoslav and the Serbian Constitution respectively (on the prohibition of the dissemination of national, racial and religious intolerance and hatred) read compatible with Article 6 (Paragraph 2) of the convention, when viewed within the context of interethnic relations.

Nevertheless, the actual implementation of these provisions turned out to be different. First, most federal provisions for national minorities, with the exception of those on the prevention of interethnic hatred and

---

[74] Council of Europe Publishing House, *Framework Convention for the Protection of National Minorities* (Strasbourg: COE, 1994).

[75] On the Serbian statutes regulating education see Law on Elementary Schools ('Zakon o osnovnoj školi', *Službeni Glasnik Republike Srbije*, 50/1992); Law on Secondary Schools ('Zakon o srednjoj školi', *Službeni Glasnik Republike Srbije*, 50/1992); Law on High Schools ('Zakon o visokom školstvu', *Službeni Glasnik Republike Srbije*, 50/1992); Law on Universities ('Zakon o univerzitetu', *Službeni Glasnik Republike Srbije*, 54/1992). On the Serbian statutes regulating public information in minority languages see: Law on Radio-Television ('Zakon o radio-televiziji', *Službeni Glasnik Republike Srbije*, 1991/48); Law on Media ('Zakon o informisanju', *Službeni Glasnik Republike Srbije*, 1991/19).

[76] On the Serbian statute regulating the official use of languages and scripts see 'Zakon o službenoj upotrebi jezika i pisama', *Službeni Glasnik Republike Srbije*, 45/91.

the right to public information in minority languages, were not included in the Serbian Constitution or any other republican legal document. This observation acquires a key significance considering Article 6 of the Yugoslav Constitution and its authorization of the Serbian republic for the regulation of a variety of issues, pertaining to its jurisdiction, by the Serbian Constitution. Therefore, there always remained an implication that certain federal provisions on national minorities might not be implemented to a proper extent. A good example, regarding the discrepancy between the federal and the republican provisions, was the field of minority education where a decline in the number of subjects taught in the minority languages was observed.[77]

There exists evidence that the number of judicial procedures in minority languages had, too, declined.[78] Moreover, the implementation of Articles 19 and 20 of the Serbian Law on the Recognized Languages and Alphabets might prove rather problematic as well, since the signposts as well as the official state's documents in quite a few parts of Vojvodina were available only in Serbian.[79] These irregularities demonstrate that not particular attention was paid, by the municipal and provincial officialdoms, to the proper implementation of the laws in question. In certain communities with a notable minority population, a small percentage of the employees at the administrative and judicial institutions knew the minority language(s) in question.[80]

Certain deficiencies were also observed in public information. The fact that all minority press institutions and electronic media in Vojvodina were state funded granted the government the opportunity to exert influence on both. This could happen through the appointment of the managerial board and the editor-in-chief at the institutions in

---

[77] Tamas Korhecz, 'The Rights of National Minorities in Vojvodina: Legal Norms and Practice', (unpublished work) (Novi Sad, 1998), 5.
[78] Ibid., 18.
[79] Samardžić Miroslav, *Položaj manjina u Vojvodini* (Belgrade: Centar za Antiratnu Akciju, 1998), 82.
[80] By mid-1990s, for example, not a single judge in the local court of Temerin was Hungarian, despite the fact that 38.08 per cent of this municipality's population was ethnic Hungarian.

question.⁸¹ However, the operation of the minority press and media in Vojvodina was not seriously obstructed during the 1990s. No minority informative institutions were ever banned or closed down. Apart from the top-level control of the minority press and media in Vojvodina, the state could ensure the loyalty of the lower staff through the practice of 'self-censorship'.⁸² Employment policy was a field where tensions occurred. By 1998, not a single president of a law court throughout Vojvodina was Hungarian; with the exception of the public prosecutor in the municipality of Senta. Moreover, the employment of individuals coming from minority backgrounds at the police and the security forces was rather low.⁸³ The new employment policy was not welcomed by the minorities in the province.

The case of Vojvodina's Hungarians, in particular, was highly compatible with the triadic nexus theory elaborated by Rogers Brubaker. The regime's nationalizing policies prompted the ethnic Hungarian elites to demand more territorial and cultural autonomy. As for Hungary's synchronized reaction, this manifested through a variety of statements by the then Conservative government in Budapest on the alleged discrimination against the Hungarian minorities in Vojvodina and elsewhere in Central Europe. The Hungarian Conservatives' 'crusade' for the rights of ethnic Hungarians in neighbouring states amplified the tension over the ethnic Hungarian minorities in Vojvodina and elsewhere (e.g. Transylvania in Romania).

Another state policy that generated tensions in Vojvodina was the military mobilization of 1991 and early 1992. Quite a few individuals coming from minority backgrounds refused to join the JNA ranks and fight for, what they regarded as, 'solely Serbian interests' in Croatia

---

[81] Poulton Hugh, 'The Hungarians, Slovaks, Romanians and Rysyns/Ukrainians of the Vojvodina', in *Minorities in Central and Eastern Europe* (London: Minority Rights Group International, 1993), 27–31, 27–8.

[82] Interview with Romanian journalist at RTS Novi Sad; 24 April 2002.

[83] Korhecz, 'The Rights of National Minorities in Vojvodina', 22–3; United Nations Economic and Social Council, *Situation of Human Rights in the Territory of the Former Yugoslavia: Special Report on Minorities*, E/CN.4/1997/8, 25 October 1996, 17.

and Bosnia-Herzegovina.[84] This amounted to a brain drain among Vojvodina's minorities. A Federal Amnesty Law benefitting persons who escaped military service (June 1996) did not reverse that process, since, by then, most draft-dodgers had well settled in their new environment.

Vojvodinian Croats were the minority group who were particularly affected by the outburst of interethnic violence in the other parts of the former Yugoslavia. The Croat community became the target of acts of violence (e.g. arson, physical assaults, attacks on religious monuments) perpetrated by incoming Serb refugees from Croatia. Between 1991 and 1995, the latter would often seek to retaliate for the maltreatment that they had previously experienced in Croatia.[85] Such incidents were witnessed in municipalities with a Croat presence, inside (e.g. Hrtkovci in Srem) and outside Vojvodina.[86] The attitude of certain political actors often fomented the tension.[87] Following the consolidation of FR Yugoslavia, the ethnic Croats lost their erstwhile status of a constituent *narod* and their collective status was to be 'readjusted'. Croatian language no longer enjoyed an official status in education, public information or any other sector. The only exception was the broadcast of a Croatian-language programme at *Radio Subotica*. The legal status of the Croatian minority in FR Yugoslavia soon became entangled with the Serbian question in Croatia. Especially since 1995, the possibilities for the concession of a legal status to the ethnic Croats in Serbia remarkably lessened. Even though the 'Agreement for the

---

[84] It is estimated that, between 1991 and early 1992, some 30,000 to 40,000 young Hungarians had fled Vojvodina in order to avoid conscription. United Nations Economic and Social Council, *Situation of Human Rights in the Territory of the Former Yugoslavia*, 17.

[85] There exist speculations that during these four years some 45,000 to 50,000 ethnic Croats fled FR Yugoslavia towards Croatia, largely intimidated by acts of violence. United Nations Economic and Social Council, *Situation of Human Rights in the Territory of the Former Yugoslavia*, 17.

[86] Ibid.; Helsinki Committee for Human Rights in Serbia, *In the Name of Humanity* (Belgrade: HCHRS, 1997), 34–5; Helsinki Committee for Human Rights in Serbia, *Minorities in Serbia* (Belgrade: HCHRS, 1998), 46–7.

[87] Vojislav Šešelj overtly called for the expulsion of Croats from Vojvodina, with the exception of those Croats who 'fought with his volunteers and these were not too many'. See this statement in *Borba*, 3 May 1992.

Normalization of the Relations between FR Yugoslavia and Croatia', signed by the two parties in August 1996, provided for the 'guarantee of the rights of the Serbs and Montenegrins in the Republic of Croatia and the Croats in FR Yugoslavia, in accordance with international law' (Item 8), little progress was observed towards either direction.

The spectrum of interethnic relations: Realities 'on the ground'

The results of the survey by Ilić and Cvejić detected a tendency towards ethnic introversion on the Serb respondents' part.[88] The relatively increased degree of suspicion towards minority groups became subject to external catalysts such as the contemporary developments in the other parts of the former Yugoslavia (most notably the fall of Krajina) and the gradual radicalization of the Albanians in Kosovo. Serbian fears over their republic's integrity, as well as their adherence to national solidarity, were subtly communicated in the same survey through the high degree of admiration towards figures associated with the Serbian ethnogenesis (e.g. Saint Sava); the nineteenth-century national awakening (e.g. Vuk Karadžić); and the unification of the Serbian lands (e.g. King Petar I Karađorđević).[89]

The responses by the Hungarian sample can be interpreted as a reaction to the nationalizing process. This seems to have triggered a counter-nationalistic attitude directed against the dominant nationality, the Serbs. When viewed through the spectrum of Brubaker's triadic nexus concept, the allegedly marginalized minority's reaction to the nationalizing policies is to adopt an equally homogenizing attitude within itself. The Hungarian opinion-formers (intellectuals and politically active individuals) avoided to stress any sort of internal cleavages (e.g. political, socio-economic and territorial)

---

[88] Ilić Vladimir and Cvejić Slobodan, *Nacionalizam u Vojvodini* (Zrenjanin: Ekspres, 1997), 181, 184–5, 188, 191–2 and 193.
[89] Ibid., 102.

and sought to present their group as homogeneous, especially as far as its grievances were concerned. In a somewhat similar fashion to their Serb counterparts, the Hungarian respondents expressed a high admiration for political figures who had defended the national rights of the Hungarians in the past (e.g. Lajos Kossuth, Sandor Petöfy) and the present (e.g. the party leaders Jozsef Kasas and Andras Agoston in Vojvodina).

The high degree of ethnic solidarity and relative introversion encountered among Slovaks can be interpreted in terms of a small group that strives to preserve its cultural identity. Slovak worries over cultural survival might have been prompted by the lack of organized political structures within the community, as well as the geographic distance of their kin-state. The observation that Slovak nationalist resurgence in Vojvodina was of an essentially cultural character is substantiated by the fact that in Ilić and Cvejić's survey most Slovak respondents expressed particular admiration towards Slovak men of art and literature, quite a few of those originated from Vojvodina.[90] As for the Romanians, a low intensity of group consciousness as well as a tendency towards conscious assimilation was observed. This incidence might have been prompted by the desire for socio-economic mobility[91] and the long-standing tradition of peaceful cohabitation between Serbs and Romanians in Vojvodina.

Neither Romanians nor Slovaks seemed to approve of the way that the province's Hungarian elites voiced their grievances.[92] On the one hand this was subject to the fear that, always bearing in mind the Hungarian minority's size and political organization, the minority discourse in Vojvodina might be dominated by the Hungarian side. The second catalyst was possibly the assessment, by the Slovak and Romanian respondents, that the vocal fashion in which the Hungarian

---

[90] Ilić and Cvejić, *Nacionalizam u Vojvodini*, 100.
[91] Some information over this issue was disclosed to the author in the course of his field research in Vojvodina (Interview with Romanian journalist at RTS Novi Sad; 24 March 2002).
[92] Ilić and Cvejić, *Nacionalizam u Vojvodini*, 163.

elites were expressing their grievances might, in the long term, generate interethnic friction in Vojvodina. An external factor that might have shaped these two groups' stance was the simultaneous ethnic Hungarian aspirations in Romania and Slovakia.

At the same time, a notable percentage of respondents opted for an increase in interethnic tolerance and mutual trust among the different communities in Vojvodina. In the smaller survey conducted by Vladimir Ilić in the early 1990s, the majority of respondents stated that they did not put high importance on the ethnicity of their partner or the ethnic composition of their workplace.[93] Apart from these, the results of another survey conducted in 1990 demonstrated that the majority of the Serb and Hungarian respondents generally held a positive view of each other.[94] One might argue that the observations of the two latter surveys can be understood by the fact that they were carried out at a time when the interethnic conflicts in the former Yugoslavia had not dramatically escalated. Still, the results of another survey, carried out throughout Serbia in 1995, demonstrate that nationalist orientation in Vojvodina remained lower than it was the case in the rest of Serbia. In addition, the Vojvodinian respondents demonstrated a more cosmopolitan attitude towards other nationalities in comparison to the respondents from Serbia proper.[95]

These ostensibly conflicting observations lead to the following conclusion. The adequate comprehension of the spectrum of interethnic relations in Vojvodina, throughout that period, consists in the detachment of the monist attitudes, which became manifest primarily on the political level, from the ethno-cultural heterophony

---

[93] Ilić Vladimir and Cvejić Slobodan, 'Vojvođani i nacionalizam', *Sociologija*, vol. XXXV, 1993, 533–47, 538–40.
[94] Seventy per cent of the Hungarian and 57 per cent of the Serb respondents stated that they held a positive view of each other. Liljana Bačević et al., *Jugoslavija na kriznoj prekretnici* (Belgrade: Institut društvenih nauka, 1991), 180, 236.
[95] Nationalist orientation was evident among 21.6 per cent of the Vojvodinian respondents (Central Serbian respondents: 41.7 per cent) whereas 36.4 per cent of the same sample demonstrated a rather cosmopolitan attitude towards other nationalities (Central Serbian sample: 18.0 per cent). Zagorka Golubović et al., *Društveni karakter i društvene promene u svetlu nacionalnih sukoba* (Belgrade: Filip Višnjić, 1995), 159, 219, 248, 252.

on the social micro-level. Collective monism manifested through the stress on group homogeneity as well as ethnic introversion and mistrust towards other groups. In regard to the Serbs, a process of political de-radicalization was soon put under way. Nevertheless, the state of crisis continued to foment sociopolitical tensions, thus deepening mistrust of everyone (e.g. politicians, institutions and 'others'). So the Vojvodinian society became more segmented and Serbs, as well as minority groups, became more introverted as a psychological mechanism of self-protection.

Besides these monist group attitudes, there co-existed a bicultural, or, more precisely, intercultural social practice. Vojvodina's ethno-cultural heterophony on the grassroots level was a by-product of the province's long-standing tradition of multiethnic cohabitation. This heterophony became institutionalized during the Communist era and was reinforced through the contraction of ethnically mixed marriages, especially in the 1970s and the '80s. Despite the inevitable political cleavages, this intercultural practice among individuals coming from different ethnic backgrounds would not radically alter during the 1990s. After all, always bearing in mind that between 1980 and 1985 approximately 27.1 per cent of the marriages in Vojvodina were mixed, it is likely that even quite a few of the respondents who demonstrated an ethno-culturally introverted attitude had relatives of a different ethnic affiliation themselves.

Despite symptoms of ethnic introversion, it would certainly not be precise to categorize the Vojvodinian society of the 1990s as a segregated one. In regard to the Serb majority, the institutional reaffirmation of Vojvodina's Serbian character did not necessarily imply that minority group identities could not co-exist with the dominant one. In other words, a more 'inclusive' version of Serbian nationalism became the case in Vojvodina. The positive grassroots climate among members of different ethnic groups primarily became evident in the more diverse parts of the province. Although the voting patterns in some of these municipalities were conditioned by the ethnic factor, still there would not be many cases that a Hungarian, say, could not understand Serbian or, vice versa, a Serb or Montenegrin could not understand, at least elementary, Hungarian.[96]

The Serbian opposition in Vojvodina

The second half of the 1990s was not a calm period for Serbia, either. This period was marked by the mounting tension between the Serbian and Montenegrin leaderships. On top of this, the friction with the West over the situation in Kosovo culminated in Serbia's bombing by NATO between spring and summer 1999. This section highlights the gradual emergence of the anti-Milošević opposition in Vojvodina. It concentrates on Vojvodina's regionalist elites, the standpoints of the Belgrade-based parties' representatives in the province, as well as the ethnic Hungarian parties. Particular attention is paid to the contribution of the Vojvodinian politicians and voters to the fall of Slobodan Milošević and the change of the political guard. This section demonstrates that *Vojvođanski identitet* ('Vojvodinian regional identity') emerged as a powerful mass phenomenon that provided a common umbrella and accommodated a multitude of anti-SPS political forces in the province.

The Serbian-Montenegrin rift, the escalation of the crisis in Kosovo and the fall of Slobodan Milošević

Throughout the second half of 1997, the dissident faction within Montenegro's ruling Party of Democratic Socialism (DPS) started to acquire a more articulate shape under the leadership of the prime minister, Milo Đukanović. The cleavage between Đukanović and the Belgrade loyalist Momir Bulatović culminated in the successful no-confidence vote submitted to the Montenegrin Assembly by the

---

[96] Jovan Komšić, *Vojvođanska iskustva i savremene dileme* (Novi Sad: Matica Srpska, 1998), 42.

former's associates and the political opposition with the aim to oust Bulatović from the Montenegrin Presidency. In the presidential elections held in October 1997, Đukanović emerged as the victor with 174,745 votes to the 169,257 won by his rival in the second round. A more definitive development took place some months later, in March 1998, when Bulatović transformed his wing of DPS into a new political party, the Socialist National Party (SNP). Đukanović's position was enhanced by the decisive victory of his DPS over SNP in the May 1998 parliamentary and municipal elections (42 to 29 seats and two-thirds of the municipalities).

Milo Đukanović was enabled to distance his policies from those of Momir Bulatović, at an early point, by a specific constitutional provision. Article 94 (Paragraph 1) of the Montenegrin Constitution (1992) enabled the Montenegrin PM to 'carry out domestic *as well as* foreign policy'. This had helped Đukanović cement some preliminary links with international organizations and foreign governments. The assumption of the Montenegrin presidency by Milo Đukanović radically altered the operation of the administrative mechanism on the level of federal politics. This resulted from the fact that, in terms of the sovereignty granted to the component republics by the Yugoslav Constitution, DPS was enabled to pursue very different policies in comparison to SPS in regard to a various areas of policymaking (e.g. the implementation of OSCE recommendations and the Dayton Agreement).

Meanwhile, throughout 1998, Serbian anxieties had intensified following Western criticism of the operations carried out by the Serbian security forces against the Kosovo Liberation Army paramilitaries. On 7 February 1999, a series of talks, involving NATO officials and representatives of the Serbian government and the Kosovan Albanians commenced in the Rambouillet chateau, France. The Kosovan Albanian delegation accepted the terms dictated by NATO. Their Serbian counterparts, on the contrary, declined NATO's conditions because they found them particularly unfavourable for their side. This resulted in a controversial NATO air campaign that lasted from 24 March until 3 June 1999. NATO's air campaign took a much higher toll on Serbia's infrastructures than on the Yugoslav military.[97] A compromise between NATO and Belgrade was reached on 3 June. In the final version of the document, signed in Kumanovo (FYR Macedonia) on the same day, the withdrawal of the Serbian army, as well as the other security forces, from Kosovo and their replacement by a NATO-led peace-keeping force was agreed upon. UN Declaration 1224 reaffirmed Kosovo as an administrative part of FR Yugoslavia. The formation of a provisional government in Kosovo, consisting of representatives of the ethnic Albanian parties, was put under way.

The post-bombing reality in Serbia was harsh. Apart from the damage inflicted on the state's infrastructure by the NATO air campaign, the indictment of Slobodan Milošević and Serbian President Milan Milutinović of war crimes by The Hague Tribunal meant that the sanctions would be prolonged as long as these two individuals remained in power. Fearful of the negative signs, the regime proceeded to constitutional amendments on the federal level. According to the amendments made to the Yugoslav Constitution on 6 July 2000, the Federal president and the deputies to the Chamber of the Republics at the Federal Parliament were to be elected directly by the Serbian and Montenegrin electorates. Another amendment made it possible for the Yugoslav president to be elected twice to that post. The driving force behind the amendments was Milošević's desire to consolidate his position for the years to come, in the event of his victory in the September 2000 ballot.

These amendments were detrimental to the equality of the component republics. Especially the direct election of the deputies to the Federal Chamber of the Republics inflicted the definitive blow on Montenegro's status, since the chamber in question was the main institutional guarantee for the equal standing of the two republics. So, it

---

[97] On this issue, see Amnesty International, 'Collateral Damage or Unlawful Killings?', A1 I INDEX EUR 70/018/2000, 6 June 2000 (http://web.amnesty.org/library/index/ENGEUR700182000); Human Rights Watch, 'Civilian Deaths in the NATO Air Campaign', Volume 12, Number 1 (D), New York, February 2000, http://www.hrw.org/reports/2000/nato/.

became obvious that an additional objective behind the constitutional revision was the ostracism of the dissident Montenegrin leadership from influential posts on the federal level. Đukanović's reaction was to declare that his government would not participate in the September federal elections but that he would not object to them taking place in Montenegro. At that point, FR Yugoslavia became the first state in the history of contemporary federalism where the one member of a two-partite federation did not recognize the validity of the federal elections but, at the same time, did not object to these elections taking place in its territory.

At the same time, a series of alignments were taking place within the bosom of the 'democratic opposition'. By summer 2000, an opposition coalition bearing the name *Demokratska Opozicija Srbije*, or DOS, (Serbian Democratic Opposition) gathered seventeen parties around the larger DS and DSS. The coalition nominated Vojislav Koštunica as its candidate for the Yugoslav Presidency. The party leaderships comprising DOS were encouraged to set aside any programmatic or other differences and form a united front, by two factors. The domestic factor was Milošević's steadily declining popularity. The external catalyst was that this time the powerful Western governments and Russia were firm, each from their own angle that Milošević no longer should remain in the leadership of FR Yugoslavia.

Consequently, 69.7 per cent of the Yugoslav electorate (Serbia: 72.5 per cent) proceeded to the poll. The higher turnout to the election, in comparison to most previous polls, served as an early indication that the Serbian electorate desired a decisive break from its recent political past. The results of the presidential elections confirmed the Socialists' decline of popularity. Vojislav Koštunica garnered 2,470,304 (50.24 per cent) to the 1,826,799 (37.15 per cent) votes won by Slobodan Milošević. The Radical candidate, Tomislav Nikolić, secured 5.88 per cent of the vote whereas SPO's Vojislav Mihajlović sank to the fourth place with a mere 2.95 per cent. In the elections for the Federal Assembly, DOS obtained 59 of the 108 mandates in the Chamber of Citizens to the 44 won by the SPS–United Yugoslav Left (JUL) coalition. As for the

Chamber of the Republics, half of the mandates (10) went to DOS and 7 to the Socialists. In a last moment attempt to rescue Milošević from defeat, the Federal Electoral Committee called for the repetition of the presidential poll, through reference to 'irregularities' committed while counting the votes. Nevertheless, following the subsequent call, on behalf of the DOS leadership, for civil disobedience the opposition supporters stormed the Republican Assembly, thus forcing the Commission to recall its decision. Vojislav Koštunica was elected the new president of FR Yugoslavia. The new order consolidated in Serbia with the December 2000 elections for the Serbian Assembly. The DOS coalition won a stunning victory, securing 176 of the 250 seats in the parliament. SPS, on the contrary, won a mere 37 seats.

Vojvodina turns against Milošević: Parties and issues

Throughout 1990, political parties with a regionalist orientation were formed in Vojvodina. These were the League of Vojvodina's Social-Democrats (LSDV), the Reformist-Democratic Party of Vojvodina (RDSV) and the National Peasants' Party. This work pays particular attention to the former two.

During the early 1990s, the League as well as the Reformists had joined the reformist pro-Yugoslav coalition GSS. In 1991, under the leadership of Nenad Čanak, a Novi Sad economist, the League presented its concept regarding Vojvodina's status within the crumbling Yugoslavia. In a document entitled 'Memorandum on Vojvodina' (23 December 1991) the party demanded the reorganization of Serbia along the lines of a confederation, within the bounds of the old Yugoslavia, where Vojvodina and Kosovo would enjoy an asymmetric status in comparison to the other Serbian regions. An alternative option, proposed in the same document, was that, as an interim solution, Vojvodina might become an 'independent, sovereign and neutral territory ... whose final status would be decided-in terms of equality-inside the spectrum of a commonly agreed territorial rearrangement within the bounds of the Socialist Federal Republic of Yugoslavia'.[98] This approach was gradually modified in the course of the groundbreaking developments in the former Yugoslavia.

The League and the Reformists gained some popularity mainly within two segments among Vojvodina's Serbian majority. One of them was some old settlers who, although acknowledging and respecting the significance of Vojvodina as the heartland of the modern Serbian national movement, still lay a stronger emphasis on Vojvodina's regional identity. These old settlers attempted to justify their regionalist stance, by reference to the different historical experience of the province in comparison to the rest of Serbia, as well as to its multiethnic composition. Consequently, these old settlers were and still are the ones to prove keener on the employment of the 'other-regarding' stereotypes on *uža Srbija* (e.g. the ones according to which Vojvodinians are regarded as more 'cultured' and 'sophisticated' than the inhabitants of Serbia proper). The same group has always emphasized the tradition of peaceful multiethnic coexistence in Vojvodina as an indication of the Vojvodinian Serbs' developed civic consciousness.

Those old settlers' support to regionalist alternatives was additionally conditioned by the economic factor. In the beginning, these old settlers saw the restriction of Vojvodina's autonomy (1990) as a detrimental move for the province's economic performance. In the long term, however, and in the process of de-legitimization of the old regime, no nostalgic allusions to the Communist era as such were made. By contrast, any demands for economic autonomy were couched in arguments over the need for administrative decentralization, in the light of a deteriorating economic situation, with a simultaneous overview of other autonomy arrangements across Europe. Still, the pattern of Vojvodinian autonomy, as promulgated during the Communist era, always served, if only subtly, as a compass. In all of this, the old settlers in question interweaved their demands for economic autonomy with references to Vojvodina's distinct historical identity. This, in turn,

---

[98] Socijal-Demokratski Front Vojvodine, *Autonomija Vojvodine Danas* (Novi Sad, 1993).

would render these old settlers prone to advocate for the restoration of Vojvodina's autonomy at all levels (political, economic and cultural).[99]

There exists evidence that these two parties found popularity among Vojvodina's colonists as well. Opinion polls and other empirical research conducted in Novi Sad demonstrated that the pro-autonomy tendencies encountered in some of the predominantly colonist-populated parts (those built after the Second World War) sometimes could be stronger than those encountered in the old settler-populated parts of the city.[100] Even further, the pro-autonomy elites themselves largely comprised second-generation colonists.[101] One explanation that can be offered regarding this trend, especially among second-generation colonists, is the influence that the state's ideology exerted on the colonists' first generation throughout the Communist era. Some of the ideological slogans adopted, especially since the mid-1970s, were those stressing Vojvodina's status as a constitutional element of the Yugoslav federation. Although the present-day demands of Vojvodina's autonomists are no longer cast within the self-management matrix, still it seems that certain aspects of the Communist era's ideological indoctrination had a subtler and further-reaching impact on quite a few second-generation colonists.[102]

Social psychology can provide an alternative explanation. According to Zdzislaw Mach, as a result of a variety of pressures from their social background (e.g. the school, the family circle and other spaces of social interaction), the second generation of migrants generally demonstrated an inclination to outbid themselves in integrating, even assimilating,

---

[99] For a brief example of this specific trend among Vojvodina's old settlers see Boarov, *Politička Istorija Vojvodine*, 240–51 (English-language summary). The author, Dimitrije Boarov, is an 'old' Vojvodinian Serb himself.
[100] Interview with historian at the University of Novi Sad; 13 March 2001.
[101] The most notable example, perhaps, is the League's leader, Nenad Čanak, an individual coming from a family background that traces its origins in Lika. This fact soon generated much criticism, even irony, on behalf of Vojvodina's pro-centralist old settlers, towards Čanak and his party. For instance, *Liga Socijal-Demokrata Vojvodine* would often be addressed, in a joking manner, as *Lika Socijal-Demokrata Vojvodine*.
[102] Interview with historian at the University of Novi Sad; 13 March 2001. Also, interview with representative of Vojvodina's Reformists; Novi Sad, 20 March 2001.

to the new environment. In the author's own words, the second generations of migrant groups often try to pose as 'more Catholic than the Pope' in their endeavour to integrate into the social environment.[103] This phenomenon was the polar opposite to the reactivation of the sentimental connection with the lands of their ancestors in Croatia and Bosnia, among other colonists, during the outburst of interethnic conflicts in the former Yugoslavia.

The regionalist opposition in Vojvodina acquired a more coherent shape from the mid-1990s onwards. In 7 December 1995, seventeen Vojvodinian parties/political groupings as well as civic groups and NGOs signed a common declaration under the title 'Manifesto for the Autonomy of Vojvodina'.[104] This document was signed by the League but, for still unknown reasons, not by the Reformist Party. The text of the manifesto expressed the following demands: a constitutional procedure for the revision of the Serbian Constitution so that Vojvodina would be recognized as 'an autonomous entity within the jurisdiction of the Republic of Serbia and FR Yugoslavia and, at the same time, as a modern European region with the competency to forge bilateral relations with other regions in the neighbouring states or elsewhere in the Continent'; the full endorsement of the individual/collective rights of the national minorities resident in Vojvodina; the recognition of Vojvodina as a 'community of citizens' (*laička zajednica*) endorsed with 'political and legal subjectivity – on the basis of the federal and republican constitutional principles – to enjoy its regional autonomy within the bounds of the Serbian republican jurisdiction'; the consolidation of Vojvodina's revised status within Serbia and FR Yugoslavia through reference to the legal acts of the international community in regard to the territory of the former Yugoslavia (e.g. the Dayton Agreement).

The Vojvodinian autonomists decided to form a united front for the November 1996 Yugoslav and local elections. A coalition named *Koalicija Vojvodina* (Coalition Vojvodina) was formed, comprising

---

[103] Mach 1989.
[104] Boarov, *Politička Istorija Vojvodine*, 228–9.

LSDV, RDSV and the National Peasants' Party. The coalition adopted a balanced platform with the objective to attract voters from all segments of the electorate. Programmatic standpoints that castigated Vojvodina's alleged economic exploitation by the central government (most of them prepared by Nenad Čanak) coexisted with the declaration that 'regardless of Vojvodina's historic and cultural particularities in relation to the rest of Serbia, the question of Vojvodina's administrative status remains, first of all, a Serbian issue' (the latter prepared by the National Peasant leader, Dragan Veselinov). The coalition's performance, though, was not very successful.

The relations between the *autonomaši* and the governing apparatus were anything but positive from the start. The SPS functionaries in Vojvodina stood firm in their position that the province's autonomy was fully endorsed and that it was not negatively affected by the constitutional reforms of 1990. Moreover, the SPS and JUL representatives saw in Vojvodina's regionalists 'potentially dangerous separatists' and 'pawns of anti-Serbian decision-making centres based abroad'.[105] Similar and more vocal was the denunciation of the *autonomaši* by SRS. In addition to the accusations of separatism and pliability to 'foreign decision-making centres', the Radicals portrayed the regionalist opposition in Vojvodina as 'the inheritors of the Comintern's interwar strategy with the aim to fragment Serbia and undermine the collective status of the Serbian *narod* in its homeland'.[106] Especially the League was accused of expanding the interwar agenda of the Comintern and CPY on Serbia.[107]

The relations between the regionalists and the Vojvodinian representatives of the Belgrade-based 'democratic opposition' were more complex. As previously mentioned, a short-lived coalition was

---

[105] As emphasized in the declaration of the 3rd Congress of the Vojvodinian SPS Committee (issued in January 1996) 'the Socialists will fight against all these local forces that aim to fragment or separate Vojvodina from Serbia, namely the League of Vojvodina's Social-Democrats, the Democratic Community of Vojvodina's Hungarians and the Democratic Union of Vojvodina's Croats'. Socijalistička Partija Srbije- Pokrajinski Odbor SPSa u Vojvodini, 'Vojvodina 2000. Korak u novi vek- Izveštaj', Novi Sad, 1996, 2.

[106] Interview with SRS representative; Novi Sad, 1 April 2002.

[107] Ibid.

established between DS and the Reformist Party of Vojvodina in the December 1992 Yugoslav and Serbian elections. On that occasion, the DS representatives in the province turned out to be flexible and agreed on a common platform with their counterparts, in which the need for Serbia's democratization combined with the demand for the restitution of certain competencies to Vojvodina. However, relations with SPO were not particularly positive. Vuk Drašković's party formally did not oppose a certain degree of autonomous jurisdiction for Vojvodina. SPO did not object to the concession of decision-making powers to Vojvodina on economic and cultural matters. According to its Programmatic Declarations, the party favoured 'the concession of broad economic authority to Vojvodina, as well as the efficient protection of the national, religious and cultural rights of the national minorities within its territory'. At the same time, though, it was stressed that the concession of any sort of jurisdiction to Vojvodina 'must not jeopardize the unity of the Serbian state or, as far as interethnic relations are concerned, the rights of the province's Serb majority'.

In this light, the SPO officials in Vojvodina did not view from a positive angle what they regarded as the 'parochial' insistence of the regionalists on the province's status. By contrast, SPO always put primary importance on the need to bring an end to the Socialists' rule in Serbia as a whole and viewed regionalist initiatives as potentially detrimental to the broader political objectives of the 'democratic opposition'. With specific regard to the Vojvodinian political landscape, the SPO functionaries often accused the *autonomaši* of fomenting unnecessary 'crypto-secessionist' tendencies and, occasionally, denounced them as 'separatists'.[108] The stance of the Vojvodinian DSS branch vis-à-vis the regionalist elites did not differentiate much from that held by SPO.

The state of friction between the representatives of the 'democratic opposition' and the regionalists, the LSDV in particular, reached a critical point in early 1998. By that time, Čanak and his party had

---

[108] Boarov, *Politička Istorija Vojvodine*, 231.

abandoned their concept of Vojvodina enjoying an asymmetric status within Serbia and started propagating the territorial reorganization of Serbia in terms of a symmetrically arranged federation (Vojvodina being one of the constituent parts). What infuriated certain representatives of the 'democratic opposition' in Vojvodina, however, was the League's proposal in its 'Declaration for a Republic of Vojvodina' (February 1998) that Kosovo must obtain republican status within FR Yugoslavia, as a means to pacify Albanian irredentist trends within that province and keep Kosovo within the 'third' Yugoslav federation.[109] In light of the increasing radicalization among Kosovan Albanians, the representatives of SPO and other opposition parties interpreted Čanak's proposal as a first step towards the southern province's secession from Serbia.

The powerful emergence of *Vojvođanski identitet* as a mass political phenomenon

Nevertheless, it was precisely during the late 1990s that the gap between the regionalists and the provincial representatives of the Belgrade-based opposition parties was gradually bridged. This had largely to do with the 'situational' reinforcement of Vojvodinian regional identity. This process took place within the bipolar interaction between Belgrade and the province and it reflected a set of grievances, on behalf of the latter, towards certain policies pursued by the former. Vojvodina's sociocultural particularities (namely, its richly diverse ethno-cultural composition) infused this identity-reinforcement process with a multidimensional character, which also comprised a sociocultural aspect besides the political and economic ones. In all of this, the role of political and economic interest groups within the province remained of vital significance.

---

[109] Also, the symbolic use of the 1980s Albanian slogan '*Kosovo Republika*' by Nenad Čanak, on the occasion of the presentation of the League's declaration in Sremska Mitrovica, generated additional tension. Ibid., 232.

Consequently, the regionalists, the League in particular, constantly employed as a key argument of their rhetoric the alleged 'plunder' of Vojvodina (in their jargon: *pljačka*) by the centre. The employment of this argument intensified, in the course of the deteriorating economic situation in the province. By the late 1990s, the representatives of the Belgrade-based opposition parties in Vojvodina also started to add a more powerful 'Vojvodinian' dimension to their agendas. The revitalized interest, on behalf of the rest of the 'democratic opposition' in Vojvodina, on issues pertaining to the province as such should not be interpreted as a political victory of the *autonomaši*. Nor should it be taken as an indication of the latter's increasing popularity among the Vojvodinian electorate, since this was not the case. Although the platforms of the various *autonomaši* circles expressed some major grievances of the province's populace, the adoption of more 'Vojvodina-specific' standpoints by the anti-SPS opposition in the province as a whole was the outcome of a more complex bottom-up process.

First of all, deficient economic management exerted a definitive impact on the political attitudes of Vojvodina's citizens. Especially the use of a considerable percentage of the province's revenues, by the republican government, in order to subsidize other less developed Serbian regions was a factor that embittered many Vojvodinians vis-à-vis the regime in Belgrade. To this one might add the broader collateral damage inflicted on Vojvodina's economy by certain policies pursued by the regime, such as the international sanctions which rendered the cross-border transactions between Vojvodina and other regions in the neighbouring states extremely problematic; the Yugoslav government's inconsistent policies on the ex-Yugoslav crisis and their consequences for Vojvodina (e.g. the influx of refugees from the interethnic wars). In the long term, these economic grievances interweaved with others of a more sociocultural nature. In other words, a notable percentage among Vojvodina's citizens became increasingly disappointed with the visible impact of the past decade's nationalist resurgence on the Vojvodinian society; namely the relative deterioration of the interethnic relations and the emergence of interethnic cleavages.

The combination of these catalysts gradually made a larger number of Vojvodinians keener on the idea that their province must enjoy greater autonomy in matters of regional administration. In almost all cases, the term autonomy implied the regional devolution of the economic administration. Apart from that, however, the very same term generated a rather abstract variety of opinions in regard to the regional devolution of the political administration.

Consequently, a variety of 'symmetric' and most commonly 'asymmetric' viewpoints over the reassessment of Vojvodina's status within Serbia and FR Yugoslavia made their appearance on the grassroots level. In spite of this diversity of viewpoints, though, what remains of primary significance is that the developments throughout the 1990s made an increasing percentage of Vojvodinians more conscious over their province's specific needs; a popular trend which was soon communicated on the political level.

Nevertheless, it should not be understood that the deterioration of the socioeconomic situation during the 1990s caused the re-emergence of Vojvodinian identity almost by default. Nor should it be understood that this bottom-up process was a mere symptom of the parochialization of sociopolitical attitudes in Serbia as a whole, as a result of the worsening material conditions. Especially in regard to the sociocultural aspect, the earlier cited results of the public surveys carried out during the 1990s indicate that the trans-ethnic substratum of the *Vojvođanski identitet* was always there, on the grassroots level. The emergence of interethnic cleavages in Vojvodina did not bring about any sort of large-scale segregation within the province and the instances of interethnic violence were certainly not as pronounced as was the case in the other multiethnic regions of the former Yugoslavia. Therefore, the deterioration of the material conditions over the 1990s was merely the trigger that made the residents of Vojvodina (Serbs and national minorities alike) regain more emphatically their regional consciousness and opt for certain changes, as perceived from a variety of angles, for the benefit of their province.

Vojvodina and Montenegro: A comparison

At this point, it would be interesting to make a qualitative comparison between the Vojvodinian case and the case of another 'situationally-reinforced' identity within FR Yugoslavia over the same period; the Montenegrin one. A common denominator between the two cases was the fact that the reinforcement of both identities was largely fuelled by unfavourable economic circumstances. In the Montenegrin case, popular grievances towards the regime in Belgrade were caused by the impact that the international sanctions had on the economic performance of Montenegro (e.g. difficulties in conducting trade with foreign states; the atrophying state of Montenegro's tourist industry). Despite their common point of departure, however, the two cases were characterized by essential differences.

By contrast to Vojvodina, in Montenegro, the reinforcement of Montenegrin identity was largely engineered from the top level downwards and from within the governing structures. Furthermore, even though Đukanović's change of course corresponded to the economic grievances of quite a few of his compatriots, there still exists some evidence that the transformation of his previous stance was conditioned by additional factors. Owing to its geographic location, Montenegro was rendered a hotspot of grey economic activity (mainly smuggling and other sanctions-busting activities) during the 1990s. In this light, the privatization policy pursued by Đukanović's government since 1997, as well as the strengthening of economic cooperation with neighbouring Italy and Croatia, should not be merely viewed as an attempt to distance Montenegro's position from the failed Serbian policies for the benefit of the former's citizens. It was also a policy dictated by the demands of certain 'grey' entrepreneurs – with access to the Đukanović circle – who saw in the aforementioned policies the solution for the gradual legalization of their semi-legal or fully illegal activities.[110] In Vojvodina, on the contrary, the regional autonomy issue and grey economic activity formed two completely separate areas.

On the other hand, there exist differences in regard to the popular bases of support of the two trends. In Vojvodina, the reinforcement of regional identity (also the various anti-autonomy standpoints) cut across the 'old settler/colonist' distinction and was irrespective of the territorial factor. In Montenegro, on the contrary, the stronghold of the reformed DPS, as well as that of the strongest proponents of a distinct Montenegrin identity, was situated along the coast; the southeast part in particular. This is the most developed part of Montenegro, where many of the locals were engaged in the tourist industry as well as the above-mentioned grey economic activities. It is also home to certain ethnic minorities (Albanians, Montenegrin Muslims) who, from their own perspectives, did not see Podgorica's differentiation from Belgrade as a negative sign. In stark contrast, the Montenegrin hinterlands were soon rendered stronghold of the anti-Đukanović opposition and home of the proponents of an essentially Serbian Montenegrin identity. On the latter occasion, the semi-clannish social organization largely accounted for the preservation of certain collective myths regarding the alleged quality of Montenegrins as the 'purest Serbs' (e.g. the state of autonomy enjoyed by the Montenegrin hinterlands in the centuries of the Ottoman conquest).

Moreover, even though the question of Vojvodina's status stirred heated debates, it never amounted to the actual polarization of the Vojvodinian society. In Montenegro, on the contrary, the split of the old DPS corresponded to a state of polarization within the society. The polarization between the pro-Bulatović and the pro-Đukanović camps reached such an extent that, just as was the case during the

---

[110] The indictment of the Montenegrin Foreign Minister Branko Perović and other Montenegrin officials with charges of illegal cigarette trading by the Italian authorities (December 1999) attests to the validity of this argument. Goati Vladimir, *Izbori u SRJ od 1990 do 1998 – Volja građana ili izborna manipulacija* (CESID: Belgrade, 2001), 142.

early 1990s in Serbia, political preferences were rendered an indicator of either 'patriotic' or 'treacherous' orientations. Consequently, it almost became fashionable for supporters of the reformed DPS to be referred to by their rivals as 'Turks' or 'pawns of the new world order' and, on the other hand, supporters of the Socialist National Party (SNP) and Bulatović to be addressed as 'Bolsheviks' or 'servants of Belgrade' by the opposing camp. The fear of civic unrest caused by this state of polarization obstructed the organization of a referendum over the question 'independence or union with Serbia?' throughout the 1990s.

Finally, the appropriation of a distinct Montenegrin identity in the 1990s, on the academic as well as the popular level, largely drew its material from similar attempts made during the Communist era. It reflected the continuation of discourses that had appeared during the 1970s and the '80s in publications such as *Ovđe* and *Stvaranje*. The renewed discourses touched upon subjects such as a presumed Montenegrin 'core' identity, through reference to certain elements of Montenegrin folk tradition, certain aspects of social organization specific to Montenegro (e.g. the semi-clannish social organization of the Montenegrin hinterlands), linguistic factors (the use of the western *ijekavica* variant in contrast to the *ekavica* spoken in Serbia) and the collective memory of old state's formations in the region (the old Kingdom of Zeta; the anti-unionist *zelenaši* dynastic notables and their followers[111]).

In Vojvodina, things were distinctly different. As already clarified, no attempts, even subtle, were made during the Communist era with the objective to promote a distinct 'core' Vojvodinian identity in relation to the Serbian one. By contrast, the image of Vojvodina as a successfully integrated multiethnic community was promoted, though always within the ideological spectrum of self-management. In a rather

---

[111] The *zelenaši* ('Greens') were supporters of the Montenegrin King Nikola Petrović who, between the late nineteenth and the early twentieth centuries, opposed Montenegro's unification with Serbia.

similar light, the revitalization of Vojvodinian identity in the second half of the 1990s never corresponded to any attempts to appropriate a Vojvodinian identity separate from the Serbian one, or the other group identities of the province. By contrast, *Vojvođanski identitet* and all the components associated with it (e.g. the space of Vojvodina through time; some common behavioural patterns adopted by all groups resident in the province) were granted the meaning of a sociocultural mosaic where the Serbs and the other groups could coexist without, at the same time, being deprived of their particularities. On the political level, the very same concept functioned as the common ground that enabled all residents of Vojvodina to share their aspirations and air some common grievances towards the central government. The only area where the respective Vojvodinian and Montenegrin issues interweaved with each other was the question of structural reorganization in FR Yugoslavia, triggered by the gradual distancing of Podgorica from Belgrade.

The standardization of the anti-SPS opposition in Vojvodina

Coming back to Vojvodina, the first attempt to conceptualize the common stance of the Serbian 'democratic opposition' on the reassessment of the province's status within Serbia was made at the meeting of the opposition representatives in Vienna, Austria (23–25 September 1999). In the communiqué of this meeting, attended by political representatives of all opposition parties, it was commonly agreed that 'the autonomy of Vojvodina within the Republic of Serbia corresponds to the interests of democratization and decentralization of Serbia as well as the preservation of its sovereignty and territorial integrity. It also represents the most suitable framework for the resolution of all issues pertaining to the national communities ... these issues are more efficiently resolved on the local level'; 'decentralization and greater autonomy for the municipalities, including the management of respective shares of revenues, is an important element of the modern democratic government; regionalization and formation of administrative districts requires taking into account interests of citizens and interests of ethnic communities'.¹¹²

Nevertheless, certain disagreements on the top level persisted between the regionalists and the representatives of other opposition parties. For instance, the SPO officials contended that the League's proposal for the restructuring of Serbia in terms of a symmetric federation might appeal to certain sections of the Vojvodinian electorate but not to the voters resident in the other parts of Serbia. Consequently, they objected to the inclusion of those or similar proposals in the opposition's central platform and, once again, underlined that the Serbian opposition should set as its top objective the effective elimination of SPS from the country's political map. In the longer term, a consensus was reached and the Platform of the Serbian Democratic Opposition (3 March 2000) included a clause according to which 'a new Serbian Constitution should be inaugurated where the elaboration of forms of administrative autonomy for Kosmet and Vojvodina, on the grounds of the two provinces' historic and cultural particularities, would be ensured'.¹¹³ The very same clause was later included in the main platform adopted by DOS in summer 2000. The epitome of these programmatic declarations was a document signed by the representatives of the victorious DOS coalition at the Vojvodinian Assembly in October 2000, where the respect to Vojvodinian autonomy was endorsed by the new government; the inauguration of a new constitutional act, endowing Vojvodina with special legislative, judicial and executive functions, was envisaged.¹¹⁴

The ethnic Hungarian parties in Vojvodina

Two of the parties that signed all aforementioned documents and later participated in DOS were the Democratic Community of Hungarians

---

¹¹² Project on Ethnic Relations, *Vojvodina: The Politics of Interethnic Accommodation* (Vienna, 23-25 September 1999; Athens, 13-15 February 2000), 37-8. These standpoints were repeated and expanded at the meeting held on 13-15 February 2000 in Athens, Greece. Ibid., 39-41.

¹¹³ Boarov, *Politička Istorija Vojvodine*, 237-8.

¹¹⁴ Ibid., 240. It should be added that this document was not signed by the representatives of DSS at the Vojvodinian Assembly.

in Vojvodina (Hungarian: *Vajdasagi Magyarok Demokratikus Kozossege*, VMDK) and the Alliance of Hungarians in Vojvodina (*Vajdasagi Magyar Szovetseg*, VMSZ). The two parties sprang from the division of the united VMDK in 1994. The VMDK was initially launched in Novi Sad on 14 February 1990, under the leadership of Andras Agoston. The party opted for a tripartite concept of autonomy for Vojvodina's Hungarians, which consisted of: personal autonomy[115]; territorial autonomy[116]; local self-administration.[117] The VMDK officials regarded their concept as a fair compromise between the right to self-determination and the principle of inviolability of national borders. A very similar concept of tripartite autonomy had been proposed, at the same time, by the Democratic Alliance of Hungarians in Romania (Cluj Declaration, October 1992).[118]

As was also the case with the Transylvanian Hungarians, the first half of the 1990s saw the powerful 'political ethnification' of Vojvodinian Hungarians (those resident in the Northern Bačka enclave, in particular) who put their overwhelming support behind VMDK. The insistence of VMDK on ethno-territorial autonomy was an additional factor that prevented the party from finding a common ground with the representatives of the Serbian 'democratic opposition' in Vojvodina. By the mid-1990s, however, certain changes occurred. By 1994, a dissenter group made its appearance within the bounds of VMDK. This group

---

[115] Personal autonomy addressed the collective legal subjectivity of the Hungarian minority; a partner-like relation to the Serbian and provincial governments. This notion addressed the vitally important fields of culture, education and public information with the aim to protect the ethno-cultural, linguistic and religious identity of the minority. Personal autonomy further entailed the formation of a Hungarian minority assembly in Vojvodina.

[116] Territorial autonomy referred to the self-government of those municipalities where the Hungarian concentration was particularly dense. This would involve the merger of the predominantly Hungarian populated municipalities into a Hungarian autonomous region; a special status entity with a separate management. This proposed autonomous region would stretch along the Kanjiza–Senta–Topola line and have its seat in Subotica.

[117] Local self-administration would be exercised in certain rural communities with a predominantly Hungarian population, along the Serbian-Hungarian border. On all these issues see VMDK, *Memorandum on Self-Administration of Hungarians Living in the Republic of Serbia* (Novi Sad, 1992).

[118] Aurelian Craiutu, 'A Dilemma of Dual Identity: The Democratic Alliance of Hungarians in Romania', *East European Constitutional Review*, Spring 1995, 43–9.

accused the leadership of arbitrary decision-making and complete disregard of the viewpoints of the lower ranks within VMDK.[119] The unbridgeable gap between the dissident group and the rest party leadership led to the expulsion of seventy-five prominent VMDK members by the latter. The expelled members founded the Alliance of Hungarians in Vojvodina in due time.

VMSZ acquired a more concrete shape as a political actor through the adoption of its 'Proposal for an Agreement on the Self-Organization of the Hungarians in Vojvodina' in January 1996.[120] The programmatic foundations of this document did not differentiate from those of the 1992 VMDK Memorandum (e.g. the concept of the tripartite autonomy). Nevertheless, whereas the concept of VMDK described the goal of ethno-territorial autonomy for Vojvodina's Hungarians, the proposal of VMSZ went one step further and drafted the way that it could be realized. Contrary to the VMDK's demand for the establishment of a 'centralized' Hungarian Assembly in Vojvodina, VMSZ proposed the establishment of five separate councils within the assembly, each of which dealing with the major areas of interest for the Hungarian community (the Political Council, Council of Education, Cultural Council, Media Council and Council of Science – Section IV, Paragraphs 1, 2, 3, 4).

The document drafted by VMSZ went one step ahead the VMDK declaration and namely proposed nine municipalities,[121] which would form the 'Hungarian Self-Governing District'; the latter being under the jurisdiction of the political council (Section V, Paragraph Aa). According to the same document, the superiors and officers in a variety of organizations within the autonomous district (the community courts, the revenue service and the police) would be appointed by the authorities of the district self-government, agreed

---

[119] Laszlo Szekeres, '*VMDK-s voltam*', *Magyar Szo*, 28 May 28–7 July 1995. Szekeres was one of the VMDK members expelled from the party in 1994.

[120] VMSZ, *Proposal for an Agreement on the Self-Organization of Hungarians in Vojvodina (The Concept of the Alliance of Hungarians in Vojvodina)*, Novi Sad, 18 January 1996.

[121] These municipalities were, namely Ada, Bačka Topola, Bečej, Čoka, Kanjiza, Mali Idoš, Subotica, Kneževac and Senta.

upon by consent of the Serbian Parliament (Section V, Paragraph B). In a further attempt to convince the Serb majority about its non-secessionist motives, the VMSZ proposal stated that the competencies of the Hungarian Autonomous District would be agreed upon between the Political Council of the Assembly of Hungarians in Vojvodina and the Serbian Parliament, and they would be regulated by law (Section V, Paragraph A). Finally, the text explicitly states that even though it should not be hindered from maintaining bilateral relations with the neighbouring municipalities in Hungary, the Hungarian Autonomous District must remain a part of the Serbian administrative structure and have essentially the same entitlements, rights and duties as the other Serbian districts (Ibid.).

Nevertheless, what essentially differentiated VMSZ from VMDK was the fact that the former placed more emphatically the Hungarian issue in Vojvodina within: the question of restoring certain competencies to the Assembly of the Autonomous Province of Vojvodina; the question of democratic changes in Serbia as a whole. With specific regard to the former, the VMSZ proposal overtly demanded that 'the autonomous provinces should gain back the right to legislate in the domains of education and culture' (Section III, Paragraph II.1).[122] Even further, the party stood firm in its position that the question of Vojvodinian Hungarians was indissolubly linked with the broader question of political changes in Serbia, by actively approaching the 'democratic opposition' and seeking cooperation with them. The first actual instance of cooperation between VMSZ and the 'democratic opposition' was at the local elections of November 1996, when the party formed a coalition with the Vojvodinian Reformists.

At the other end of the spectrum, VMDK repeatedly set as top priority the question of ethnic Hungarian autonomy within Vojvodina and regarded the issues of Vojvodinian autonomy and the democratization of Serbia as separate questions, primarily concerning

---

[122] It should be added that this demand, as put in the text, did not regard exclusively the Hungarians of Vojvodina but the Slovaks, the Ruthenes and the Romanians as well (Section III, Paragraph III.2).

the Serbs in Vojvodina and the rest of Serbia. Furthermore, VMDK were more interested in presenting their standpoints to the international community (e.g. international and European organizations such as the OSCE) and seeking support from the Hungarian government in Budapest, instead of engaging into any sort of negotiations with representatives of the Serbian political elites.[123]

The dichotomy of the policies pursued by VMSZ and VMDK witnessed a notable political development within the Hungarian community: The emergence of intra-minority pluralism and its gradual prevalence over the persistence of groupness, which was triggered by the process of political ethnification and was typical of Vojvodina's Hungarian minority until the mid-1990s. In turn, the vocal rejection, on behalf of the Hungarian political elites, of any sort of cooperation with the Serbian political elites (on the top as well as on the grass-roots level) gave its way to more flexible alternatives, which opted for macro-level changes in the Serbian political landscape that could have a positive impact on the minority group micro-level. Consequently, even though the political preferences of most ethnic Hungarians in the northern Bačka enclave still rotated around ethnic parties, the Hungarian political map in Vojvodina no longer was monolithic.

This fully contrasted with the contemporary case of the Transylvanian Hungarians and their political elites, whose political introversion and groupness persisted throughout the decade. An additional difference between the Hungarian minority cases in Vojvodina and Transylvania was the fact that in the former case the alternative policies pursued by VMSZ effectively broke the erstwhile prevalent triadic nexus relation among the minority, the Serbian state and Hungary. In other words, the Hungarian political elites progressively opted for the improvement of the minority's status through political changes on the Serbian macro-level, instead of seeking support from Budapest. This process

---

[123] Ildiko Arpasy, *The Hungarians in Vojvodina: Political Condition of a Minority in a Nationalizing State* (MA Thesis, Central European University Press, Budapest, 1996), 40, 43, 62.

culminated with the final cooperation of both ethnic Hungarian parties with the Serbian opposition.

Even more significant is the fact that these developments on the elite level found a positive response from the grassroots level. This initially manifested in the 1996 Yugoslav elections where VMSZ won 81,310 votes and three seats in the Chamber of Citizens of the Federal Assembly. On the other hand, VMDK won a mere 46,807 votes and no representatives on the federal level. The results in the provincial elections held in the same year were even more positive for VMSZ. Of 120 seats in the Vojvodinian assembly, VMSZ won thirteen (10.8 per cent) and the VMDK only one (0.8 per cent). Political analysts interpreted these results as a punishment of the VMDK leadership for the 1994 purges and their intra-party authoritarianism. Nevertheless, it seems more likely that the results of the 1996 electoral contest were a reward to VMSZ's more articulate concept of autonomy and its more pragmatic strategy that, apart from minority rights, opted for a 'Vojvodina for all' inside a democratic Serbia.

Vojvodina and Kosovo: A comparison

At this point, it would be interesting to proceed to a qualitative comparison between the cases of Kosovo and Vojvodina and the political attitudes of their Albanian and Hungarian populations, in the second half of the 1990s. With regard to Kosovo, comparative evidence from other cases of interethnic conflict demonstrates that hegemonic control is not always a successful instrument for managing ethnic differences. This instrument often marginalizes the moderate segments within the ethnic community in question, it simultaneously bolsters radicals and ultimately hinders prospects for peaceful accommodation in the future.[124] Indeed, in Kosovo, the Serbian top-level policies resulted in

---

[124] On the Northern Irish case, see Brendan O' Duffy, 'British and Irish Conflict Regulation: From Sunningdale to Belfast. Part I: Tracing the Status of Contesting Sovereigns, 1968–1974', *Nations and Nationalism* 5, no. 4 (1999): 529–33.

the radicalization of the Albanian community, a development that saw the gradual outflanking of Ibrahim Rugova and his passive resistance policies by KLA.[125] In Vojvodina, on the contrary, the policies of the Serbian nationalizing state were much subtler. Therefore, there was no serious chance that the large-scale radicalization of the Hungarian, or any other ethnic, community might be triggered 'from above'.

On the other hand, a key difference between the political attitudes of the Vojvodinian Hungarians and the Kosovan Albanians was the continuous participation of the former in the state's political arena and the boycott of all sorts of mainstream political activity (e.g. elections at all levels) by the latter. In Vojvodina, participation in the state's political life was the case with all minority groups. The overwhelming success of the boycott in Kosovo was not merely an indication of successful mass mobilization by the 'parallel' elites; it also relied on a sociological factor. This factor was the prevalence of a highly collectivist social ethos among Kosovo's Albanians. This, in combination with the persistence of a highly patriarchal as well as extended family ethos within the same community, might make the participation in the boycott appear (in accordance with a homocentric circles pattern) as the moral thing for an individual to do with respect to the family and the extended kin, the local community and the ethnic group as such.[126] The combination of all aforementioned catalysts also accounted to a large extent for the

---

[125] For further information on Ibrahim Rugova's LDK, its passive resistance agenda and the 'parallel' political organizations in Kosovo see Sqhelzen Maliqi, 'The Albanian Movement in Kosova', in *Yugoslavia and After*, 138–54; Janusz Bugajski, *Ethnic Politics in Eastern Europe: A Guide to Nationality Policies, Organizations and Parties*, New York: The Center for Strategic and International Studies (1994), 153–6. On the origins, the formation and the increasing popularity of KLA among the ethnic Albanian masses, see Tim Judah, 'A History of the Kosovo Liberation Army', in *Kosovo: Contending Voices on Balkan Interventions*, ed. William Joseph Buckley (Cambridge: Eerdmans Publishing, 2000), 108–15.

[126] Similar patterns of grassroots political behaviour are encountered among the semi-clannish Ghegs of Northern Albania. On certain occasions, a political candidate's clan background can be of primary significance for his popular appeal. A typical example is the vast support channelled towards Sali Berisha, the leader of the Democratic Party of Albania, by the Northern Albanian electorate at the first Albanian multiparty elections (March–April 1991). Sali Berisha belongs to the powerful Gheg clan of the Berishas.

high degree of political homogeneity among the Kosovan Albanians[127] and, following the community's radicalization process, the unequivocal support channelled towards KLA.

In the Vojvodinian Hungarian case, on the contrary, neither a high degree of internal political homogeneity (especially since the mid-1990s) nor any indications of ethnic radicalization were the case. In regard to the latter, no demands, even subtle, were ever raised by the Hungarian political elites in Vojvodina for the secession of the northern Bačka enclave from Serbia. Especially during the second half of the 1990s, the Vojvodinian Hungarian elites would always try to maintain a responsible and balanced stance with regard to ethnic issues pertaining not only to the micro-level of the province but the Serbian/Yugoslav macro-level as well.[128]

Finally, the most essential difference between Vojvodina and Kosovo was that, in the former case, the persistence of the transethnic substratum of *Vojvođanski identitet*, as a mass phenomenon, effectively preserved the character of Vojvodina as a multiethnic space. This was definitely the factor that brought Vojvodina's political elites together, regardless of the ethnic divisions. By contrast, in the case of Kosovo, a combination of ethnic segregation on the grassroots level and unbridgeable standpoints between the political actors involved (the Serbian state and the Albanian 'parallel' elites) resulted, first, in the extreme aggravation of the crisis and, following NATO's intervention, the transformation of the southern province into a mono-ethnic and mono-cultural society.

---

[127] Even though the 'parallel' political landscape in Kosovo comprised nearly eighteen parties, Rugova's LDK enjoyed the support of over 95 per cent of Kosovan Albanians throughout most of the 1990s.

[128] In the eve of the NATO bombing, the VMSZ presidium issued a declaration in which it was stressed that 'the resolution of the Kosovo question can only be achieved by means of negotiations'. The party condemned the incoming air campaign against Serbia as unacceptable because 'it would sink the country into even greater misery and endanger the lives of *the entirety* of its citizens, including the Hungarians of Vojvodina'. The party equally castigated 'Slobodan Milošević's decade-long domestic policy of defying the entire world'. On this issue, see the 'Statement by the Presidium of the Alliance of Hungarians in Vojvodina Regarding the Situation in Kosovo', 24 March 1999 (http://www.hhrf.org/kosovo.htm).

The change of the political guard in Serbia: The contribution of the Vojvodinian voters

The Yugoslav elections of 1996 in Vojvodina were marked by the decisive victory of the SPS–JUL–ND coalition. The 'left' coalition garnered 35.57 per cent of the vote (371,875 votes and 12 mandates in the Federal Chamber of Citizens) to the 15.57 per cent (163,659 votes and 3 mandates) won by *Zajedno* and the 18.96 per cent (199,390 votes and 6 mandates) won by the SRS. As for the regionalist *Koalicija Vojvodina*, it garnered 6.53 per cent of the total vote (68,669 votes) and secured two seats at the federal parliament.

The results of the 1996 federal elections in Vojvodina can be interpreted, first of all, through reference to 'objective' factors that were of a crucial significance throughout Serbia. The most noteworthy was the inability of *Zajedno* to overcome its internal inconsistency and project a solid and convincing image to the Serbian electorate. On the other hand, the performance of the anti-SPS opposition in the provincial elections that were held at the same time was largely affected by the electoral legislation. First, the application of an absolute majority system enabled SPS to secure 67.2 per cent of the seats (74 out of 110) at the Vojvodinian assembly with only 23 per cent of the total vote (236,414 out of 1,025,103). Moreover, in the same contest, a peculiar two-round majority system was applied in the election of the premier of the Vojvodinian assembly. The peculiarity of that system, in comparison to the procedure applied in the federal and municipal elections, rested in the fact that it was three (instead of 2) candidates, winning the greatest number of votes, who entered the second round. Therefore, it became fairly obvious that the application of this system aimed at weakening the possibilities of a serious challenge to SPS's rule on the provincial level. As the actual outcome of the poll demonstrated, it was highly improbable that the two other candidates could gain in their own right as many votes as the SPS one.

However, the victory of *Zajedno* in the 1996 municipal elections in Novi Sad served as an early indication that Novi Sad and the other major urban centres in the province would soon become the strongholds of the 'democratic opposition' in Vojvodina. Apart from Novi Sad, *Zajedno* also won the local councils in the industrial centre of Kikinda, the small borderline town of Vršac and, although not winning the contest, had a decent performance in Sombor, Pančevo and Zrenjanin (Table 12). What served as an additional indication of the increasingly dominant political trends in the Vojvodinian capital and the other major urban centres was the particularly successful mobilization of their population in the course of the autumn–winter 1996 protests.

Table 12 Electoral results by number of votes at selected municipalities in Vojvodina

Novi Sad

Parties	Local 1996	Yugoslav 1996	Serbian 1997	Serbian Presidential 1997 (Third round)
SPS	32,742			48,234
SPS–JUL–ND		39,124	30,794	
SRS	30,203	36,567	40,835	20,584
SPO			12,624	
DSS	1,493			
ZAJEDNO	37,064	28,141		
KOALICIJA VOJVODINA	6,695	29,016	27,995	
VMDK	1,867			
VMSZ				
Others	28,992	7,048	16,546	

Pančevo

Parties	Local 1996	Yugoslav 1996	Serbian 1997	Serbian Presidential 1997 (Third round)
SPS	17,996		18,049	24,994
SPS–JUL–ND		27,028		

Parties	Local 1996	Yugoslav 1996	Serbian 1997	Serbian Presidential 1997 (Third round)
SRS	5,950	12,590	17,687	22,484
SPO			11,359	
ZAJEDNO	17,180	14,240		
KOALICIJA VOJVODINA			4,500	
VMDK	315	1,438		
VMSZ				
Others	17,488	4,925	4,654	

Zrenjanin

Parties	Local 1996	Yugoslav 1996	Serbian 1997	Serbian Presidential 1997 (Third round)
SPS	19,105			28,529
SPS–JUL–ND		21,653	18,154	
SRS	11,563	12,676	19,438	22,289
SPO			5,892	
ZAJEDNO	15,220	9,464		
KOALICIJA VOJVODINA	4,498	12,800	10,722	
VMDK	36			
VMSZ		3,129	1,032	
Others	16,553	7,362	7,930	

Kikinda and Vršac (local elections, 1996)

Parties	Kikinda	Vršac
SPS	8,661	
SRS	7,624	2,069
ZAJEDNO	8,810	9,073
KOALICIJA VOJVODINA	4,556	
VMDK	339	

Parties	Kikinda	Vršac
VMSZ	432	
Others	7,431	13,503

Sremska Mitrovica

Parties	Local 1996	Yugoslav 1996	Serbian 1997	Serbian 1997 (Third round)
SPS	13,834			19,614
SPS–JUL–ND		18,557	14,498	
SRS	10,006	12,007	16,197	18,880
SPO			6,791	
ZAJEDNO	8,558	9,480		
KOALICIJA VOJVODINA			4,598	
VMDK				
VMSZ				
Others	10,458	3,605	2,971	

Stara Pazova

Parties	Local 1996	Yugoslav 1996	Serbian 1997	Serbian Presidential 1997 (Third round)
SPS	8,900			11,022
SPS–JUL–ND		11,736	7,273	
SRS	6,270	8,423	10,972	11,758
SPO			3,290	
ZAJEDNO	4,636	4,654		
KOALICIJA VOJVODINA			1,724	
VMDK				

Parties	Local 1996	Yugoslav 1996	Serbian 1997	Serbian Presidential 1997 (Third round)
VMSZ				
Others	7,069	2,193	1,927	

Sombor

Parties	Local 1996	Yugoslav 1996	Serbian 1997	Serbian Presidential 1997 (Third round)
SPS	12,987			21,426
SPS–JUL–ND		17,924	13,079	
SRS	8,345	10,285	15,109	15,940
SPO			3,180	
ZAJEDNO	12,573	9,445		
KOALICIJA VOJVODINA			4,646	
VMDK	1,826			
VMSZ	399	3,668		
Others	9,128	3,976	6,589	

Kovin

Parties	Local 1996	Yugoslav 1996	Serbian 1997	Serbian Presidential 1997 (Third round)
SPS	8,300			9,930
SPS–JUL–ND		9,197	6,727	
SRS	1,995	3,092	4,443	6,429
SPO			3,190	
ZAJEDNO	5,202	3,253		
KOALICIJA VOJVODINA			1,420	
VMDK	558			
VMSZ		741		
Others	2,578	1,851	1,206	

Alibunar

Parties	Local 1996	Yugoslav 1996	Serbian 1997	Serbian Presidential 1997 (Third round)
SPS	6,059			8,866
SPS-JUL-ND	801	6,106	4,470	
SRS		1,860	2,828	4,334
SPO			1,835	
ZAJEDNO	1,902	1,980		
KOALICIJA VOJVODINA			2,108	
VMDK				
VMZS			307	
Others	3,651	2,034	836	

Vršac

Parties	Yugoslav 1996	Serbian 1997	Serbian Presidential 1997 (Third round)
SPS			13,808
SPS-JUL-ND	10,821	8,922	
SRS	4,753	7,838	9,658
SPO		2,872	
ZAJEDNO	5,227		
KOALICIJA VOJVODINA		5,167	
VMDK			
VMSZ	771		
Others	3,128	1,596	

Subotica

Parties	Local 1996	Yugoslav 1996	Serbian 1997	Serbian Presidential 1997 (Third round)
SPS	8,482			37,583
SPS-JUL-ND		17,955	11,946	
SRS	7,515	5,394	10,033	11,801

Parties	Local 1996	Yugoslav 1996	Serbian 1997	Serbian Presidential 1997 (Third round)
VMSZ				
Others	7,069	2,193	1,927	

Sombor

Parties	Local 1996	Yugoslav 1996	Serbian 1997	Serbian Presidential 1997 (Third round)
SPS	12,987			21,426
SPS–JUL–ND		17,924	13,079	
SRS	8,345	10,285	15,109	15,940
SPO			3,180	
ZAJEDNO	12,573	9,445		
KOALICIJA VOJVODINA			4,646	
VMDK	1,826			
VMSZ	399	3,668		
Others	9,128	3,976	6,589	

Kovin

Parties	Local 1996	Yugoslav 1996	Serbian 1997	Serbian Presidential 1997 (Third round)
SPS	8,300			9,930
SPS–JUL–ND		9,197	6,727	
SRS	1,995	3,092	4,443	6,429
SPO			3,190	
ZAJEDNO	5,202	3,253		
KOALICIJA VOJVODINA			1,420	
VMDK	558			
VMSZ		741		
Others	2,578	1,851	1,206	

Alibunar

Parties	Local 1996	Yugoslav 1996	Serbian 1997	Serbian Presidential 1997 (Third round)
SPS	6,059			8,866
SPS-JUL-ND	801	6,106	4,470	
SRS		1,860	2,828	4,334
SPO			1,835	
ZAJEDNO	1,902	1,980		
KOALICIJA VOJVODINA			2,108	
VMDK				
VMZS			307	
Others	3,651	2,034	836	

Vršac

Parties	Yugoslav 1996	Serbian 1997	Serbian Presidential 1997 (Third round)
SPS			13,808
SPS-JUL-ND	10,821	8,922	
SRS	4,753	7,838	9,658
SPO		2,872	
ZAJEDNO	5,227		
KOALICIJA VOJVODINA		5,167	
VMDK			
VMSZ	771		
Others	3,128	1,596	

Subotica

Parties	Local 1996	Yugoslav 1996	Serbian 1997	Serbian Presidential 1997 (Third round)
SPS	8,482			37,583
SPS-JUL-ND		17,955	11,946	
SRS	7,515	5,394	10,033	11,801

Vojvodina in the 1990s

Parties	Local 1996	Yugoslav 1996	Serbian 1997	Serbian Presidential 1997 (Third round)
SPO			2,483	
ZAJEDNO	1,785	5,172		
KOALICIJA VOJVODINA			2,562	
VMDK	6,362			
VMSZ	14,023	24,112	18,819	
Others	28,863	13,199	15,551	

Čoka

Parties	Local 1996	Yugoslav 1996	Serbian 1997	Serbian Presidential 1997 (Third round)
SPS	1,750			4,130
SPS–JUL–ND		1,888	1,276	
SRS	750	880	1,759	1,701
SPO			484	
ZAJEDNO		333		
KOALICIJA VOJVODINA		350	529	
VMDK	670			
VMSZ	244	2,087	1,431	
Others	4,234	1,990	1,953	

Temerin

Parties	Local 1996	Yugoslav 1996	Serbian 1997	Serbian 1997 (Third round)
SPS	2,184			5,271
SPS–JUL–ND		3,673	2,888	
SRS	3,754	3,907	4,770	5,301
SPO			1,014	
ZAJEDNO	1,753	2,171		
KOALICIJA VOJVODINA			1,338	

Parties	Local 1996	Yugoslav 1996	Serbian 1997	Serbian 1997 (Third round)
VMDK	3,412			
VMSZ		664		
Others	2,526	3,398	3,552	

Ada

Parties	Local 1996	Yugoslav 1996	Serbian 1997	Serbian Presidential 1997 (Third round)
SPS	403			5,446
SPS–JUL–ND		1,024	940	
SRS	97	427	835	2,085
SPO			493	
ZAJEDNO	692	619		
KOALICIJA VOJVODINA		435	763	
VMDK				
VMSZ	3,234	4,027	3,477	
Others	5,110	2,871	2,129	

Source: http://www.cesid.org.

Apart from that, no notable changes in the local bases of support of other political forces became evident in the November 1996 elections. SRS, for instance, remained powerful – though not dominant – in the municipalities of Srem where a dense concentration of colonists and refugees is observed (Table 12). Moreover, the voting procedure in the northern Bačka and Banat municipalities with a Hungarian local majority once again took place in ethnic terms at all levels (Table 12). Finally, *Zajedno* remained quite popular in certain predominantly old settler-populated municipalities (though not to the extent that DEPOS was some years ago), whereas the regionalists still proved themselves a noteworthy political force in quite a few ethnically mixed constituencies (Table 12). Overall, the 1996 elections in Vojvodina can be regarded as 'elections of continuity' by most aspects.

Almost identical was the case at the 1997 Serbian elections. In these elections, the 'left' coalition won 28.81 per cent of the vote and elected twenty-two mandates to the Serbian parliament. SRS came second with 28.52 per cent of the vote (21 mandates) and SPO had a disappointing performance with 9.73 per cent of the vote and only four mandates to the Serbian parliament. An interesting incidence was the rather decent performance of the *Koalicija Vojvodina* (11.37 per cent of the vote). As for the presidential race, in most constituencies, it turned into a question of SPS-ND-JUL versus the Radicals. Finally, VMSZ won 5.15 per cent of the total vote.

As far as the negative performance by SPO was concerned, it had to do with Vuk Drašković's increasingly discredited image as the leader of the 'democratic opposition' throughout Serbia. On the other hand, the Radicals' startling performance was much subject to the fact that, as a result of the DSS's boycott of the procedure, no moderate nationalist option was available in these elections. This, in combination with the SPO's diminishing popular appeal, might have accounted for the diversion of a certain percentage of voters, who had previously voted for *Zajedno*, towards SRS. With specific regard to the SRS voters, a larger percentage among them (especially in Srem) voted for the party in the 1997 Serbian elections than in the 1996 Yugoslav ones (Table 12). Quite similar was the case in 1992, when a larger percentage of the Radicals' voters in Vojvodina voted for them in the Serbian elections than in the Yugoslav ones, which were held at the same time. Therefore, it seems that a greater percentage of SRS voters in Vojvodina were interested in their party securing a firmer place in the Serbian parliament, largely because of the way that the constitutional structure of Serbia and FR Yugoslavia was set up.

As far as the performance of *Koalicija Vojvodina* was concerned, one explanation that can be given is that it was also affected by the boycott of the elections by certain parties. In other words, it is quite likely that a certain percentage of voters previously affiliated to DS voted for the regionalist coalition. A complementary explanation that can be offered is that, in terms of what was earlier mentioned, a greater number of Vojvodinians had started becoming increasingly dissatisfied with Belgrade's policies on the province by then. The ostensibly illogical electoral geometry applied in the 1997 contest might have claimed an additional number of votes from the regionalists.[129] Vojvodina was divided into seven electoral districts (i.e. Subotica, Zrenjanin, Pančevo, Sombor, Novi Sad, Vrbas, Sremska Mitrovica), the constituent municipalities of which often had no geographic connection to each other. The most plausible explanation that can be offered, in regard to this gerrymandering, is that it formed an attempt by the regime to counterbalance the powerful support channelled towards the anti-SPS opposition, including SRS, in certain parts of Vojvodina (e.g. Bečej and its surrounding municipalities in Bačka, as far as the 'democratic opposition' was concerned). After all, the local and Yugoslav elections held one year earlier had adequately demonstrated that a notable percentage of urban residents in Vojvodina harboured either pro-SRS or pro-'democratic opposition' sympathies.[130]

At this point, it might be useful to highlight that the period between the 1993 and the 1997 Serbian elections saw the steady decrease in the voters' turnout to the procedure. In the 1996 Yugoslav elections, the percentage of the Vojvodinian electorate who proceeded to the poll was 66.68 per cent. One year later, a mere 62.13 per cent of the province's registered voters participated in the Serbian elections. As far as the latter case is concerned, it is always likely that the opposition's call for a boycott found some appeal among Vojvodinian voters. Still, it is even more likely that a greater percentage of Vojvodinian citizens had become, just as was the case throughout Serbia, disillusioned with their country's political elites. However, it seems that, irrespective of any boycott tactics, abstention from polling did particular harm to the opposition parties in Vojvodina.[131]

The effective projection of the growing dissatisfaction with the regime's policies in Vojvodina, on the electoral patterns encountered in

---

[129] Boarov, *Politička Istorija Vojvodine*, 231–2.
[130] This explanation is supported through reference to the way that the Novi Sad electoral unit was set up. In a city populated by over 400,000 inhabitants, an electoral unit consisting of merely 257,000 voters and electing just 9 representatives was finally formed.
[131] On this issue, see the results of an empirical survey conducted by the Sociology Department at the University of Novi Sad in the late 1990s, in 'Umorni od lidera' (http://www.medijaklub.cg.yu).

the province, was subject to two kinds of catalysts: macro-level and micro-level ones. With regard to the former, the most notable was the process of bridging the programmatic and ideological differences within the 'democratic opposition', which culminated into the formation of DOS. In Vojvodina, specifically, this development was further encouraged by the aforementioned reawakening of the unifying substratum of Vojvodinian identity, on the grassroots level, and its endorsement in the platform employed by DOS in the province. This provided the key to the coalition's decisive victory in Vojvodina, since it managed to melt the diverse pockets of anti-SPS, and at the same time not particularly sympathetic to SRS either, opposition (the pro-opposition urbanites, the regionalist trends encountered in the ethnically mixed settlements, the anti-regime disposition of the Hungarians and other minorities)[132] into a viable political movement (Table 13). Therefore, the paradoxes of previous contests, when the 'democratic opposition' could not capitalize on the electorate's apparent discontent with the regime's policies because of its high degree of fragmentation, were not repeated.

The results of the 2000 electoral contest 'spoke for themselves'. In stark contrast to the previous elections, over 70 per cent of Vojvodina's

Table 13 The results of the Yugoslav parliamentary elections (September 2000) at the Vojvodinian electoral units

Subotica

Parties	Votes	%	Mandates
SPS–JUL	21,742	18.61	1
Civic Alliance of Subotica-Vojvodinian Opposition	7,176	6.14	0
Communist Alliance of Yugoslavia in Serbia-Communists of Subotica	2,278	1.95	0

(Continued)

---

[132] On the grievances of Vojvodina's Slovaks towards the governing apparatus, see Juraj Bartos, 'Izbori 2000: I Slovaci su rekli DOSta', *Reflektor*, nos. 13–14 (2001): 3–5.

Parties	Votes	%	Mandates
SRS	8,436	7.22	0
DOS	45,878	39.20	2
SPO	877	0.75	0
Ecological Party of Vojvodina	2,888	2.47	0
VMDK	9,247	7.92	0
VMSZ	18,377	15.73	0

Zrenjanin

Parties	Votes	%	Mandates
SPS–JUL	61,951	27.80	2
VMDK	14,717	6.60	0
SRS	26,870	12.06	0
VMSZ	29,391	13.19	1
New Communist Party of Yugoslavia	2,053	0.92	0
DOS	76,561	34.36	2
Vojvodinian Coalition for Yugoslavia	4,614	2.07	0
Radical Party of the Left 'Nikola Pašić'	2,433	1.09	0
Party of Natural Law	1,260	0.57	0
SPO	2,998	1.35	0

Pančevo

Parties	Votes	%	Mandates
SPS–JUL	54,701	30.12	1
DOS	96,464	53.12	3
New Communist Party of Yugoslavia	3,839	2.11	0
SPO	6,819	3.76	0
VMDK	3,107	1.71	0
SRS	16,660	9.17	0

Sombor

Parties	Votes	%	Mandates
SPS–JUL	43,853	36.42	1
SPO	3,484	2.89	0
SRS	15,234	12.73	0
DOS	55,991	46.50	2
VMDK	1,748	1.45	0

Novi Sad

Parties	Votes	%	Mandates
Civic Group for a Better Serbia	6,282	3.31	0
SRS	31,862	16.81	1
SPO	5,690	3.00	0
Serbian Radicals	2,054	1.08	0
SPS–JUL	44,989	23.68	1
DOS	94,791	50.00	2
VMDK	1,927	1.02	0
New Communist Party of Yugoslavia	1,170	0.62	0
Radical Party of the Left 'Nikola Pašić'	897	0.47	0

Vrbas

Parties	Votes	%	Mandates
SPS–JUL–ND	50,431	35.36	1
DOS	63,262	44.36	2
SRS	21,106	14.80	0
SPO	2,978	2.09	0
VMDK	4,839	3.39	0

Sremska Mitrovica

Parties	Votes	%	Mandates
SPO	9,042	5.16	0
Radical Party of the Left 'Nikola Pašić'	5,570	3.18	0
SRS	30,288	17.28	1
SPS–JUL	59,694	34.06	1
DOS	70,664	40.32	2

registered voters participated in the poll – a sign that a strong desire for change was evident. Moreover, in the elections for the Yugoslav president, Koštunica secured 57 per cent of the vote in Vojvodina to the 29 per cent won by Milošević. At the same time, in the elections for the Federal Chamber of Citizens, DOS secured 55 per cent of the vote to 33 per cent garnered by the SPS–JUL coalition. The victory of the united opposition was even more overwhelming in the elections for the Vojvodinian Assembly where DOS won 117 out of the 120 seats. On the latter occasion, the application of absolute majority (3 candidates on the second round) ultimately backfired at the Socialists. Finally, in the local elections, DOS was victorious in 38 out of the 45 municipalities in Vojvodina.

In addition to the Socialists' defeat, the performance of the Radicals was not successful either. The SRS was left with no representatives at the Vojvodinian assembly, whereas its performance at all levels was disappointingly low, even at its electoral strongholds in Srem. This was a sign that the Vojvodinian electorate had been literally de-radicalized and was keener on the reintegration of Vojvodina and Serbia with the rest of the world rather than on the politics of groupness and ethno-cultural introversion. Finally, the active participation of protesters from Novi Sad and other Vojvodinian cities at the civil disobedience acts organized in Belgrade (5 October 2000) served as an additional indication of the dominant political trends in Vojvodina.[133] A new political era had dawned for the province, even though various problems persisted.

---

[133] Dragan Bujošević and Ivan Radovanović, *October 5: A 24-Hour Coup* (Belgrade: Media Centre Press, 2000), 312.

4

Vojvodina Going through Transition (the 2000s)

This chapter places Vojvodina inside the broader spectrum of Serbia's regionalization during the first decade after the year 2000. This consists in an overview of the actual developments in regard to the administrative status of Vojvodina within Serbia which stretches from the inauguration of the *Omnibus* law (2002) all the way to the adoption of the new statute for Vojvodina (2009). Simultaneous attention is paid to Serbia's regionalization as viewed from the perspectives of the local political elites in the province. Then, this chapter sets in context the grassroots outlooks on regional identity and the state of interethnic relations in Vojvodina during that period. Of particular importance is to underline how the question of restituting Vojvodina's autonomous competencies interweaved with and became entangled into other crucial policymaking areas for Serbia, namely the developments in Kosovo and the readjustment of the Serbian-Montenegrin relations.

The *Omnibus Zakon* (Omnibus law) for Vojvodina: Adoption, content and implementation

An early indication of the new government's disposition vis-à-vis the Vojvodinian question was the inauguration of the *Omnibus Zakon* in February 2002. The initial draft was presented to the Vojvodinian assembly on 14 December 2001. The final approval of the new law by the Serbian Parliament was preceded by the emergence of certain cleavages. Apart from the accusations, brought forward by SPS and SRS, that the new law would be a step towards the break-up of Serbia certain disagreements arose within the provincial DOS circles.[1] The Vojvodinian DSS representatives judged that the circumstances were not yet ripe for the reassessment of Vojvodina's status within Serbia. They added that Serbia had issues of a more vital importance to take care of, such as the redefinition of its relations with Montenegro and the evaluation of the new prospects that had opened for the Kosovan question. Even though the DSS representatives agreed that the question of Vojvodina had to be entrenched in novel foundations, they still contended that this issue had to be settled within the bounds of a new Serbian Constitution and not partially. Therefore, when the voting for the approval of the *Omnibus* law was called at the Vojvodinian assembly, the DSS representatives voiced their reservations over the draft. By contrast, the representatives of DS, as well as those of LSDV, the Reformists and VMSZ voted in favour of the draft.

The law's dispatch to the Serbian parliament for its final approval generated further disagreements. At the initial parliamentary session on the *Omnibus Zakon*, on 22 January 2002, over 300 amendments (most of them drafted by SPS and SRS delegates) were proposed.[2] Even though most of these amendments were rejected in due time, the Serbian government proposed thirty amendments on the draft. Most of these amendments were proposed by the DSS delegates. First of all, objections were raised in regard to the financing of projects organized in Vojvodina from the provincial budget. Moreover, some MPs expressed their objections in regard to the draft's suggestions on: Vojvodina organizing its provincial plan for agriculture; the appointment of a provincial ombudsman with the task to supervise the arrangement of the educational system in Vojvodina.

The recommendation of the amendments generated friction between the Serbian parliament and the executive council of the

---

[1] 'SPS protiv omnibus zakona: Korak ka razbijanju Srbije', *Glas Javnosti*, 20 January 2002.
[2] 'Više od sto amandmana na "omnibus" zakon', *Glas Javnosti*, 22 January 2002; 'Autonomaški apetiti', *Velika Srbija* (the SRS monthly journal), February 2002, 36–7.

Vojvodinian assembly. The latter made clear to Belgrade that they would not accept any restrictive amendments on the draft document. They also warned the republican government that any serious tension between the two sides over the *Omnibus Zakon* might pose a challenge to the internal cohesion of the DOS coalition as such.[3] The fact that at that time the DSS representation at the provincial executive council was weak, served as an additional factor that enabled the Vojvodinian *autonomaši* to voice their disagreements with the Serbian government more emphatically. Soon, a compromise was reached between the two sides. The amendment on the provincial ombudsman of education was recalled, by the Serbian government, whereas modifications were made to the other amendments. Consequently, on 28 January 2002, the Vojvodinian assembly declared that they unanimously accepted all other twenty-nine amendments on the law. When the document was returned to the republican parliament for its final approval, on 4 February 2002, 118 MPs voted in favour of the law, 72 voted against, 42 held their reservations over the proposed text and 1 representative abstained from the procedure. With specific regard to DOS, the DSS representatives held their reservations.

The law conceded to the Vojvodinian assembly a set of competencies, which extended to over twenty areas.[4] Article 57 provided for the institution of an ombudsman appointed by the Vojvodinian assembly in accordance with the relevant Serbian law.[5] In regard to education, official use of alphabets/languages and public information quite a few competencies were conceded to the province. As far as elementary and middle-level education was concerned, Articles 12 and 13 authorized the responsible provincial organs to: issue educational programmes and textbooks in the languages of national minorities; allow for the arrangement of teaching programmes in the languages of ethnic

---

[3] 'Omnibus zakon neće oboriti Vladu Srbije', *Dnevnik*, 14 January 2002.
[4] For a full text-version of the *Omnibus Zakon* (including an explanatory section), see http://www.vojvodina.com/prilozi/omnibus.htm.
[5] The first provincial ombudsman was appointed on 23 December 2002.

minorities in such cases that less than fifteen pupils per school were native speakers of a minority language (Articles 12.4, 12.5, 12.8, 13.6 and 13.11). Furthermore, Articles 12, 13, 14 and 15 enabled the responsible provincial organs to found elementary, middle-level and high schools, as well as universities or new departments at the already existing universities (Articles 12.1, 13.1, 14.1 and 15.1). Finally, Article 16 (Paragraphs 11 and 14) allowed for the establishment of administrative-supervisory boards, as well as for the organization of inspections to all educational institutions.

In regard to the official use of the recognized languages and alphabets in Vojvodina, Article 18 (Paragraphs 1 and 2) authorized the responsible provincial organs to guarantee the official use of the recognized languages and their alphabets throughout the territory of the autonomous province; appoint a supervisory board with the task to carry out inspections, regarding the actual implementation of this article's terms. As far as the sector of public information was concerned, Article 19 (Paragraphs 5 and 6) enabled the provincial organs to appoint the director and the other members of the administrative-supervisory boards at those informative and broadcasting institutions under the immediate jurisdiction of the autonomous province (e.g. RTS Novi Sad); carry out the relevant inspections at the local radio and television stations, as well as any other provincial institution in the field of public information.

As clarified in the explanatory section, attached to the legal document, the *Omnibus Zakon* was basically drafted with the aim to secure the more efficient execution of certain administrative functions on the provincial level. It was noted that, since the inauguration of the 1990 Constitution, little actual progress had occurred in the field of the autonomous provincial administration. In some cases, on the one hand, many of the legal decisions enacted by the Serbian Assembly for Vojvodina were not applied properly. On the other hand, at some instances, certain republican enactments over the autonomous province actually reduced Vojvodina's capacities to a symbolic level. The authors of the *Omnibus Zakon* concluded that this law signified the initial step towards the inauguration of the new Serbian Constitution and the definitive settlement of the province's status.[6]

In regard to the official use of the minority languages and alphabets, it was estimated that the closer communication between the provincial organs and the local minorities would ensure a quicker response by the former to any requirements of the latter. The role of the supervisory board was particularly stressed. As far as public information was concerned, it was underlined that, as specified in the relevant clause of the *Omnibus Zakon*, RTS Novi Sad was to become an independent legal subject with regard to the territorial, cultural, linguistic and other specificities of Vojvodina.[7] However, as clarified in the basic clauses of the legal document, the provisions of this law were always to be applied in harmony with the Serbian Constitution and the republican legislation (Articles 1, 2 and 3). The requirement for the provincial organs to have reached a previous agreement with the relevant republican ministries was reminded in various parts of the *Omnibus Zakon* (e.g. Articles 12.7 and 13.11, on the issue of textbooks in the minority languages).

As far as the finance of the above-mentioned projects was concerned, following a *modus vivendi* between the Serbian government and the Vojvodinian executive council, in most cases they were to be financed jointly by the provincial and the republican budget. For example, Article 17 dictated that all administrative and supervisory functions on educational matters were to be either fully or partially funded by the provincial budget. Nevertheless, Articles 12.7 and 13.11 on national minority education stated that the execution of certain tasks in that given area was, on certain occasions, to be financed either partially or wholly by the republican budget. Finally, in regard to agriculture, Article 42 (Section b, Paragraph 1) authorized Vojvodina to arrange special projects for the protection, use and organization of arable land and fund them from its own budget. However, it was added that the

---

[6] 'Razloži za Donosenje Zakona i Ciljevi koji se Ostvaruju', *Omnibus Zakon*, 14 December 2001.
[7] Ibid., 'Objasnenje Osnovnih Pravnih Instituta' (1, 2, 3 and 4).

execution of all such agricultural projects must be carried out in firm accordance with the uniform agricultural planning of the republic. A top issue that emerged soon after the inauguration of the *Omnibus Zakon* was the financial question. In other words, there was an urgent need for the rebalancing of the provincial budget, regarding the percentage of the provincial income to be transferred to the republican coffers in Belgrade and the percentage to be invested on regional projects in accordance with the law. By the time that the proposal for the *Omnibus Zakon* was drafted by Vojvodina's executive council, the provincial secretary for finance, Đorđe Misirkić, estimated that in the event that a compromise was reached between the republican and provincial organs around 27 to 33 billion dinars would be required for the execution of regional projects. The Serbian minister of finance, Božidar Đelić, suggested that a slightly lower amount (i.e. 25 to 30 billion dinars) should be invested on the same purpose.[8] Nevertheless, when the final decision was reached over this issue, in late June 2002, the actual amount agreed upon, by the provincial secretariat for finance and the Serbian Ministry of Finance, was 9 million dinars.[9]

The financial debate over the *Omnibus Zakon* and the inauguration of the law as such generated certain disagreements within DOS in Vojvodina. Nenad Čanak, for instance, assessed that little would change regarding the central government's control over the economic potential of Vojvodina.[10] A certain discontent, though from a different angle, was expressed by the DSS. Dejan Mihajlov, DSS group-representative at the Serbian Assembly, stated that 'the new law is the fruit of new conflicts that have resulted from the imprecise distribution of authority' and repeated that the Vojvodinian question should be resolved 'within

---

[8] Milena Putnik, 'Omnibus Zakon ili vraćanje autonomije: Prenete nadležnosti ali ne i novac', 24 December 2001, http://www.aimpress.org. By March 2001, Vojvodina had accumulated around 6.5 billion dinars from taxes and other sources of income. Approximately 4.5 billion dinars of this total were siphoned towards the republican budget, whereas less than 57 million dinars were returned to the Vojvodinian coffers.

[9] Dimitrije Boarov, 'Ustavnoj povelj ususret: Ima neka tajna veza', July 2002, http://www.helsinki.org.yu.

[10] 'Referendum i u Vojvodini', Medija Klub Podgorica, 2002. http://www.medijaklub.cg.yu.

the bounds of a new Serbian Constitution, not separately'.[11] Mihajlov's statements echoed the mood of the entire DSS Vojvodinian committee. At the other end of the spectrum, the late Zoran Đinđić greeted the new law and stressed that 'decentralization and the restoration of Vojvodina's true autonomy is one of the most important tasks in the agenda of the new government'.[12] A very similar position on the matter was held by DS's Đorđe Đukić at the provincial assembly, during the drafting of the law.[13] Furthermore, the Reformists regarded the *Omnibus Zakon* as a sign that the issue of Vojvodinian autonomy still existed and added that this autonomy should increase in the near future.[14] The reactions of VMSZ were very positive as well.[15]

In an overall assessment, the *Omnibus Zakon* signified a small but notable step towards the gradual acquisition of more extensive competencies by Vojvodina. The new law reinforced Vojvodina's asymmetric status within Serbia, even though Belgrade retained some authority over the finances. One can comprehend the importance of the *Omnibus Zakon* in the following sense: it was the first occasion since the constitutional reforms of 1990 that the Vojvodinian executive council drafted and submitted a legal text on its administrative jurisdiction to the Serbian Assembly and that text was largely accepted.

One year later, in March 2003, the new constitutional charter of the state's union between Serbia and Montenegro was inaugurated. With specific regard to Vojvodina, the charter's preamble stated that the component republic of Serbia also comprised 'the Autonomous Provinces of Vojvodina and Kosovo and Metohija-the latter currently being under an international administration according to the UN Resolution 1244'.[16] This was a formal recognition of Vojvodina's status

---

[11] 'Vojvodina je dobra vest za Srbiju', *Dnevnik*, 5 February 2002.
[12] 'Omnibus Vojvodina, Srbija u Evropi', *Dnevnik*, 23 January 2002.
[13] 'Omnibus Zakon za sada je dovoljan', *Glas Javnosti*, 10 December 2001.
[14] 'Vojvodina je dobra vest za Srbiju', *Dnevnik*. Also, the relevant article in the daily *Danas*, 20 March 2002, http://www.danas.co.yu.
[15] 'Klali vola za kilo mesa', *Bulevar*, 8 February 2002.
[16] 'Ustavna Povelja Državne Zajednice Srbija i Crna Gora, 2003', Srbija i Crna Gora: Direkcija za Informisanje, 2003. http://www.gov.yu.

as a constituent part of the Republic of Serbia. Nevertheless, no other references to the autonomous provinces were made elsewhere in the document. This, in combination with the fact that the Serbian organs still retained primacy over most issues pertaining to the republic's jurisdiction, served as a reminder that Vojvodina's final status would only be resolved through the inauguration of the new Serbian Constitution.

Vojvodina's political elites and the question of regionalization in the early 2000s

At this point, it would be interesting to outline the standpoints of the political elites in Vojvodina on the question of the province's status during the early 2000s. Particular attention is paid to the two most popular parties back then, with an appeal all over Serbia (DSS and DS); and to the League and the Reformists from the pro-autonomists.

The DSS Committee in Vojvodina regards the province as the hearth of the modern Serbian national movement, whereas the Vojvodinian Serbs are viewed as the pioneers of modern Serbian nationalism. The short-lived *Vojvodstvo Srpsko* of 1848–9 as well as the struggles of Jaša Tomić and other Vojvodinian Serb political figures for the national unification of the *prečani* Serbs with Serbia proper, are regarded with particular respect.[17] By contrast, the system of autonomies established within the Socialist Federal Republic of Yugoslavia is viewed from a particularly negative angle. The DSS Vojvodinian representatives argue that this system merely signified the implementation of the Yugoslav Communists' interwar ideological platform with the aim to weaken the political sovereignty of the Serbian nation within Yugoslavia. The 1974 Constitution especially is regarded as a document which 'set up a model of autonomies incompatible with any European or universal precedents

---

[17] Dejan Mikavica, 'Vojvodina kao Politički Program', *Srpska Atina* (the journal of the DSS Novi Sad committee), February 2002, 3–12.

in the fields of legal theory and political practice'. It is further added that in accordance with the 1974 arrangements three constitutional areas were set up in Serbia, the two of which (Kosovo and Vojvodina) were granted more extensive competencies than the remaining one (Serbia proper).[18] In this light, even the 1990 Serbian Constitution was viewed as an arrangement that maintained certain aspects of the Communist constitutional order.[19]

Therefore, in regard to the broader question of regionalization in Serbia, the DSS representatives in Vojvodina and in Serbia as a whole seem to be keen on a unitary solution. The main standpoints of the party on the regional question were outlined in DSS's *'Osnovna načela za novi Ustav Republike Srbije'* ('Basic Principles for the New Constitution of the Republic of Serbia'). First of all, this document declared the territory of Serbia 'united and inalienable'. The official language recognized was Serbian in the Cyrillic script. The respective languages and alphabets of the national minorities were to be officially used in those territories where a national minority forms the local majority. Furthermore, the rights (individual and collective) of national minorities were to be codified in the state's legislation on civil rights and freedoms. The option of positive discrimination, in favour of individuals coming from a minority background was also endorsed.

This document proposed the establishment of six regions with their respective seats at the capital Belgrade, Kragujevac, Niš, Novi Sad, Užice and Priština – following the final settlement of Kosovo's status. The Serbian Assembly was to be bicameral, comprising a Chamber of Citizens and a Chamber of Regions. The latter was given a right of veto over decisions of the former that might prove detrimental to the status of a region. The regional parliament was endorsed to enact the regional statute, whereas the main executive organs of the region were to be its government and president. In regard to financial autonomy,

---

[18] Dejan Mikavica, 'Kome Treba Vojvođanski KomunističkiUstav?', 2002, http://www.dssns.org.yu.

[19] Dejan Mikavica, 'Vojvodina kao Politički Program', 10–11.

every region was entitled to arrange its budget and have a say over which taxes should remain local and which should be directed towards the republican coffers. Nevertheless, a republican mechanism should supervise the equal economic development of all regions. As far as legislative authority was concerned, the regional parliament was to enact certain regional laws in a variety of areas (e.g. agriculture, regional planning, natural resources). Nevertheless, in case the republican government considered that a proposed regional law was not in harmony with the republican legislation (e.g. in case it jeopardized civil rights within a region or it attributed that region a higher legal status in comparison to the rest) it would be enabled to test the law's validity before the Republican Constitutional Court prior to its application. Finally, all regional courts of justice were to operate in full harmony with the republican judicial system.[20]

The proposal of the whole arrangement was theoretically entrenched in the necessity to safeguard the territorial integrity of Serbia and the national rights of Serbs in their homeland. Moreover, it was made clear that the DSS opposes the concession of any kind of 'special status' that might encourage ethnic segregation or separatist tendencies. Finally, in regard to the functional aspect, the asymmetric option was rejected on the grounds that 'Serbia is a small and poor country and cannot afford to finance any "parallel" governmental entities.' By contrast, the gradual strengthening of local self-government was proposed as a more pragmatic and effective solution.[21] Even though the DSS proposal seemed quite unitary in its conceptualization, still it favoured decentralization in a number of areas. This was particularly the case with its allowance for vetoes at the republican parliament, the degree of regional financial autonomy, as well as the authorization of the regions to proclaim certain laws pertaining to their jurisdiction (not merely the issuing of sub-legal acts). Furthermore, the six regions proposed by the

---

[20] Demokratska Stranka Srbije, 'Osnovna načela za novi Ustav Republike Srbije', 2001, 2–3, 10–14.
[21] Milovan Mitrović, 'Politika Demokratske Stranke Srbije u Vojvodini', 22 April 2002, http://www.dssns.org.yu.

DSS would follow at least some historical divisions, so therefore might potentially form the basis of future regionalist demands. However, the DSS officials tended to offset this probability in a rather dubious manner by arguing that in Serbia there do not exist historically established regions as it is the case in, say, Spain or Italy.[22]

Meanwhile, DS did not present an articulate platform on the question of regionalization in Serbia. In the party's political programme it was mentioned that Vojvodina is a region with specificities of a historical, cultural, geographic and national character. It was further recommended that the Republic of Serbia should devolve part of its authority (e.g. in economy, education, exploitation of natural resources, minority rights, public information) to the province, as long as these functions did not resemble the attributes of a state. It was also suggested that Vojvodina should be granted the appropriate fiscal and executive authority.[23]

The party's relaxed attitude towards the issue of Vojvodinian autonomy had gained some popularity for DS among the province's pro-autonomist parties and groupings. On certain occasions, though, DS firmly rejected certain demands by the regionalist elites as detrimental to the state's interest. The party's policy of tactical adjustments over the Vojvodinian question had resulted from its intention to keep the 'democratic forces' in the province together. However, a question that remained unanswered is where, exactly, the DS's lenience towards asymmetric alternatives ended and where those of the party's consideration of the broader state's interest began. DS's manoeuvring between these two poles occasionally generated criticism over the party's alleged inconsistency, from the League of Vojvodina's Social Democrats all the way to DSS.[24]

---

[22] Interview with DSS representative; Novi Sad, 15 March 2001.
[23] See the political program of the DS at: http://www.demokrata.org.yu/srpski/program/politicki.html.
[24] DS had been also accused of displaying an equally 'chameleonic' attitude vis-à-vis the management of interethnic relations in Vojvodina, thereby, frequently switching from lenient to more reserved outlooks on minority rights (Interview with sociologist at the University of Novi Sad; 14 November 2005).

The League's greatest gain from the nomination of posts within DOS in autumn 2000 was the appointment of Nenad Čanak to the position of president of the Vojvodinian assembly. According to the League's agenda, Vojvodina is characterized by such a degree of ethno-cultural diversity that is difficult to encounter anywhere else in Europe. As a result of these regional specifics, the provision of certain institutional guarantees was prescribed. These provisions were, namely, a bicameral parliament (consisting of a Chamber of Citizens and a Chamber of Nationalities) and a Vojvodinian Constitution arranged by the Vojvodinian assembly. The territorial autonomy of Vojvodina's sub-regional units (Srem, Bačka, the Banat) was also endorsed.

In regard to Serbia's constitutional rearrangement, federalization was proposed as the most appropriate option. According to LSDV, Serbia should be rearranged in terms of a democratic federal state whose units would enjoy a high degree of autonomy. The League proposed the establishment of six units drawn in accordance with their political interests, historical particularities, economic features and demographic factors. The units proposed were Vojvodina, Šumadija, Southeast Serbia, the greater Belgrade area, the Sandžak and Kosovo – following the settlement of its status. This 'democratic federal Serbia' was to be endowed with a bicameral parliament comprising a Chamber of Citizens and a Chamber of the Federal Units. The competencies assigned to the central government were to be national defence, foreign policy, monetary policy and other macro-economic issues. The primacy of the Chamber of Citizens was also endorsed.[25]

At this point, a similarity by default between the programmes of the League and DSS becomes apparent, namely the arrangement of an equal number of units in accordance with almost the same criteria. Especially in regard to functional and demographic catalysts, it seems that both parties found the drawing of units consisting of 2,000,000 residents on average as an efficient option. But this is where the similarities between

---

[25] Liga Socijal-Demokrata Vojvodine, 'Republika Vojvodina: Put mira razvoja i stabilnosti', March 1999, 1–4.

the programmes of the two parties ended. In regard to the powers that the central government should retain, according to LSDV, the picture looked much closer to the very minimalist arrangement of the Serbia-Montenegro union – thus implying some sort of loose union of regions with extensive self-government.

The very use of the term 'federalization' by LSDV implied the concession of more extensive competencies, even though not explicitly clarified in its programme. Perhaps it should be noted that the employment of the term 'federalization' in the party's programme was not to be taken literally, but mainly as a means to emphasize deep decentralization. After all, the application of a genuine federal structure in a country as small and as poor as Serbia would not sound as a rational proposal, at the first place. Finally, even though at a first glance symmetric, the League's programme mentioned that the six units would be granted 'a higher or lower degree of autonomy in comparison to each other'.[26] This, in combination with the institutional provisions proposed for Vojvodina, would leave much room, if only implicitly, for the attribution of a higher status to the province.

The Reformist Democratic Party of Vojvodina emphasized the historical and other particularities of Vojvodina in relation to the rest of Serbia. The Reformists also underlined, more emphatically than the League, the internal subdivision of Vojvodina into the, equally historical, sub-regions of Srem, Bačka and the Banat. In this sense, they argued that Vojvodina differentiated from other European regions.[27] By contrast to LSDV, the Reformists openly stood for the asymmetric regionalization of Serbia. The party envisaged the establishment of 'a state of autonomous provinces and regions' in Serbia. It was underlined that the autonomy of these regions and provinces should be explicitly defined in the Serbian Constitution. The areas in which the autonomous provinces, by their acts, independently and thoroughly would regulate certain decisions should be clarified as well. Also, the

[26] Ibid., 3.
[27] Interview with RDSV representative; Novi Sad, 20 March 2001.

constitutionality of the provincial legal acts should be assessed by the single Constitutional Court of the republic. The central competencies of the Serbian government would be national defence, foreign policy, state security, criminal law, monetary policy and other macro-economic issues.

In the specific case of Vojvodina certain institutional provisions were recommended. In accordance with the province's internal subdivision, a power-sharing model of autonomy was proposed, in which the provincial government in Novi Sad would share its authority with sub-governments established in Srem, the Banat and the rest of Bačka. Finally, RDSV opted for the utilization of certain aspects of the 1974 arrangements that might still be applicable today.[28]

Nevertheless, none of the two pro-autonomy parties was particularly popular then. The League, in particular, would not succeed in augmenting its public appeal, in the years to come, despite its continuous participation in the provincial institutions and decision-making organs. There can be given quite a few explanations in regard to this occurrence. First of all, as a result of the wide diversity of popular views over what 'autonomy' means, the agendas of the pro-autonomy parties might not necessarily correspond to the way that many Vojvodinians perceived decentralization or regionalization. Second, both parties had often been accused of being too 'region-centered' and monopolized by their leaders (e.g. Nenad Čanak's focal position within the League). In regard to the former allegation, Vojvodina's status within the broader political context of Serbia and Montenegro was not adequately addressed in their programmes. To these might be added allegations regarding the inefficient staffing of LSDV and RDSV alike. Finally, the previous association of quite a few individuals among the pro-autonomist elites with the reformist branch of the old LCY (also, their frequently nostalgic allusions to the post-1974 era) might have

---

[28] Ibid.; Radosavljević Duško, 'Autonomy of Vojvodina: Challenges and Perspectives', in Open University Subotica, *Essays on Regionalization* (Subotica: Agency for Local Democracy, 2001), 151-6.

discouraged quite a few Vojvodinians who opted for a definitive break from whatever they perceived as remnants of Titoism.

The Serbian Constitution of 2006 and Vojvodina's status

As it was stated in the *Omnibus* law's explanatory section, this document simply signified a step towards the inauguration of the new Serbian Constitution and the definitive settlement of Vojvodina's status. In practice, however, this objective became entangled into the fuzzy and multifaceted web of geopolitics within the ex-Yugoslav space. The main areas of concern were the redefinition of Serbian-Montenegrin relations; Kosovo's locus within Serbia since 1999. Especially with regard to the latter, Serbian policymakers concentrated their efforts on negotiations with the international community, hoping to secure Kosovo's maintenance within Serbia, while pending the definitive settlement of the province's status. Correspondingly, Serbian constitutional theorists and policymakers started favouring centralized options for Serbia's regional restructuring with only some room for functional decentralization and limited financial autonomy.[29] This dominant trend among Belgrade's political circles was reflected in the new Serbian Constitution, which was inaugurated on 8 November 2006.

At this point, it should be noted that the period prior to the inauguration of the new Constitution saw the drafting of certain proposals for Serbia's symmetric regionalization. For the purposes of this work, attention is paid to Pavle Nikolić's recommendations.[30] Nikolić, a constitutional theorist at Belgrade University, advocated for the dissolution of the autonomous provinces of Vojvodina and Kosovo

---

[29] Zorica Radović, 'Srbija kao država regiona', Forum za Etničke Odnose, *Prinčipi ustavne deklaracije* (Belgrade: Forum za Etničke Odnose Publikacije, 2000), 30–48; Zoran Bačić, Mijatović Boško, Aleksandar Simić and Zorica Radović, *Regionalizacija Srbije* (Belgrade: Centar za Liberalno-demokratske Studije Publikacije, 2003).

[30] *Dnevnik*, 2 February 2004.

and the establishment of thirteen regions with equal competencies. As part of this arrangement, Vojvodina was to be divided into the sub-regions of Srem, the Banat and Bačka. Nikolić contended that symmetric regionalization would ensure the administrative autonomy of all Serbian regions whereas, on the contrary, asymmetric regionalization would generate inequalities and tensions. Especially the existence of the two autonomous provinces in Serbia was judged, by the author, as an out of date reminder of the 1946 arrangement. In a similar vein to the DSS proposal (2001), Nikolić called for the concession of an equal degree of fiscal autonomy to all regions plus their entitlement to veto certain governmental decisions that might prove detrimental to their jurisdiction. However, as a result of functional considerations, the author proposed the formation of thirteen regions instead of DSS's six. Nevertheless, the Serbian policymakers' top objective remained the formal affirmation of Kosovo's locus (within its existing limits) inside the bounds of the Serbian republic. This amounted to no room for such 'symmetric' considerations.

Indeed, the Preamble of the Constitution defines Kosovo and Metohija as 'an integral part of the territory of Serbia with substantial autonomy'.[31] In addition, Part VII designates Kosovo, together with Vojvodina, as one of Serbia's autonomous provinces with all the rights and obligations prescribed (Articles 182–187). With specific regard to Vojvodina, Article 184.3 dictates that 'the budget of the autonomous Province of Vojvodina shall amount to at least 7 per cent in relation to the budget of the republic, bearing in mind that three-sevenths of the budget of the autonomous province of Vojvodina shall be used for financing the capital expenditures'. This provision signifies a departure from the 1990 Constitution and establishes the preconditions for regulated fiscal autonomy. Nevertheless, Article 184 does not make it explicitly clear whether the autonomous provinces are allocated a right of taxation or not. In addition to this, Article 177 specifies that

[31] For a full-text version of the 2006 Serbian Constitution, see 'Ustav Republike Srbije', *Službeni Glasnik Republike Srbije*, br. 98/06. For a commentary on the Constitution, see Venice Commission, *Opinion on the Constitution of Serbia*, Opinion No. 405/2006.

'local self-government units (*opštine*) shall be competent in those matters which may be realized, in an effective way, within a local self-government unit, and autonomous provinces in those matters which may be realized, in an effective way within an autonomous province'.

However, nowhere in the new Constitution are the relations within the triadic nexus that comprises the Serbian government, the autonomous provinces and the *opštine* precisely defined and regulated. This leads to the conclusion that the new Constitution informally strengthened local self-government in an attempt to counterbalance any potential aspirations by the autonomous provinces (namely Vojvodina) to enhance their status. The strengthening of local self-government has often formed part of the political bargaining, on the national governments' behalf, with the objective to place a check upon larger regional institutions (e.g. Spain in the 1980s). In the case of the new Serbian Constitution, this argument gains greater weight if the previous articles are read in combination with Article 97 which places the jurisdiction and operation of both autonomous provinces and *opštine* under the auspices of the Serbian government (once again, though, not clearly defined). Lastly, Article 182.3 allows for the establishment of new autonomous provinces if so decided in a referendum. At this given moment, though, it is hard to predict how this clause might bring about a long-term 'symmetricization' of Serbia's regionalization. In an overall assessment, the 2006 Serbian Constitution relatively enhanced Vojvodina's control over its revenues but not Vojvodina's asymmetric status as such. In practice, the 2006 Constitution favoured decentralization over asymmetric regionalization.

Rapid developments in Serbian politics and the European dimension

The provisions of the new Serbian constitution for Vojvodina caused dissatisfaction among a variety of interest groups in the province. As expected, this was particularly the case with the League of Vojvodina's

Social Democrats and other regionalist groupings. As already stated, neither the League nor any other pro-autonomy parties had been particularly popular in Vojvodina. This also became evident in the results of the May 2008 elections for the Vojvodinian assembly, where the 'Together for Vojvodina' coalition (led by Nenad Čanak) garnered a mere 8.2 per cent of the vote.

Nevertheless, the year 2008 saw radical realignments at the governmental level in Serbia. As illustrated throughout this work, Serbian elite politics have long been dominated by short-term interests and characterized by a high degree of fragmentation and fluidity. Numerous coalitions have been formed and swiftly dissolved as a result of conflicting standpoints, disagreements in decision-making or even personal antipathies. This is what happened when Boris Tadić's and Vojislav Koštunica's positions on Kosovo's unilateral declaration of independence (17 February 2008) clashed; a disagreement which brought about the May 2008 elections. The fear of losing the elections to SRS rendered DS flexible even to alliances with the League and the Sandžak minority parties. The League's participation in the governing structures after May 2008 enhanced this party's bargaining potential in regard to the reinforcement of Vojvodina's asymmetric status. To this objective, Čanak and his associates were also encouraged by indications that the popular mood in Vojvodina had been constantly swinging towards asymmetric or highly devolved options.[32]

In light of these new circumstances, a number of DS policymakers in Belgrade and Novi Sad started regarding allegations over 'secessionist' trends in Vojvodina as rather exaggerated. DS policymakers were soon encouraged to adopt a more positive outlook on the restitution of certain competencies to the Vojvodinian assembly, in an attempt to placate the EU and enhance Serbia's prospects for accession to the Union; respond to the popular demands in Vojvodina for the reinforcement of the

---

[32] NVO Diferentija Niš, Istraživanje o stavovima građana regiona Srbije prema toleranciji, suočavanju s prošlošću, decentralizaciji, i prepoznavaju osnovnih demokratskih vrednosti (2009), Niš, 14; Zsölt Lazar, Vojvodina amidst Multiculturality and Regionalization (Novi Sad: Mediterran Publishing, 2007), 51–60.

province's status. In regard to the former objective, the more favourable disposition, on Belgrade's behalf, towards the restitution of autonomous competencies to Vojvodina was greeted with satisfaction in Brussels. This was reflected in the positive remarks that Serbia's regionalization process had received in the EU progress reports for 2009 and 2010.[33]

Moving to the 'external front', Serbia's path towards the EU has long been paved with obstacles. Since 2000, the pressures on the Serbian government to cooperate with the Hague Tribunal had generated tensions between the two sides. This even led to the suspension of the EU–Serbia negotiations (3 May 2006). Radovan Karadžić's arrest (21 July 2008) reopened the way to Serbia's accession to the European structures. This culminated with the country's formal application to the EU (22 December 2009).

EU advisors have not exerted overt and intense pressures on Serbia in regard to Vojvodina's status and regionalization per se. No universally agreed-upon and binding 'European' guidelines on regionalization are in force, at the first place, either. In 1997, the Council of Europe issued the *Draft European Charter on Regional Self-Government*. This signified an attempt to introduce some universal standards on the implementation of regionalization and the allocation of administrative capacities to regional authorities. Nevertheless, this draft charter was never officially approved due to the objections, by certain COE and EU member-states, to its prerogatives. In spite of this, the Council of Europe and certain bodies operating under the umbrella of the EU have highlighted the necessity for European states to devolve part of their authority towards the regional and local self-government levels, in a balanced and coordinated manner; reach a *modus vivendi* over the percentage of the regional revenues channelled towards the central coffers.

With specific regard to Vojvodina, these guidelines acquired particular significance considering that Vojvodina is a rich agricultural

---

[33] European Commission, *Serbia 2009 Progress Report*, SEC (2009) 1339; European Commission, *Serbia 2010 Progress Report*, SEC (2010) 1330.

region which has been participating in a number of EU-sponsored cross-border cooperation schemes such as the 'Banat' (or DKMT) Euro-region.[34] Despite the absence of any serious pressures on Belgrade, the EU's informal engagement over Serbia's regionalization and Vojvodina's status had been rather active. EU advisors held a series of meetings with their Serbian counterparts. In the course of these sessions, the former outlined to the latter the benefits of enhancing Vojvodina's administrative competencies in light of Serbia's accession to the European structures. EU advisors particularly stressed that the extension of the province's capacities could contribute to the more efficient management of ethnic relations 'on the spot'. They underlined that this could also facilitate Vojvodina's fruitful participation in a number of EU-sponsored cross-border cooperation schemes. Lastly, they emphasized that, in the long term, the strengthening of the administrative institutions in Vojvodina could operate as an efficient mechanism for the local management and distribution of the Structural Funds.

The new statute for Vojvodina (2009) and its political significance

The outcome of this intersection between domestic and external catalysts was the inauguration of the new statute for Vojvodina. The draft version of this document was ready, as early as mid-August 2008.[35] The drafting board comprised Vojvodinian DS-affiliates, local academics and constitutional theorists involved in pro-autonomy workshops (e.g. the Novi Sad Centre for Regionalism). The Vojvodinian assembly approved this document after a heated session on 15 October

---

[34] Vassilis Petsinis, 'The Banat Euro-Region: Prospects and Obstacles', in *The Borders of Europe*, New Europe College and Goethe Institute Bucharest (Bucharest: University of Bucharest Publishing, 2007).

[35] 'DS: Novi statut Vojvodine,' *Dnevnik*, 21 August 2008.

2008.³⁶ As Bojan Pajtić, a DS-member and president of the executive council at Vojvodina's assembly, stated: 'the Communist-era system of autonomies was embedded in an one-party state structure .... The new statute brings about a novel concept of autonomy, always considering that Vojvodina aspires to become a European region and have more effective control over its resources'.³⁷

Nevertheless, not everyone shared this state of euphoria. A number of DSS and SRS deputies voiced their dissatisfaction with the draft statute and regarded it as 'unconstitutional' and a document which builds up a 'state within a state'.³⁸ The objections by a considerable segment of Belgrade's political elites (including some DS-affiliates) to the draft statute delayed this document's ratification by the Serbian parliament for nearly a year. The approval process commenced on 24 November 2009, and the statute was finally approved by the Serbian parliament on 30 November.³⁹ Of all amendments, only a number of amendments proposed by the Socialists were accepted. The statute was officially proclaimed on 14 December 2009, in Novi Sad and put into force on 1 January 2010.

In accordance with Article 185 of the Serbian Constitution, this document is formally designated as a statute and not a separate constitutional act. In practice, however, the new statute concedes numerous competencies to the Vojvodinian assembly. Article 33 of the statute designates the Vojvodinian assembly as the 'highest organ and the institution with norm-setting powers in the autonomous province of Vojvodina'. Article 47 designates the government at the

---

[36] The 89 deputies of the DS-spearheaded governing coalition at the Vojvodinian assembly voted in favour of the new statute. Meanwhile, the 21 DSS and SRS deputies voted against. On this issue, see 'Novi Statut Vojvodine', *BBC Srpski*, 15 October 2008. For a full-text-version of the statute, see 'Statut Autonomne Pokrajine Vojvodine', *Službeni List AP Vojvodine*, br. 17/2009.

[37] 'Poslanička većina podržala statut Vojvodine', *Građanski List*, 15 October 2008.

[38] Ibid.; 'DSS i SRS nude svoje verzije Statuta', *Radio-televizija Vojvodine*, 15 October 2008.

[39] The 137 deputies of the ruling coalition voted in favour of the new statute, whereas 24 deputies from the DSS and New Serbia voted against. The SRS deputies abstained from the procedure. On this issue, see 'Prošla autonomija', *Večernje Novosti*, 30 November 2009.

Vojvodinian assembly as the highest executive organ. The use of the term *government* instead of 'executive council', which was in force before, implies an upgraded status – if only at the symbolic level. Article 34 authorizes the assembly to have its say on constitutional amendments that can have an impact on Vojvodina. Article 18 authorizes either the Vojvodinian assembly or government to appeal to the Constitutional Court in the event that a republican law infringes upon the statute. Although Article 34 does not concede *separate* legislative competencies to the assembly (except issuing the statute plus certain declarations and resolutions of regional significance), the two aforementioned provisions are of great significance since they safeguard the premises of the province's autonomy. Another significant provision is the provincial ombudsman with the task to supervise the proper implementation of the statute and other relevant legislation (Article 61). As far as judicial autonomy is concerned, Article 34 authorizes the assembly to organize the network of courts throughout Vojvodina.

A question of vital importance was the financial one. Article 62 reiterates the clause with regard to the ratio between the Vojvodinian and the republican budget, as stated in Article 184.3 of the Constitution (7 per cent of the republican budget). Article 63 enables Vojvodina to: finance projects within its territory from the provincial budget; have its own taxation system. Nevertheless, the same article dictates that it must be implemented in accordance with a special law on Vojvodina's finances. In principle, Articles 62 and 63 provide plenty of space for financial autonomy. Another provision of major importance is Vojvodina's authorization to establish its regional bank (Articles 29 and 34). Moreover, Article 16 specifies that Vojvodina can sign agreements on financial cooperation with foreign agents in its own right; have its representatives in Brussels and other European regions. The former clause reads like a 'reformulated reminder' of certain provisions in the 1974 Vojvodinian Constitution which also enabled the province to arrange financial deals with foreign agents. Here, it should be kept in mind that since 2002, Vojvodina has been participating in the Assembly of European Regions (AER) in Brussels. This is an independent network and interest-association of regions.[40]

The statute significantly enhances the protection of minority rights and enables provincial organs to manage this issue 'on the spot'. The statute's preamble upgrades the collective status of national minorities to that of national communities (*nacionalne zajednice*). Articles 6 and 7 reaffirm Vojvodina's multiethnic physiognomy and equality among all ethnic groups; provide for the implementation of positive discrimination with the aim to safeguard minority identities.[41] Article 23 reaffirms the dual dimension of minority rights (individual as well as collective), whereas Article 26 safeguards the use of minority languages in education and public information.

An institutional provision of major importance is the establishment of a Council for National Communities at the assembly (Article 40). This thirty-member body is to consist of representatives of the largest minorities in Vojvodina; concentrate on the implementation of the clauses on minority education, cultural activities and the official use of minority languages. Similar provisions were included in the *Law for the Protection of the Rights and Freedoms of National Minorities* which was inaugurated in February 2002 within the framework of the Serbian-Montenegrin loose federation.[42] Therefore, it seems that the statute's drafting committee modified and incorporated certain guidelines of this law to their document. Finally, Article 17 sets the preconditions for the establishment of the Vojvodinian Academy of Sciences (VANU). Throughout this arrangement, the statute stresses its locus within Serbia's constitutional framework and reaffirms Vojvodina as an indivisible part of Serbia (Articles 1 and 64).

---

[40] Through its participation in AER, Vojvodina expects to gain from the knowledge exchange with developed European regions, such as Lombardy and Catalonia, in a number of areas (e.g. financial management and infrastructural issues). For more information on AER, see: https://aer.eu/.

[41] It should be added that Article 6 restored the collective legal status of the ethnic Croat community.

[42] Vassilis Petsinis, 'Vojvodina's National Minorities: Current Realities and Future Prospects', *Spaces of Identity* 3[1], no. 2 (2003): 8–11.

As one might expect, the new statute did not leave everyone satisfied. In the one end of the spectrum, DSS and SRS representatives, as well as certain constitutional theorists, interpreted the statute as a document which concedes Vojvodina nearly the attributes of a state. Particularly bitter were the reactions of the pro-centralists in regard to Vojvodina's designation as a 'European region' (Article 1), its authorization to cooperate with other European regions, fiscal autonomy and the establishment of VANU. Nevertheless, all these allegations were exaggerated. The designation 'European region' implies that Vojvodina is a region where European civic values prevail; not a separate entity within Europe. Moreover, there is nothing unconstitutional with Article 16 on foreign cooperation since the very same provision for Vojvodina is included in Article 181 of the Serbian Constitution. As far as financial autonomy is concerned, this was a demand shared among almost the entirety of Vojvodina's citizenry and not exclusively the regionalists. This is not hard to grasp, taking into consideration the mismanagement of the province's revenues, by the central government, during the 1990s. Lastly, regional academic associations operate in various European states; whether unitary (France), federal (Germany) or 'regionalized' (Italy).

In the opposite end of the spectrum, the League and other pro-autonomists complained that the new statute does not really touch on legislative and judicial powers; neither does it resolve the financial question.[43] At this point, it should be noted that the 1974 system of autonomies still serves as a, if merely symbolic, compass for many Vojvodinian autonomists albeit not openly admitted. Nevertheless, nowadays, the concession of extensive legislative and judicial powers to Vojvodina, along the lines of the 1974 arrangement, might lead to Serbia's confederalization. The introduction of such parallel structures is

---

[43] *Dnevnik*, 16 October 2009: A statement by Nenad Čanak on the new statute for Vojvodina.

not something that a small and not particularly wealthy state like Serbia could afford. This argument gains greater weight, considering Serbia's 'state-shrinkage' after the dissolution of the Serbian-Montenegrin state union (21 May 2006) and the loss of Kosovo. As it occurred in Spain during the 1980s, there is also a serious possibility that such an option would anger other Serbian regions who might protest that Vojvodina gets a very preferential treatment.

Otherwise, the new statute is compatible with the European standards on contemporary regionalization. For the purposes of this work, attention is paid to the guidelines of the *Draft European Charter on Regional Self-Government* (Council of Europe 1997). This may not be a legally binding document but it still has a 'framework value' for setting up some basic standards on the devolution of authority towards the regional level within the European space.

For a start, the new statute is consistent with the draft charter's clauses which affirm the locus of regional institutions within the administrative and constitutional frameworks of the state that they belong to (*Draft European Charter on Regional Self-Government*; Preamble, Article 8); and encourage inter-regional cooperation throughout the Continent (ibid.; Preamble, Article 11).

In accordance with Article 1.2 of the draft charter, the new statute precisely defines the scope of regional self-government for Vojvodina. This is equally the case in regard to the designation of the regional competencies, the affirmation of their free function and assignment to the regional bodies responsible (ibid.; Articles 4, 12.1 and 12.2). Furthermore, the new statute authorizes Vojvodina to participate in decision-making processes of vital interest, at the macro-political level (ibid.; Article 9.1); guarantees its representation in the relevant European institutions (ibid.; Article 10.1). As far as finance and the management of regional resources are concerned, the new statute precisely specifies the boundaries of Vojvodina's financial autonomy (ibid.; Article 14) and establishes a regional taxation system (ibid.; Article 15). Lastly, the new statute safeguards the boundaries of Vojvodina's autonomy and the regional ombudsman functions as an adequate supervisory mechanism (ibid.; Articles 16, 17 and 19).

The new statute for Vojvodina was drafted and came into force with a rather long delay, amid what has been seen as Serbia's 'state-shrinkage'. In regard to the extent of autonomous jurisdictions, one might argue that the new statute somewhat resembles more closely the arrangement for the 'special' Italian regions. In principle, this document strengthens Vojvodina's asymmetric status within Serbia and comes to fill in certain ambiguities in the 2006 Constitution. The traumatic experience of the 1990s had rendered the safeguard of Vojvodina's autonomous jurisdiction an imperative. Furthermore, it became essential that the Vojvodinian assembly should pass legal measures of direct importance to the province (e.g. its statute and other relevant legislation) *jointly* with the republican parliament and not under full subordination to the latter. Especially the concession of fiscal autonomy to Vojvodina became an urgent necessity, in order to reverse the aftermath of economic mismanagement during the 1990s. This is equally valid in regard to the more efficient management of minority issues on a more regionalized basis and 'on the spot'.

Public outlooks on Vojvodina's regional identity and the state of interethnic relations

At this point, it would be interesting to highlight the public outlooks of Vojvodina's citizens towards regional identity and the climate of interethnic relations during the early part of the 2000s. A general trend observed in most public surveys was a preference towards the asymmetric and/or substantially decentralized options (Tables 14, 15 and 16) in regard to Vojvodina's administrative status within Serbia. This trend was highly subject to the deterioration of the socio-economic conditions during the 1990s. Hence, the overwhelming stress on the questions of economic autonomy and the improvement of the province's economic capacities in several opinion polls (Tables 15, 16 and 17).

Table 14 What should Vojvodina's administrative status be?

A similar degree of autonomy to what was the case according to the 1974 constitutional arrangement	33.1% of the respondents
The same as it is today	22.7% of the respondents
More autonomy within Serbia but less than it was the case according to the 1974 constitutional arrangement	17.6% of the respondents
Republic within FR Yugoslavia	6.4% of the respondents
No autonomous jurisdictions whatsoever	6.3% of the respondents
Independent state	4.2% of the respondents
Something else	4.5% of the respondents
I do not know	5.2% of the respondents

Source: Milka Puzigaca and Aleksandar Molnar, *Istraživanje javnog mnenja: Autonomija Vojvodine* (Novi Sad: SCAN, 2001), 1–19 (Sample size: 1,422 respondents).

Table 15 What kind of status should Vojvodina enjoy?

The existing status	13.9% of the respondents
Economic, political and cultural autonomy within the Republic of Serbia	57.9% of the respondents
Republic within the State's Union of Serbia and Montenegro	9.8% of the respondents
Independent state	0.8% of the respondents

Source: Zsölt Lazar and Radivoj Stepanov, 'Odnos Vojvođana prema ustavnopravnom statusu Vojvodine', in *Kultura u proćesima razvoja, regionalizacije i Evrointegracije Balkana* (University of Niš [Institute of Sociology], 2003) (Sample size: 516 respondents).

Table 16 What should Vojvodina's administrative status be?

Vojvodina should become an independent state	1.18% of the respondents
Vojvodina should remain part of FR Yugoslavia	14.71% of the respondents
Vojvodina should be granted economic and political autonomy within Serbia	28.24% of the respondents

(Continued)

Vojvodina should have a greater say over the management of its income resources	34.71% of the respondents
The existing status	12.35% of the respondents
No autonomous jurisdictions whatsoever/ establishment of a centralized state	8.82% of the respondents

Source: Novosadska Novinarska Škola, *Nacionalistička vrednosna orijentacija kao faktor otpora prema autonomiji Vojvodine* (Novi Sad: NNS, 2001), 34 (Sample size: 170 respondents).

Table 17 Vojvodina is denied the right to finance projects within its territory from the provincial budget. Would this be a good arrangement?

No, because in this way Vojvodina would be robbed of its provincial income	68.9% of the respondents
Yes, because in this way Serbia would have greater control over Vojvodina's income resources	9.3% of the respondents
Some alternative arrangement would be better	9.9% of the respondents
I do not know	11.9% of the respondents

Source: Puzigaca and Molnar (2001, p. 9).

Meanwhile, certain ambiguities persisted in regard to the other areas of institutional autonomy (Table 18). The entire concept of 'autonomy' remained rather vague for quite a few Vojvodinians, even though the general climate regarding the reinforcement of Vojvodina's autonomy beyond the economic sector was rather positive. Even though positively pre-disposed towards the prospect of regional autonomy, the majority of Vojvodinians still believed that the best path towards strengthening Vojvodinian autonomy was through constant negotiation with Belgrade's political elites over the achievement of a compromise over this issue.[44] This could have been an additional factor that accounted for the low public appeal of the pro-autonomy parties.

[44] Milka Puzigaca and Aleksandar Molnar, *Istraživanje javnog mnenja: Autonomija Vojvodine* (Novi Sad: SCAN, 2001), 12.

Table 18 What kind of meaning does the term *autonomy* have for you?

A negative one	16.47% of the respondents
A vague and unclear one	44.12% of the respondents
A not particularly clear one	27.65% of the respondents
A very clear and positive one	11.75% of the respondents

Source: Novosadska Novinarska Škola (2001, p. 34).

As far as the reserved or negative attitudes towards the prospect of autonomy were concerned, these had been subject to the gradual fragmentation of the old Yugoslavia and its negative repercussions on the ethnic Serb communities. Although, as already clarified, the question of Vojvodinian autonomy is qualitatively different to the various secessionist trends witnessed all over the former Yugoslavia throughout the 1990s, the negative consequences of the latter seemed to have left their mark on the political outlooks of quite few Serbs in the province. This sensitivity over questions of regional autonomy was also subject to the memories of the 1974 constitutional arrangements, which many Serbs in Vojvodina and elsewhere tended to perceive as, perhaps, the root of all evils in regard to the troubles in the former Yugoslavia. In addition to these, the positive stance of quite a few Vojvodinian Montenegrins and other colonists towards more centralized state's structures (Table 19) seemed to be an additional by-product of the psychological turmoil involved in the interethnic warfare across the former Yugoslavia. Especially incidents such as the ethnic cleansing of the Serb community in the Croatian Krajina (1995) had exerted a definitive and largely personalized impact on them.

Furthermore, the high degree of parochial affiliation observed in these public surveys originated from a feeling of uncertainty.[45] It became evident that the disintegration of the old Yugoslavia, the international isolation and widespread poverty made the citizens of Vojvodina

---

[45] Zsölt Lazar and Dušan Marinković, 'Regional Identity: Vojvodina's Urban Public Research Survey', in *Essays on Regionalisation*, 184–5.

Table 19 What should Vojvodina's status within Serbia be (broken down in accordance with national affiliation)?

National affiliation	Existing status	Economic and cultural autonomy within Serbia	Republic within FR Yugoslavia	Independent state	Total
Serbs	77 23.4%	202 61.4%	37 11.2%	13 4.0%	329 100.0%
Montenegrins	19 65.5%	6 20.7%	4 13.8%		29 100.0%
Croats	10 24.4%	25 61.0%	5 12.2%	1 2.4%	41 100.0%
Hungarians	12 23.5%	24 47.1%	11 21.6%	4 7.8%	51 100.0%
Others	23 35.4%	27 41.5%	11 16.9%	4 6.2%	65 100.0%

Source: Zsolt Lazar and Dušan Marinković, 'Regional Identity: Vojvodina's Urban Public Research Survey', in *Essays on Regionalization*, 181.

incline more to their local communities where they felt more intimately rooted. In this light, the high degree of affiliation with the Republic of Serbia, on behalf of many respondents who settled in Vojvodina during the 1990s (mostly refugees), serves as an indication that the war evicted persons from Croatia and Bosnia-Herzegovina perceived the Serbian republic as a safe haven and shelter from persecution. In regard to the higher importance attached to social tolerance and personal security by refugees,[46] this derived from their relative social marginalization and instances of confrontation with the locals over the allocation of scarce job opportunities.

The public survey *Istraživanje javnog mnenja: Autonomija Vojvodine*, conducted by the Novi Sad SCAN agency throughout 2000 and 2001, had observed a generally positive disposition among Vojvodinians towards the official use of minority languages and their alphabets; relations between Vojvodina's ethnic minorities and their kin states; institutional guarantees for ethnic minorities (Table 20).[47] The results of this opinion poll serve as an additional indication that in the case of Vojvodina we have to do with *intercultural* instead of multicultural cohabitation. In the latter case, contacts among ethnic groups exist on a formal level and are mostly of a political and economic nature (e.g. the case of Bosnia-Herzegovina prior to the recent conflict). In the case of Vojvodina, however, it seems that there exist ethnic group cultures but beside these cultures there exists a common cultural substratum which becomes manifest in the form of Vojvodinian regional identity. It is precisely this regional identity that is one of the main factors influencing the presence of common denominators. Regional identity establishes common human values, developed as significant or even existential by diverse ethnic groups. On such an occasion, the part played by similar living conditions, historical links and mutual reliance, as well as the common future perspectives should be taken into account.

---

[46] On this issue see the results of the opinion poll in Ibid., 179.
[47] Puzigaca and Molnar, *Istraživanje javnog mnenja*, 11 and 15.

Table 20 Should the Assembly of the Autonomous Province of Vojvodina comprise a Chamber of National Communities where the major national communities in the province will be equally represented (broken down in accordance with national affiliation)?

National affiliation	Yes, with full-fledged jurisdiction	Yes, but only as a body which will decide over questions pertaining to the equality of national communities	No	I do not know	TOTAL
Serbs	15.5% of the respondents	37.7% of the respondents	31.4% of the respondents	15.4% of the respondents	100.0%
Croats	26.7% of the respondents	53.3% of the respondents	3.3% of the respondents	16.7% of the respondents	100.0%
Hungarians	45.7% of the respondents	39.4% of the respondents	2.9% of the respondents	12.0% of the respondents	100.0%
Montenegrins	9.1% of the respondents	31.8% of the respondents	50.0% of the respondents	9.1% of the respondents	100.0%
Slovaks	40.6% of the respondents	30.4% of the respondents	5.8% of the respondents	23.2% of the respondents	100.0%
Romanians	47.1% of the respondents	23.5% of the respondents		29.4% of the respondents	100.0%
Ruthenes	22.2% of the respondents	22.2% of the respondents	33.3% of the respondents	22.2% of the respondents	100.0%
Others	20.6% of the respondents	36.5% of the respondents	23.8% of the respondents	19.0% of the respondents	100.0%

Source: Puzigaca and Molnar (2001, p. 15).

This notion of intercultural cohabitation manifests itself in various shapes in the Vojvodinian everyday life and experience. Intermarriage among different ethnic groups remains a common occurrence in the urban as well as the rural settlements. In most cases, catalysts such as the workplace or the neighbourhood still seem to take precedence over ethno-cultural or religious cleavages. Furthermore, in certain multiethnic rural communities the locals often celebrate religious and other *seoške* ('village') feasts together, regardless of their ethno-cultural affiliation and regardless of whether the religious festivities are Eastern Orthodox or Roman Catholic.[48] This is not to say that Vojvodina is anywhere near the American melting pot. By contrast, the ethnic communities in Vojvodina have preserved a certain degree of integrity, insisting on their own distinctive identities.[49] In Vojvodina, this often becomes obvious on the grassroots level through the persistence of certain auto-stereotypes (images of the self) and hetero-stereotypes (images of others). All sorts of group stereotypes represent oversimplified views on the characteristics of ethnic groups. In social science, what is oversimplified cannot be regarded as valid. On the popular level, though, it seems that the persistence of mutual stereotypes has somewhat facilitated the preservation of the distinctiveness of the ethnic communities in Vojvodina.[50]

On the other hand, the negative stance towards the prospect of making further concessions to the province's minority groups became subject to the fragmentation of the old Yugoslavia; the resurgence of militant irredentist nationalism (e.g. the ethnic Albanian case); the negative impact of the recent conflicts on the Serbs in Kosovo and the other parts of ex-Yugoslavia. Finally, the relative reluctance of quite a

---

[48] Interview with sociologist at the University of Novi Sad; 13 March 2001 – Interview with representative of the Serbian Orthodox Church; Novi Sad, 18 March 2001.
[49] Interview with sociologist at the University of Novi Sad; 14 November 2005.
[50] For example, the dominant group stereotype about Serbs is that they are generally open and joyful people but not very punctual. The Hungarians, on the other hand, are regarded as precise, gentle and hard-working people but not particularly 'temperamental'. Some information over these stereotypes was disclosed to the author in the course of his field research in Vojvodina (interview with sociologist/interview with historian at the University of Novi Sad; 13 March 2001).

few ethnic Hungarians towards the initiatives of VMSZ and VMDK for northern Bačka may be interpreted as a fear that the concession of autonomy within Vojvodina according to the ethno-territorial principle might resurface cleavages and tensions potentially detrimental to the state of intercultural understanding in the province.[51]

Some worrying signs: The 'ethnic incidents' of the mid-2000s

Between 2003 and 2005, a spate of incidences often categorized as 'ethnic' took place in Vojvodina. These incidences ranged from hate graffiti to acts of vandalism directed against churches or graveyards.[52] In most cases, however, they involved violent clashes between individuals or groups of youths belonging to different ethnic affiliations (most commonly, Serbs and ethnic Hungarians or Croats).

On this occasion, the impact of external catalysts comes to the fore again. The recent wars for secession in the former Yugoslavia were largely conditioned by the concept that internal political stability and socio-economic progress 'equal' national homogeneity. This drive towards national homogenization in the breakaway Yugoslav republics often escalated to violent excesses in the course of the latest conflicts. The equation of internal stability with national homogeneity soon found acceptance among international policymakers as well. This was reflected, for instance, in the constitutional structuring of Bosnia-Herzegovina along the lines of ethnic partition by the Dayton Agreement. With specific focus on the Serbs, they had also been target of the aggressive drive towards national homogenization in the other parts of the former Yugoslavia. In regard to the Serbs of Vojvodina, the presence of a considerable number of Serb refugees in the province serves as a constant reminder of what many Vojvodinian Serbs perceive

---

[51] Puzigaca and Molnar, *Istraživanje javnog mnenja*, 16.
[52] Dinko Gruhonjić, 'Gde je Vojvođanska tolerancija išla?' *Građanski list*, 21 October 2003.

as the 'historical injustice' against the Serbian nation. This was not solely the case with the 1995 'Operation Storm' or the developments in Bosnia-Herzegovina over the 1990s but also the 'silent' ethnic cleansing of the Serbs from Kosovo since 1999.[53] Therefore, a greater percentage of Serbs in Vojvodina and Serbia as a whole had come to adhere to the principle 'internal stability=national homogeneity', thus indirectly condoning acts of ethnic intolerance. Despite the non-negligible significance of the external dimension, however, the part played by domestic political actors also possessed pivotal significance.

In the case of Vojvodinian Hungarians, of particular importance was the stance held by the two ethnic Hungarian parties. Both VMDK and VMSZ were quick on their feet to label these incidents as a well-orchestrated campaign with the aim to terrorize ethnic Hungarians. These two parties also tried to promote their case in international forums, such as the OSCE, though with little success. On the Vojvodinian micro-level, the VMDK and VMSZ officials informally declared a 'state of emergency' for the ethnic Hungarian community. Meanwhile, both parties tried to pose as the only agents with the ability to defend the Hungarian community's interests under these adverse circumstances. At a first instance, this stance resulted in the temporary deterioration of the relations between the two ethnic Hungarian parties and their regional partners among the Serbian mainstream parties (namely DS). Moreover, this functioned as an additional catalyst that contributed to the temporary intensification of ethnic solidarity and *groupness* among Vojvodinian Hungarians; an increase in ethnic segmentation in certain Vojvodinian towns with a predominantly Serbian and ethnic Hungarian population (e.g. Temerin and Stari Bečej in Bačka).[54]

In regard to the Serbian majority, the key part was played by SRS. Between 2003 and 2004, the then party leader, Tomislav Nikolić, and

---

[53] OSCE, *Ninth Assessment of the Situation of Ethnic Minorities in Kosovo* (Period covering September 2001 to April 2002), 2002; Human Rights Watch, *Failure to Protect: Anti-minority Violence in Kosovo (March 2004)* 16, no. 6 (July 2004): 30–53, 62–5.
[54] Interview with academic specialist in ethnic relations; University of Belgrade, 18 November 2005; Áron Léphaft, Ádám Németh and Péter Reményi, 'Ethnic Diversity and Polarization in Vojvodina', *Hungarian Geographical Bulletin* 63, no. 2 (2014): 143–54.

Vojvodinian Radical functionaries sought to gain political capital out of violent incidents in which the victims were Serbs and the perpetrators Hungarians or other 'ethnics'. Such occurrences were swiftly interpreted as the shape of things to come for Vojvodinian Serbs and placed within the broader framework of 'shrinkage of Serbdom', together with the expulsion of Serbs from the Croatian Krajina and the Serbian emigration out of Kosovo.[55] This rhetoric obviously aimed at declaring a 'state of emergency' and increasing the party's mobilizing potential among the Serbian majority. The strategy of the Radicals found some appeal among the refugees from Croatia and Bosnia; largely owing to the vulnerability of this segment as well as its traumatic and easily manipulated collective memory. According to empirical evidence, quite a few refugees had active involvement in the incidences earlier described.[56]

This issue requires some further elaboration. Especially in the light of the broader socio-economic antagonism, ethnic Serb refugees occasionally perceived Vojvodinian Hungarians as the intruding 'other' in terms of ethno-cultural categorization. The refugees perceived Vojvodina, and by extension Serbia, as a safe haven from persecution where they could live together with the rest of their 'ethnic kin'. Therefore, from the refugees' perspective, their needs should be granted greater priority in comparison to those of ethnic minorities.[57] For Vojvodinian Hungarians, on the contrary, the Serb refugees were external intruders and usurpers of scarce employment opportunities and social benefits. Nevertheless, these 'ethnic incidents' did not succeed in bringing about and cementing a state of ethnic segregation in Vojvodina's multiethnic settlements. According to reports by the Serbian government as well as external observers, the intensity of 'ethnic incidents' in Vojvodina had started to enter a steady phase of decline since late 2004. According

---

[55] http://www.srs.org.yu/izbori/ns.htm.
[56] Ilić Vladimir, *Manjine i izbeglice u Vojvodini* (Belgrade: Helsinki Committee for Human Rights in Serbia, 2001).
[57] Interview with expert in ethnic relations at the Hungarian Academy of Sciences (Budapest), 13 April 2008.

to the same reports, the main underlying cause behind these incidents was the frustration of a considerable percentage among the Vojvodinian youth with the deteriorating standards of living. Field research in the towns of Sombor, Kikinda, Novi Sad and Subotica demonstrated that competition for employment had been the major underlying cause behind 'ethnic' tensions on the regional and local micro-levels.[58]

---

[58] Centre for Development of Civic Society, 'Ethnic Incidents in Vojvodina after Internationalization', May 2004, 1–6, http://www.cdcs.org.yu/docs/internat_engl.doc; Interview with expert in ethnic relations at the Hungarian Academy of Sciences (Budapest), 13 April 2008.

5

Vojvodina Today: Between New Challenges and Opportunities

This chapter positions Vojvodina inside the context of the latest political developments in Serbia and Europe. Particular attention is paid to the predominance of President Aleksandar Vučić and the ruling Serbian Progressive Party (*Srpska Napredna Stranka*, SNS), as well as to the prospects for Serbia within its trajectory of accession to the EU. This chapter also casts its focus on the current state of political affairs in neighbouring states (namely Hungary) and assesses their ramifications upon ethnopolitics within the province. An additional objective is to briefly discuss powerful regionalisms in the Continent (the 'new' Catalan question and, to a secondary degree, the case of Italy's *Lega Nord/ Northern League*) and isolate the main aspects which differentiate such cases from regionalism in Vojvodina. Lastly, this chapter touches upon the recent arrival of war refugees from the Middle East and measures the impact that this novel development can exert on social stability and inter-group relations in the province. Of essential importance is to highlight whether and how Vojvodinian regional identity, as a trans-ethnic substratum, can withstand the new challenges and benefit from the new opportunities.

Aleksandar Vučić and SNS as preponderant political actors in Serbia: The implications for Vojvodina

SNS was officially launched on 21 October 2008. It was set up by leading figures within the old SRS (former SRS chairman Tomislav Nikolić and Aleksandar Vučić) who had departed from the party, between late 2007 and early 2008, on grounds of tactical disagreements with the nationalist hardliners. These cadres and their factions had suggested that the most efficient way for SRS to capitalize on the cleavages among their rivals in the centre/centre-right (DS, DSS and SPO) and consolidate a firmer foothold on the political mainstream should have consisted in a lesser emphasis on nationalism; a greater stress on the reformation of the economy; the conditional endorsement of Serbia's accession process to the EU. SNS soon evolved from a splinter group into a full-fledged party with a, conservative, centre-right agenda.[1] It pledged to maintain an equal distance from east and west and endorsed accession to the EU under the fundamental premise that Serbia's national interests in its neighbourhood (Kosovo and *Republika Srpska*) are effectively safeguarded.

Following Boris Tadić's tenure in office as president of the Republic (2004–12), Serbia's centrist and liberal forces (namely DS) have been continuously shrinking as a result of their inability to project a convincing alternative to the electorate. In light of the global economic crisis, the 'Third Way' prerogatives, espoused by DS until recently, quickly lost their popular appeal also in Serbia. To this should be added allegations of corruption against the party during its term in the government.[2] Further along the right angle of the spectrum, the decision of DSS to form a coalition with the more nationalistic *Dveri* ('Gates') for the latest parliamentary elections (24 April 2016) did not succeed in enhancing the party's political weight. Meanwhile, the 'new' SRS has been marginalized into a peripheral actor with a low political significance. As an aggregate of these circumstances, SNS has come to dominate a political continuum that ranges from the fringes of the liberal centre all the way to the conservative right. The results of the last

---

[1] Vassilis Petsinis, 'Competing Conservatisms in Serbia and Croatia', *Open Democracy*, 11 July 2017, https://www.opendemocracy.net/author/vassilis-petsinis.

[2] These allegations culminated with the departure of Boris Tadić from DS in January 2014. On this issue, see https://www.b92.net/eng/news/politics.php?yyyy=2014&mm=01&dd=30&nav_id=89173.

parliamentary and presidential elections (7 April 2017) clearly testify to the party's preponderance in Serbian politics.[3]

In its preamble, the party programme (2011) defines SNS as a 'political organization with a clear democratic orientation' and sets three primary areas of concern: 'protection of the vital national interests; promotion of human rights; real and accelerated economic development.'[4] SNS does not dedicate a separate section of its programme to Vojvodina per se. However, elsewhere in the text, the party clarifies that, as far as the territorial arrangement of Serbia is concerned, it opts for the model of functional decentralization. In greater detail, SNS specifies that it encourages the uniform development of all parts of the state, which also takes into consideration their regional and local particularities, and which should be built around the major urban centres (Belgrade, Novi Sad etc.).

The party envisages the municipal units of local administration as the main vehicle towards the implementation of the decentralization process.[5] It further contends that SNS stands for the equal development of all parts of the state and that every administrative unit must be drawn in correlation with the financial and infrastructural needs of the others. In addition, the party-programme pledges to accelerate the return of ethnic Serb refugees to Croatia, as well as the restitution of their immobile property, and enhance the economic cooperation between *Republika Srpska* and the Republic of Serbia. The absence of any concrete and extensive references to Vojvodina, in combination with the schematic outline of functional decentralization, implies that SNS favours a symmetric and unitary pattern of territorial organization instead of an asymmetric and regionalized one.

In the parliamentary elections of 2014 and 2016, the electoral attitudes of Vojvodinian voters seem to have become subject to the

---

[3] SNS garnered 48.25 per cent of the vote in the latest parliamentary elections (2016) and Aleksandar Vučić 55.06 per cent of the vote in the latest presidential elections (2017).
[4] Srpska Napredna Stranka, *Bela Knjiga Programom do Promena* (Belgrade: SNS, 2011), 2–3.
[5] Ibid., 46.

macro-political catalysts which are relevant throughout the whole of Serbia. As previously mentioned, especially during the tenure of Bojan Pajtić as president of the executive council at Vojvodina's assembly, DS had held a favourable stance vis-à-vis the extension of the administrative jurisdiction and the enhancement of Vojvodina's asymmetric status within Serbia. Until the parliamentary, presidential and provincial elections of 2012, this had enabled DS and Boris Tadić to garner the majority of the vote among the Vojvodinian electorate (Table 21). Nevertheless, the long-term inability of DS to concretize and project a new image to Serbian voters also claimed its toll on the party's performance in Vojvodina. Meanwhile, despite their continuous representation in the Vojvodinian assembly and the provincial administrative organs, LSDV and the Vojvodinian regionalists kept on suffering from the impediment of a poor and inadequate staffing. The steady growth of SNS's public appeal culminated with the party's overwhelming victory in the most recent elections for the Vojvodinian assembly (24 April 2016) (Table 22).

The gradual emergence of SNS as a potent political actor across Serbia reinvigorated the pro-unitary forces in the province and rekindled their pressures for a revision of the 2009 statute on the autonomy of Vojvodina.

Table 21 The results of the elections for the assembly of the autonomous province of Vojvodina (May 2012)

Party	Leader	%	Seats
DS coalition	Bojan Pajtić	48.33	58
SNS coalition	Tomislav Nikolić	18.33	22
SPS coalition	Ivica Dačić	10.83	13
LSDV	Nenad Čanak	8.33	10
VMSZ	István Pásztor	5.83	7
SRS	Vojislav Šešelj	6.30	5
DSS	Vojislav Koštunica	3.33	4
Liberal Democratic Party	Čedomir Jovanović	0.83	1

Source: http://www.cesid.rs/.

Table 22 The results of the elections for the assembly of the autonomous province of Vojvodina (April 2016)

Party	Leader	%	Seats
SNS coalition	Maja Gojković	44.48	63
SPS coalition	Dušan Bajatović	8.86	12
SRS	Đurađ Jakšić	7.66	10
DS coalition	Miroslav Vasin	7.24	10
LSDV	Branislav Bogaroški	6.43	9
'Enough!'	Svetlana Kozić	5.54	7
VMSZ	István Pásztor	4.88	6
VMDK	Tamás Korhecz	1.71	2
Green Party	Branislava Jeftić	1.14	1

Source: http://www.cesid.rs/.

This resulted in a new round of tensions between LSDV and the pro-unitary camp which comprised DSS, the reformed SPS and SNS. DSS, in particular, took the statute to the Republican Constitutional Court in autumn 2013. At a first instance, the Court judged that two-thirds of the statute was not in accordance with the Serbian Constitution.[6] In the long run, though, a compromise was reached between the Republican Constitutional Court and the Vojvodinian assembly. Consequently, an amended version of the statute was inaugurated on 22 May 2014.[7] The amendments were approved at the assembly by the vote of 91 out of the 113 members in total.[8]

The changes in the new version of the statute touched upon subjects of a mostly symbolic dimension and a slightly more condensed version of the 2009 document was produced. Throughout the amended text,

---

[6] Jelena Džankić and Christina Isabel Zuber, 'Serbia and Montenegro: From Centralization to Secession and Multi-Ethnic Regionalism', in *Regional and National Elections in Eastern Europe: Territoriality of the Vote in Ten Countries*, ed. Arjan H. Schakel (London: Palgrave Macmillan, 2017), 221–2; Jovan Komšić, 'Autonomism in Vojvodina', *Südosteuropa* 61, no. 3 (2013): 335–40.

[7] 'Statut Autonomne Pokrajine Vojvodine', *Službeni List AP Vojvodine*, br. 20/2014.

[8] https://inserbia.info/today/2014/05/assembly-of-vojvodina-adopts-provincial-statute/.

Novi Sad was re-designated from 'capital city' (*glavni grad*) into 'seat of the provincial organs' (*sedište pokrajinskih organa*) (Article 10) whereas 'the government of Vojvodina' (*vlada Vojvodine*) was replaced by the more neutral 'provincial government' (*pokrajinska vlada*) (Article 44). Furthermore, the amendments maintained the right of Vojvodina to cooperation with organizations and agencies based abroad but underlined that 'Vojvodina may cooperate with corresponding territorial communities and other forms of autonomy in other countries as part of Serbia's foreign policy, and will be under the obligation to respect Serbia's territorial integrity and legal order' (Article 16). However, a symbolic dispute between LSDV and SNS, which persists up to date, is the one over the patterns of Vojvodina's regional flag (Figures 1 and 2).[9]

Overall, the amendments of 2014 did not result into the actual curtailment or the significant reduction of Vojvodina's administrative autonomy. Nor has Serbia's SNS-led government displayed any intentions to cancel or further revise certain terms in the statute on provincial autonomy. From a broader angle, SNS's tenure in office has demonstrated that the party is rather keen on a tactical and situationally adaptive pattern of policymaking with the objective to maintain a favourable balance vis-à-vis a wide range of interest groups and stakeholders.[10] Nevertheless, the efficient implementation of the statute has frequently become entangled into complications of a legal as well as a constitutional nature. For a start, it has often not been feasible to precisely calculate the 7 per cent of the republican budget for Vojvodina as stipulated in Article 57. This 'vagueness' has occasionally led several interest groups among the Vojvodinian regionalists to accuse the Serbian government of deliberately miscalculating the share

---

[9] SNS favours a flag and coat of arms modelled in accordance with those displayed during the *Vojvodstvo Srpsko* of 1848. LSDV opts for the more recent version which comprises the Serbian tricolour plus three stars (each for the sub-regions of Bačka, Srem and the Banat). On this issue, see https://www.blic.rs/vesti/politika/sta-stoji-iza-spora-oko-novog-grba-i-zastave-vojvodine/d385t88.

[10] On this issue, see Vassilis Petsinis, 'Enter Serbia's "Orbán"? Aleksandar Vučić and his Catch-all Politics', *Open Democracy*, 28 June 2017, https://www.opendemocracy.net/author/vassilis-petsinis.

Figure 1 Vojvodina's regional flag and coat of arms favoured by SNS.

Sources: http://www.skupstinavojvodine.gov.rs/: The official website of Vojvodina's provincial assembly.

Figure 2 Vojvodina's regional flag favoured by LSDV.

Sources: http://www.skupstinavojvodine.gov.rs/: The official website of Vojvodina's provincial assembly.

of the republican budget allocated for Vojvodina.[11] More importantly, as previously mentioned, it remains an imperative that the Serbian Constitution defines more concretely and anchors more firmly the locus of Vojvodina's asymmetric status inside Serbia's constitutional order.[12] In spite of these shortcomings, though, the statute on the autonomy of Vojvodina still preserves Vojvodina's asymmetric status within Serbia and remains consistent with the European standards on regionalization.

The management of interethnic relations and the domestic ramifications of external developments

However complicated and nonlinear, Serbia's accession process to the EU has corresponded to rapid developments in the institutional and legal infrastructure for the protection of minority rights. As early as July 2008, the Ministry of Human and Minority Rights came into existence as a full-fledged institution on the republican level. Moreover, the provisions of the statute for Vojvodina on minority rights are anchored inside the relevant clauses of the Serbian Constitution on the public use of minority languages, the prohibition of discrimination and the relations of minorities with their kin states (Articles 75–80). In addition, the Serbian laws on local self-government (2002), the official use of minority languages (amended in 2005) and prohibition of discrimination (2009) also contribute to the arrangement of an articulate infrastructure for the protection of minority rights.[13] Meanwhile, the political programme of SNS fully subscribes to

---

[11] Dimitrije Boarov, 'Podrivanje Vojvodinu: U Ustavnom Tunelu', *Vreme*, 1136, 11 October 2012. The urgent necessity to standardize the legislation over the finances of Vojvodina has also been highlighted by the European Commission. On this issue, see European Commission, *Serbia 2018 Report*, 17 April 2018, SWD (2018), 8.

[12] Komšić, 'Autonomism in Vojvodina', 335–40.

[13] Vassilis Petsinis, 'Minority Legislation in Two Successor States: A Comparison through the Lens of EU Enlargement', *Baltic Worlds*, no. 1 (2012): 31–5.

safeguarding the collective rights and freedoms of ethnic minorities as these are stipulated in the state legislation (education, political representation, public use of minority languages and cross-border links to the kin states).[14]

With specific regard to the political engagement of Vojvodina's ethnic Hungarian parties (VMSZ, in particular), this still consists in a preference to the politics of consensus over the politics of confrontation. Capitalizing on the state of fragmentation in Serbian politics since the fall of Slobodan Milošević and prior to the consolidation of SNS, VMSZ has been participating in a series of government coalitions with larger Serbian parties on the republican as well as on the provincial level. Most recently, following the results of the 2016 elections for the Vojvodinian assembly, the party has been steadily cooperating with the local SNS committee over a broad range of policy areas.[15] Since 2000, this pattern of engagement has facilitated VMSZ to promote their standpoints and demands on minority rights from within the halls of power. At the same time, although this document still maintains a great symbolic value, VMSZ appears to place a secondary importance to the tripartite concept of ethno-territorial autonomy as the fundamental premise for planning the party's policymaking. Throughout the last decade, this lesser emphasis on the various concepts of ethno-territorial autonomy and the higher stress on a gradualist strategy of cooperation with the larger political actors have been characteristic of several other ethnic Hungarian parties across the Carpathian basin (e.g. the *Most-Híd*/'Bridge' party in Slovakia).

---

[14] Srpska Napredna Stranka, *Bela Knjiga Programom do Promena*, 44–5.
[15] It should be noted that the party chairman, István Pásztor, currently serves as president at the executive council of the provincial assembly. For more on this issue, see https:// www.blic.rs/vesti/vojvodina/blizu-dogovora-i-socijalisti-u-vladi-vojvodine-uz-sns-i-svm-mirovic-moguci-premijer/mn7dysc.

Coming back to Brubaker's *triadic nexus* theory, the political developments in the ethnic minority's external homeland can exert direct and crucial repercussions upon the political attitudes of the minority within the state where it resides. The situation of the ethnic Hungarian minorities across the Carpathian basin, as well as the extension of political rights to ethnic Hungarians from the neighbouring states who reside in Hungary, has long formed a focal concern among a string of Hungarian governments and Hungary's main parties. On certain occasions, the question of minority rights for ethnic Hungarians fomented tensions between Budapest and neighbouring governments (e.g. Hungary's objections during Romania's EU accession process and its opposition to the Slovak Language Law of 2009). Since 2010, the preponderant Hungarian premier, Viktor Orbán, and his ruling FIDESZ have been consolidating their concept of *illiberal democracy*. The EU's apprehension over the state of democratic freedoms in Hungary, as well as Viktor Orbán's strident opposition to the EU's refugee quotas arrangement, has largely shifted the lens of the Hungarian government's grievances from the neighbouring states towards Brussels.

Further along the right angle of the political spectrum, Jobbik (*Jobbik Magyarországért Mozgalom*/Movement for a Better Hungary) stands as the second most popular party after the 2018 parliamentary elections. In addition to its militant pattern of political engagement within Hungary, Jobbik firmly cushions its scope inside the political culture of Hungarian nationalism. In its political manifesto (2010), Jobbik espouses an ethno-nationalist instead of a civic agenda and specifies that the party's political scope is 'not defined by the borders of our country but by the borders of our nation'.[16] Moreover, it is made clear that one of the party's main objectives is 'the reincorporation into the national body of both Western and Carpathian-basin Hungarians'

---

[16] Jobbik-The Movement for a Better Hungary, *Radical Change: A Guide to Jobbik's Parliamentary Electoral Manifesto for National Self-Determination and Social Justice* (Budapest: Jobbik, 2010), 15.

whereas, elsewhere in the text, Hungary is referred to as 'the territorially-maimed, mother-country'.[17]

Within the context of these programmatic standpoints, Jobbik has also demonstrated its interest in becoming active and setting up a representation office in Vojvodina. Between 2014 and 2016, Jobbik MPs based in Hungary (namely, István Szávay) had been engaged in attempts to open offices for the party, first, in Subotica and later in Senta (northern Bačka).[18] These endeavours were repeatedly thwarted by the local authorities on the grounds that the Serbian legislation prohibits the operation of political parties and organizations which serve foreign interests in the territory of Serbia.[19] However, there exist allegations that Jobbik's representation office in Senta has still been operating on an informal basis.[20] The memories from the 'ethnic incidents' of the mid-2000s are rather fresh. Consequently, any prospects towards the political engagement of a radical right-wing party with a revisionist and virulently ethno-nationalist profile do not leave out promising implications for the state of social stability and interethnic relations in Vojvodina. At this given moment, it is not an easy task to make further-reaching and accurate assessments in regard to the opportunity structures for Jobbik to evolve into a potent political actor among the ethnic Hungarian community.

Nevertheless, empirical research, conducted on the political preferences of 'trans-border'[21] ethnic Hungarians across the Carpathian basin, hints that, whereas FIDESZ has succeeded in claiming the lion's share of their vote, Jobbik has not yet managed to gain a momentum

---

[17] Ibid., 20.
[18] https://www.jobbik.com/istvan_szavay_opens_representative_office_in_vojvodina_too.
[19] https://dailynewshungary.com/serbian-court-calls-on-jobbik-to-close-local-office/.
[20] http://www.rtv.rs/sr_lat/vojvodina/kancelarija-jobika-u-senti-jos-radi_682736.html.
[21] This term denotes those ethnic Hungarians from one of Hungary's neighbouring states who have been awarded Hungarian citizenship but still maintain connections with their native places of origin. In accordance to the 2011 national census, 251,136 ethnic Hungarians (13 per cent of the total population) resided in Vojvodina (Table 23).

Table 23 The ethnic structure of the population in Vojvodina (2011 census)

Nationality	Numbers	%
Serbs	1,289,635	66.76
Hungarians	251,136	13.00
Slovaks	50,321	2.60
Croats	47,033	2.43
Roma	42,391	2.19
Romanians	25,410	1.32
Montenegrins	22,141	1.15
Bunjevci	16,469	0.85
Ruthenes	13,928	0.72
Yugoslavs	12,176	0.63
Macedonians	10,392	0.54
Ukrainians	4,202	0.22
Muslims	3,360	0.17
Germans	3,272	0.17
Albanians	2,251	0.12
Slovenes	1,815	0.09
Bulgarians	1,489	0.08
Gorani	1,179	0.06
Russians	1,173	0.06
Bosnjaks	780	0.04
Vlachs	170	0.01
Others	6,170	0.35
Regional affiliation	28,567	1.48
Non-defined	81,018	4.19
Unknown	14,791	0.77
TOTAL	**1.931,809**	**100**

among this specific segment of the electorate.[22] This pattern is equally valid in the case of Hungarian voters who originate from Vojvodina. More importantly, as early as January 2014, the VMSZ chairman, István Pásztor, warned Jobbik, on the occasion of the party's attempt to inaugurate its representation office in Subotica, that 'we do not need anyone, not a single one, who comes from Hungary to ignite fire with their irresponsible behavior, and then go home' and added that 'Vojvodina's Hungarians have never been and will never become protagonists in either Serbian or Hungarian nationalism'.[23] Lastly, in addition to the prohibition of ethnic discrimination, Serbia's legal infrastructure comprises an articulate platform against the dissemination of hate speech and the incitement of ethnic hatred. Selected aspects of this legislation were also activated as part of the endeavour to hinder Jobbik from opening its representation offices.[24] The aggregate of these sociopolitical and legal realities, in combination with Vojvodina's long-standing heritage of harmonious coexistence, hints that the opportunity structures for Jobbik's successful engagement in the province currently do not seem particularly encouraging.

Vojvodina amid the powerful awakening of European regionalisms

The last few years have witnessed the virulent resurgence of regionalist movements across the Continent. Within certain political environments, the reinvigorated engagement of regionalist parties seems to coincide with the simultaneous and varying impact of the economic crisis (the cases of Spain, Italy and, to a lesser extent,

---

[22] Szabolcs Pogonyi, *Extra-Territorial Ethnic Politics, Discourses and Identities in Hungary* (London: Palgrave Macmillan, 2017), 104–5.
[23] http://www.vesti-online.com/Vesti/Srbija/377296/Pastor-Jobiku-Ne-vrsljaj-po-Vojvodini.
[24] In particular, see Article 317 of the Criminal Code of Serbia (amended in 2012) against the instigation of ethnic, religious and racial hatred and intolerance at http://www.legislationline.org/documents/id/18732.

Belgium). The evolutionary trajectories of regionalist movements in the political map of contemporary Europe are highly diverse, complicated and idiosyncratic. Moreover, the political physiognomies of regionalist parties and groupings may also remarkably vary and range from the radical left all the way to the far right. In light of this complex landscape, it is not the aim of this book to highlight the internal distinctions and qualitative differences among European regionalists. Instead, the chief objective here is to isolate the main aspects which differentiate selected European regionalisms from the case of Vojvodina. Considering that the variants of Spanish and Italian regionalisms and regionalization have functioned as pivotal points of reference for this book, particular attention is paid to the latest developments in Catalonia and, to a secondary extent, *Lega Nord* and 'Padanian' regionalism.

For a start, whereas Vojvodina remains the richest part of Serbia with a developed agricultural industry, Catalonia is Spain's second richest region after the Basque Country. Both regions comprise urban centres which are characterized by a socially liberal ethos and a vibrant commercial, as well as cultural, entrepreneurship within the bounds of their respective states (Novi Sad and Barcelona). It does not come as a surprise that Nenad Čanak and other leading cadres of LSDV immediately voiced their endorsement to the Catalan referendum for independence (October 2017) and rushed to underline what they perceived as the common denominators between Catalonia and Vojvodina.[25] In addition to the apparent similarities, though, there exist notable qualitative differences between the two cases.

Throughout the last decades, Catalan regionalism has succeeded in fashioning an increasingly *civic* profile. In the long run, regionalists, as well as overt proponents of Catalan independence, succeeded in attracting the first generation of internal migrants from other parts of

---

[25] http://www.politika.rs/sr/clanak/389917/Canak-u-Barseloni-Situacija-je-dosta-cudnovata.

Spain (e.g. Andalusia) to their ranks.[26] Nevertheless, one cannot argue that this development has effaced the *core*, ethno-cultural, component of Catalan regionalism.[27] Instead, Catalan regional autonomy and its institutions are still legitimized through reference to the constitutional clause that the Catalans are one of Spain's *historical nationalities*. Hence, the pronounced stress on the institutional promotion of Catalan language and culture by the *Generalitat* (Catalan assembly) which, on certain occasions, intensified the cleavage between the proponents of independence and the Spanish government.[28] By contrast, Vojvodina's asymmetric status and its institutional infrastructure are still legitimized along the necessities to accommodate the economic specificities, manage interethnic relations and guarantee social stability within a highly diverse part of Serbia. This provides plenty of room towards the accommodation of a rich mosaic of micro-identities whereas pro-autonomy leanings still cut across ethnic lines in the province.

Furthermore, alongside its powerful sociocultural and sociopsychological dynamics, the orchestration of Catalan regionalism has long and primarily revolved around certain political parties. At this given moment, the dominant pro-independence coalition at the *Generalitat* ('Together for Yes') comprises parties as diverse as the nominally centrist/centre-right Democratic European Party of Catalonia and the leftist ERC. By contrast, although one should not underestimate the endeavours by LSDV and other Vojvodinian regionalists towards safeguarding the province's asymmetric status, the political engineering of Vojvodinian regionalism has not been primarily revolving around parties with an explicitly 'Vojvodinian' profile. Instead, especially since 2000, various local politicians have engaged towards preserving and

---

[26] For instance, Oriol Junqueras, the leader of the leftist, pro-independence, Republican Left of Catalonia (ERC) originates from an Andalusian family background. For a more extensive discussion over this issue, see Ivan Serrano, 'Just a Matter of Identity? Support for Independence in Catalonia', *Regional and Federal Studies* 5 (2013): 523–45.

[27] Thomas Jeffrey Miley, 'Against the Thesis of the "Civic Nation": The Case of Catalonia in Contemporary Spain', *Nationalism and Ethnic Politics* 13, no. 1 (2007): 1–37.

[28] Henry Miller et al., 'Language Policy and Identity: The Case of Catalonia', *International Studies in Sociology and Education* 6, no. 1 (1996): 113–28.

enhancing Vojvodina's asymmetric status from within the structures of the larger Serbian parties. The case of DS, during Bojan Pajtić's tenure as president of the executive council at the provincial assembly, serves as a representative example.

Moreover, the 'new' Catalan question also appears to be subject to catalysts which do not bear any particular or direct relevance to the cases of Vojvodina and Serbia as a whole. The most noteworthy of them is the decisive impact of the economic crisis across the EU memberstates from Southern Europe and the negative toll that the EU's austerity policies have been claiming on the Catalan economy. It is precisely within this context of the 'pro-austerity versus anti-austerity' debate that the question of Catalonia's status acquires an additional dimension which further polarizes and radicalizes the pro-independence and the pro-union segments in the local society.[29] In the course of autumn 2017, a variety of leftist initiatives across Europe channelled their unequivocal support towards the 'Together for Yes' coalition and perceived Catalan independence as one more battlefield in the struggle of the European peoples against austerity.[30] This is indicative of the powerful external ramifications of the 'new' Catalan question as well as the ways that it interweaves with the toll of the economic crisis across Southern Europe.

By contrast, one cannot discern any drastic intersections between the Vojvodinian question and the European economic crisis. In addition, the divergent opinions over Vojvodina's status do not polarize the local society and, as it became obvious in the compromise over the amendments of 2014, the politics of consensus still prevail in the provincial assembly. Most importantly, as repeatedly stressed, Vojvodina's *autonomaši* circles and groupings never endorsed

---

[29] To this one should add the successful campaigning by ERC and the smaller Popular Unity Candidacy (CUP) with the objective to embed the question of Catalan independence inside their anti-austerity platforms on the EU's monetary policies across the European south. On this issue, see https://www.politico.eu/article/austerity-fuels-catalan-disaffection/; https://www.theguardian.com/world/2015/sep/29/catalan-seccession-anti-austerity-party.

[30] For a brief example of this line of thought among the European left, see the analytical commentary by Boaventura de Sousa Santos for *Critical Legal Thinking*, http://criticallegalthinking.com/2017/09/28/the-left-and-catalonia/.

secessionist inclinations or put Serbia's territorial integrity under scrutiny. In this specific light, one might argue that Nenad Čanak's hurried and unequivocal endorsement of the pro-independence faction in Catalonia runs the risk of generating undesirable connotations and associations for LSDV among certain sections of the Vojvodinian electorate.[31]

The last decade has also seen the consolidation of right-wing regionalist movements and parties with an overtly Eurosceptic and xenophobic profile such as *Vlaams Belang* (Flemish Interest) in Belgium and *Lega Nord* in Italy. Taking into account the rapid and steady transformation of the latter into a political organization with a 'pan-Italian' profile and appeal, one might seriously scrutinize the extent to which *Lega* can still be regarded as a regionalist party. For the purposes of this work, though, a, if only schematic, comparison between Vojvodina and 'Padania' would suffice to illustrate that whereas the former is a European region with a deeply embedded identity and historical origins, the latter has been a situationally adaptive, if not utterly artificial, geographic construct.[32] More importantly, by stark contrast to *Lega*'s Euroscepticism, Vojvodinian regionalist parties and groupings have long espoused a pro-EU orientation whereas Vojvodina still participates in the Brussels-based Assembly of European Regions (AER) as well as cross-border cooperation schemes under the auspices of the EU (e.g. the Danube–Kris–Mures–Tisa, or 'Banat', Euroregion).

---

[31] Nenad Čanak repeatedly stated that Catalonia's future status must be decided inside the framework of the Spanish constitutional order. Nevertheless, the Catalan flag had been flying from the LSDV's headquarters throughout the duration of the Catalan referendum in October 2017. For more on this issue, see https://www.blic.rs/vesti/politika/katalonska-zastava-na-sedistu-lsv-canak-znak-solidarnosti-sa-gradanima-cije-se-pravo/z5yj1rw.

[32] Throughout the 1990s, the geographic limits of 'Padania' coincided in the *Lega*'s party pamphlets with the territory of the Po Valley. In the longer run, though, this concept came to comprise the entire Northern Italy, plus a few territories of Central Italy, largely as part of the party's endeavour to expand its bases of support. For a more analytical treatise of this subject, see Benito Giordano, 'The Contrasting Geographies of "Padania": The Case of the Lega Nord in Northern Italy', *Area* 33, no. 1 (2002): 27–37; 'A Place Called Padania? The Lega Nord and the Political Representation of Northern Italy', *European Urban and Regional Studies* 6, no. 3 (1999): 215–30.

Lastly, *Lega* has recently succeeded in consolidating its 'pan-Italian' appeal, by large, on the basis of its anti-immigration/xenophobic platform and via the capitalization on the public grievances over the impact of the refugee crisis across Italy.[33] The following section illustrates that, by contrast, the political mobilization against the influx of refugees in Vojvodina and Serbia, as a whole, has been much less intensive in comparison to other parts of Central and Eastern Europe (namely, the 'Visegrad Four' group of states).

Vojvodina and the 'new' refugee question in Central and Eastern Europe

Since the second half of 2015, the countries of Central and Eastern Europe started sensing, however remotely, the repercussions of the refugee crisis. The refugee waves from Greece to Hungary, via the corridor through the former Yugoslavia, and their temporary concentration in Budapest were a unique experience which swiftly impacted upon these societies' perceptions as well as actual management of *otherness*. Especially the gradual consolidation of the Islamic State and its militant Salafism in Syria and Iraq intensified the public apprehension over the potential export of asymmetric threats to their region among many Central Europeans. In light of these new realities, a series of political actors started building their platforms along the *virtual* politics of (anti-) immigration. This term addresses the alarmism over the 'imminent threat of Islamization', in the rhetoric of various political actors across Central and Eastern Europe, despite the actual absence (or minuscule presence) of Muslim war refugees in these societies.

The first endeavours to capitalize on popular insecurities over the refugee question were carried out by the populist and radical right

---

[33] For a more extensive discussion over this topic, see Stella Gianfreda, 'Politicization of the Refugee Crisis? A Content Analysis of Parliamentary Debates in Italy, the UK and the EU', *Italian Political Science Review* 48, no. 1 (2018): 85–108.

but were not restricted within this angle of the party spectrum. In due time, the political mainstream in the 'Visegrad Four' group of states virulently opposed the European Commission's refugee redistribution plan and its directive for the proportional allocation of war-displaced persons to each EU member-state on the basis of fixed quotas. These objections were frequently cushioned inside the *cultural* argument. Viktor Orbán, in particular, rushed to accuse the European Commission of 'irresponsibility', underlined that 'Europe and European culture are rooted in Christian values' and judged that 'there is no alternative, and we have no option but to defend Hungary's borders'.[34] Further to the north, Slovakia's Premier, Robert Fico, attempted to draw tentative comparisons between the refugee and the Roma questions arguing that if the social integration of the Slovak Roma has been so complex, the social integration of Muslim migrants would be tantamount to impossible.[35] The standoff between the 'Visegrad Four' governments and the European Commission culminated with Viktor Orbán's decision to seal Hungary's southern borders with Serbia (15 September 2015) and Croatia (17 October 2015). Empirical surveys, conducted across the 'Visegrad Four' states, hinted at the clear resonance between the tough line of the national governments over the EU's redistribution plan and the reserved public outlooks on the refugee crisis.[36] Further to the northeast, opinion polls have detected a comparable sentiment of apprehension, vis-à-vis the admission of war refugees, among the local societies in the Baltic States.[37]

---

[34] https://www.theguardian.com/world/2015/sep/03/migration-crisis-hungary-pm-victor-orban-europe-response-madness.

[35] https://www.politico.eu/article/migrants-are-central-europes-new-roma-refugees-viktor-orban-robert-fico/.

[36] On Hungary, see http://www.pewresearch.org/fact-tank/2016/09/30/hungarians-share-europes-embrace-of-democratic-principles-but-are-less-tolerant-of-refugees-minorities/. On Slovakia, see https://www.euractiv.com/section/central-europe/news/study-cautious-slovaks-take-eu-approach-to-refugees/.

[37] On Estonia, see http://news.gallup.com/poll/216377/new-index-shows-least-accepting-countries-migrants.aspx. On Latvia, see https://eng.lsm.lv/article/society/society/majority-of-latvians-against-taking-in-refugees.a195952/.

The locus of Serbia inside these new realities is rather idiosyncratic and complicated. On the one hand, Serbia is not an EU member-state. This means that the country is not bound to the conditions of the EU refugee resettlement scheme although it has been receiving financial assistance from the EU towards the management of the migration flows.[38] On the other hand, by September 2017, approximately 4,146 refugees and other migrants had been stranded inside the country (many of them along the Serbian-Hungarian borderline in northern Bačka) as a result of the Hungarian government's decision to shut the southern border.[39] By contrast to the 'Visegrad Four' leaderships, the Serbian government never resorted to anti-refugee rhetoric along the lines of the *cultural* argument. However, on 3 October 2016, Serbia also decided to close its borders to the migrants and the then President Tomislav Nikolić, as well as the Minister of Labour Aleksandar Vulin, underlined that the state possessed neither the logistics nor the technical infrastructure to accommodate an additional number of refugees.[40]

The main objective in this section is to concentrate on the sociocultural aspects of the presence of war-displaced persons in Vojvodina and assess the new realities that this may engender for the state of inter-group relations and social stability in the province. The primary sources are the observations of empirical surveys conducted by research institutes and human rights NGOs in localities with a high concentration of refugees and other migrants all over Serbia.[41] The results of the empirical survey conducted jointly by UNHCR and CESID (September 2014) across the country detected overall high levels

---

[38] Approximately €80 million have been allocated by the European Commission and the EU member-states to assist Serbia in effectively managing the migration waves. For this figure, see http://ec.europa.eu/echo/files/aid/countries/factsheets/serbia_en.pdf.

[39] Ibid.

[40] https://visegradpost.com/en/2016/10/03/serbia-closes-her-borders-to-migrants/.

[41] In May 2015, a total of 13,148 foreign nationals had expressed their intention to seek asylum in Serbia. By the end of 2017, the total number of refugees, asylum seekers and other migrants stationed in the territory of Serbia dropped to 4,000 with more than 90 per cent of them accommodated in state-managed accommodation centres. For these figures, see Belgrade Centre for Human Rights, *Human Rights in Serbia* (Belgrade: BCHR, 2015), 50; European Commission, *Serbia 2018 Report*, 35.

of empathy and understanding, among the respondents, in regard to the reasons why asylum seekers moved there and their desire to stay in Serbia[42]; a general agreement, among the respondents, that the Serbian state should improve living conditions for asylum seekers and refugees stationed within its territory[43]; generally relaxed outlooks vis-à-vis the prospects for the establishment of refugee accommodation centres in the respondents' neighbourhoods.[44]

These observations largely resonate with those of another empirical survey, conducted by the Friedrich Ebert Foundation across the country throughout 2016 (including the Vojvodinian localities of Subotica and Šid), which detected: a higher stress on humanitarian than on 'securitized' attitudes, among the respondents, vis-à-vis the arrival of refugees[45]; overall relaxed outlooks on the prospects for refugees to become members of the local communities, in the longer run[46]; a more pronounced stress on the economic than on the cultural obstacles to the social integration of the newcomers.[47] With specific regard to the two Vojvodinian localities where refugees are accommodated (Subotica and Šid), a series of micro-surveys, conducted by the Ana and Vlade Divac Foundation throughout 2016, observed generally high levels of compassion and understanding, among the respondents, in regard to the reasons why asylum seekers fled there (namely, war)[48]; a satisfactory degree of daily contacts between the newcomers and locals[49]; optimism

---

[42] UNHCR, *Izvestaj sa istraživanja javnog mnenja: Stav građana Srbije prema tražiocima azila* (Belgrade: UNHCR/CESID, September 2014), 13 and 15. This survey was conducted in southern and central districts of Serbia.
[43] Ibid., 24 and 25.
[44] Ibid., 34 and 39.
[45] Friedrich Ebert Foundation (Serbia), *Studija o Izbeglicama: Srbija 2016* (Belgrade: Friedrich Ebert Stiftung, 2016), 7 and 8.
[46] Ibid., 14.
[47] Ibid., 19–20.
[48] Ana and Vlade Divac Fondacija, *Stavovi građana Srbije prema izbeglicama* (Belgrade: USAID/Ana and Vlade Divac Foundation, June 2016), 1 and 2; Ana and Vlade Divac Foundation, *The Attitudes of Serbian Citizens towards Refugees: Key Findings of the Third Wave of Survey* (Belgrade: USAID/Ana and Vlade Divac Foundation, 2016), 5 and 6.
[49] Ibid. (June 2016), 2; Ibid. (2016), 8.

towards the prospects for the long-term integration of refugees in the local communities.⁵⁰

These strikingly more favourable outlooks on refugees in comparison to the 'Visegrad Four' societies, which persisted through the closure of the Hungarian-Serbian border, have, first of all, been subject to catalysts that pertain throughout the territory of Serbia. The most important of them is that, by contrast to the 'Visegrad Four' governments, Serbia's major political parties did not endeavour to weaponize the refugee question, and incorporate culturally essentialist or Islamophobic speech, within the context of potential disagreements with the European Commission over the management of the crisis. This is not to contend that there were no political actors who voiced their staunch opposition to the accommodation of refugees in Serbia, such as the SRS leader, Vojislav Šešelj,⁵¹ and several DSS/*Dveri* local committees including the one in Pančevo.⁵² Nevertheless, the sociopolitical repercussions of such statements cannot compare to the systematic mobilization against the influx of refugees which was coordinated by the populist and radical right across Central Europe between 2015 and 2016 (e.g. Jobbik and, further to the north, the 'Our Slovakia' party).

From a more socio-psychological angle, the high levels of empathy expressed in all relevant surveys, on the grounds that the refugees had fled their hearths because of the war and in order to avoid

---

[50] Seventy-seven per cent of the respondents in Subotica and 69 per cent in Šid expressed their optimism towards the long-term social integration of refugees (June 2016). Moreover, 87 per cent of the respondents in Subotica and 82 per cent in Šid judged that Serbia had accepted refugees more positively in comparison to other countries (December 2016). For these figures, see Ibid. (June 2016), 1; Ana and Vlade Divac Fondacija, *Stavovi građana Srbije prema izbeglicama* (Belgrade: USAID/Ana and Vlade Divac Foundation, December 2016), 2.

[51] On 15 March 2017, Vojislav Šešelj had stated that 'following Viktor Orbán's example, I would erect a barbwire fence and if this was not sufficient, I would set up minefields along the border'. On this issue, see http://www.rts.rs/page/stories/sr/story/2660/izbori-2017/2679047/seselj-ogradom-ili-minskim-poljem-smanjiti-priliv-migranata.html.

[52] On 26 September 2016, the DSS local committee issued a statement according to which the party does not object to the refugees crossing through Pančevo but opposes their long-term settlement in the municipality. It was added that the culprit for the war in Syria is not Serbia but NATO and the EU; therefore, the most developed EU member-states must accommodate the refugees. For this statement, see http://www.dss.rs/dss-protiv-trajnog-naseljavanja-migranata-u-pancevo/.

persecution, have been of decisive significance. This appears to have alleviated the impact of potentially negative connotations generated by the Muslim religious affiliation among many of the newcomers or, even worse, their indirect association with the older conflicts in Bosnia and Kosovo. To this one might add the widespread persistence of popular narratives within the Serbian society, according to which both the former Yugoslavia and the Middle East have equally fallen victims to the 'geopolitical antagonisms and the machinations of global powers'. Lastly, Yugoslavia's participation in the non-aligned movement and the widespread cooperation with the secular regimes of the Arab world (including Syria and Iraq) must have also contributed to the development of more receptive and compassionate outlooks on refugees, at least among the older generation in the society.

With specific regard to Vojvodina, not so long ago, the province succeeded in accommodating and largely integrating the refugee waves from Croatia, Bosnia and, since 1999, Kosovo. As also highlighted in the empirical surveys, one crucial difference between the current and the previous newcomers is that, by contrast to the ethnic Serb refugees of the 1990s, the 'new' migrants possessed neither a command of the Serbian language nor kin-networks within the local society.[53] More importantly, the main bulk of refugees and other migrants still perceive that they are on transit to the West and usually do not foresee the prospects of a long-term stay in Vojvodina or elsewhere in Serbia.

At this given moment, though, one can single out two major factors which have contributed to the successful, first-stage, reception of the migrants and which, if necessary, can also contribute to their longer-term inclusion to the local society. The one of them is the highly professional and well-coordinated mobilization of the civic society and the provincial, as well as municipal/local, institutions of government towards the objective to accommodate the newcomers.[54] The other

---

[53] UNHCR, *Izvestaj sa istraživanja javnog mnenja*, 21–2.
[54] Friedrich Ebert Foundation (Serbia), *Studija o Izbeglicama*, 20–1; Belgrade Centre for Human Rights, *Human Rights in Serbia*, 50.

is the absence of a systematic endeavour by local political actors, originating either from the Serbian majority or from one of the ethnic minorities, with the objectives to mobilize the society and obstruct the accommodation of refugees in Vojvodina.

Lastly, Vojvodina's higher living standards and more developed infrastructures in comparison to other parts of Serbia can provide the necessary financial incentives towards the more effective inclusion of the refugee population. Especially considering the constant mobility and decline in the numbers of refugees accommodated in the province, it is rather precarious to make solid and longer-term predictions about the prospects for the social integration of this recently arrived segment. Nevertheless, and in light of Serbia's persistent economic and other shortcomings, the local society has undoubtedly made a sound contribution towards the initial reception of war-displaced persons.[55] This acquires an even greater significance, taking into account the alarmism and prevalence of the *virtual* politics of (anti-)immigration in other societies of Central and Eastern Europe despite the much lower presence of war refugees therein.

Vojvodina as a *European* region: What comes next?

Serbia's party landscape has long been fluid and highly malleable. The multiparty map of the 2000s was gradually replaced by the preponderance of SNS and Serbian president, Aleksandar Vučić. Despite SNS's pro-unitary leanings, this party's consolidation was not accompanied by any attempts to further revise or restrict Vojvodina's administrative jurisdiction beyond the latest amendments to the statute on provincial autonomy (2014). The statute on the autonomy of Vojvodina preserves Vojvodina's asymmetric status within Serbia,

---

[55] Quite a few refugees also expressed their satisfaction with their reception by the local authorities and society. On this issue, see https://www.theguardian.com/world/2017/aug/08/eu-refugees-serbia-afghanistan-taliban.

remains consistent with the European standards on regionalization and provides an adequate roadmap for further developments in the future. At this given moment, though, it remains an imperative that the Serbian Constitution defines more concretely and embeds more solidly the locus of Vojvodina's asymmetric status inside Serbia's constitutional order. The most urgent necessity is to standardize the legislation over the finances of Vojvodina and concretize more transparently the calculation of the budget's percentage allocated for the provincial coffers.

In regard to the climate of interethnic relations, the political actors who represent Vojvodina's largest minority group (the ethnic Hungarians) appear to prioritize the politics of consensus over the politics of confrontation. Following a widespread trend among ethnic Hungarian parties across the Carpathian basin, VMSZ focuses on a gradualist strategy of cooperation with the larger political actors towards the more effective promotion of the ethnic Hungarian minority's standpoints and demands from within the halls of power. This lesser emphasis on the tripartite concept of ethno-territorial autonomy, in combination with the existence of an articulate legislation on minority rights and Vojvodina's long-standing heritage of harmonious coexistence, considerably limits the opportunity structures for the successful engagement of nationalist actors originating from Hungary (namely Jobbik) among the ethnic Hungarian community.

By contrast to resurgent European regionalisms which are embedded into a *core*, ethno-cultural, component (e.g. the 'new' Catalan question), Vojvodinian regionalism is still legitimized along the necessities to accommodate the economic specificities, manage interethnic relations and guarantee social stability within a richly diverse part of Serbia. This provides plenty of room towards the accommodation of a rich mosaic of micro-identities whereas pro-autonomy leanings cut across ethno-cultural lines in the province. Furthermore, Vojvodinian regionalists never espoused secessionist trends, or put Serbia's territorial integrity under scrutiny, whereas the divergent opinions over Vojvodina's administrative status do not polarize or radicalize the local society.

From a broader and longer-term angle, this book is an additional contribution towards the more extensive and in-depth study of the under-researched multiethnic regionalisms in Southeast Europe. Alongside Vojvodina, the Croatian region of Istria represents one more case where multiethnic regionalism, as a bottom-up movement, united a multitude of local micro-identities, preserved social stability and successfully withstood the nationalizing pressures emanating from Zagreb during the 1990s.[56]

Moreover, by contrast to European regionalisms with an explicitly anti-immigrant and xenophobic agenda (e.g. *Lega Nord* and 'Padanian' regionalism), no political actors, originating either from the Serbian majority or from one of the ethnic minorities, endeavoured to systematically mobilize the local society against the latest influx of migrants. Instead, the recent arrival of the refugee waves saw the highly professional and well-coordinated mobilization of the civic society and the provincial, as well as municipal/local, institutions of government towards the objective to accommodate the newcomers. As it was also the case with the Serb refugees during the 1990s, Vojvodina's society has demonstrated that it is capable of integrating newcomers even under particularly adverse circumstances. From a more functional angle, the refugee crisis, if only subtly, provides an additional argument in favour of Vojvodina's autonomous jurisdiction so that such urgent issues can be managed efficiently and 'on the spot'.

Since the fall of Slobodan Milošević, Serbia's trajectory to the EU has been complicated, nonlinear and subject to a variety of uneven catalysts (e.g. the normalization of bilateral relations with Kosovo and cooperation with the Hague Tribunal). Most recently, the decision of the European Commission to freeze the EU's enlargement process further prolongs the anxiety and uncertainty over Serbia's prospects to finally join the Union. This decision was taken amid the threatening spectrum of the economic and the refugee crises in the EU interior, as well as

---

[56] Instead of multiethnic, Dejan Stjepanović defines the pattern of Istrian regionalism as *plurinational*. On this issue, see Dejan Stjepanović, *Multiethnic Regionalisms in Southeastern Europe* (London: Palgrave Macmillan, 2018), 49–100.

Russia's gradual emergence as a potent contender in the east. From a further-reaching perspective, it would not be a wise idea for Brussels to postpone for an indefinite period of time and additionally complicate the EU accession process of Serbia and the Western Balkans as a whole. This argument acquires greater weight in light of the simultaneous and systematic engagement by powerful and illiberal actors across the region (namely, Russia in Serbia; and Turkey in Albania and Bosnia).[57]

With specific regard to Vojvodina, it is a multiethnic society that, throughout history, has proven its capacity to withstand the impact of war and interethnic strife. Moreover, Vojvodina is 'traditionally' outward looking (as already exemplified in the way that the nineteenth-century Vojvodinian Serb political elites and intelligentsia made successful use of Western political and ideological currents), less nationalistic, and its ethnic minorities can function as a bridge to neighbours and beyond. However stereotypical this might seem at first, it is not an exaggeration to claim that Vojvodina can still reassume the potential towards leading Serbia 'back to Europe'. This, however, is also conditional upon the genuine intention of the EU not to bring about, even by default, a new era of prolonged isolation for Serbia and the Western Balkans. Especially Vojvodina's example of harmonious multiethnic cohabitation may have plenty of useful lessons to teach to several other multiethnic societies, both in the eastern and the western part of the Continent.

---

[57] On Russia's engagement in the Western Balkans, see Dimitar Bechev, *Rival Power: Russia in Southeast Europe* (New Haven, CT and London: Yale University Press, 2017), 51–85.

Bibliography and Other Sources

English language sources

Monographs, doctoral theses and dissertations

- Arpasy, Ildiko. 'The Hungarians in Vojvodina: Political Condition of a Minority in a Nationalizing State'. MA Dissertation, Central European University Press, Budapest, 1996.
- Banać, Ivo. *The National Question in Yugoslavia: Origins, History, Politics*. Ithaca, NY: Cornell University Press, 1984.
- Batt, Judy and Kataryna Wolczuk. *Region, State and Identity in Central and Eastern Europe*. London–Portland: Frank Kass, 2002.
- Bechev, Dimitar. *Rival Power: Russia in Southeast Europe*. New Haven and London: Yale University Press, 2017.
- Bilandžić, Dušan. *Management of the Yugoslav Economy (1945–1966)*. Belgrade: Dnevnik, 1967.
- Buckley, William Joseph, ed. *Kosovo: Contending Voices on Balkan Interventions*. Cambridge: Eerdmans Publishing, 2000.
- Bugajski, Janusz. *Ethnic Politics in Eastern Europe: A Guide to Nationality Policies, Organizations and Parties*. New York: The Center for Strategic and International Studies, 1994.
- Bujošević, Dragan and Ivan Radovanović. *October 5: A 24-Hour Coup*. Belgrade: Media Centre Press, 2000.
- Burg, Stevan L. *Conflict and Cohesion in Socialist Yugoslavia: Political Decision Making Since 1966*. New Jersey: Princeton University Press, 1983.
- Cohen, Lenard J. *Broken Bonds: The Disintegration of Yugoslavia*. Colorado: Westview Press, 1993.
- Connor Walker. *Ethnonationalism: A Quest for Understanding*. London: Routledge, 1993.
- Crampton, R. J. *Eastern Europe in the Twentieth Century*. London: Routledge, 1994.
- Djilas, Aleksa. *The Contested Country*. California: Harvard University Press, 1991.
- Elazar, Daniel J., ed. *Federalism and Political Integration*. Jerusalem: Jerusalem Institute for Federal Studies, 1979.

Galantai, J. *Trianon and the Protection of Minorities*. New York: Atlantic Studies on Society and Change No. 70, 1992.
Glenny, Misha. *The Fall of Yugoslavia: The Third Balkan War*. London: Penguin, 1992.
Helsinki Committee for Human Rights in Serbia. *In the Name of Humanity*. Belgrade: HCHRS, 1997.
Helsinki Committee for Human Rights in Serbia. *Minorities in Serbia*. Belgrade: HCHRS, 1998.
Janjetović, Zoran. *Between Hitler and Tito: The Disappearance of the Ethnic Germans from Vojvodina*. Belgrade: Institut za Savremenu Istoriju, 2000.
Judah, Tim. *The Serbs: History, Myth and the Destruction of Yugoslavia*. New Haven and London: Yale University Press, 2000.
Kann, R. H. *The Multinational Empire: Nationalism and National Reform in the Habsburg Empire (1848–1918)*, vol. 2. New York: Octagon, 1983.
Keating, Michael. *State and Regional Nationalism*. Cheltenham: Elgar, 1988.
Keating, Michael. *The New Regionalism in Western Europe*. Cheltenham: Elgar, 1998.
Keating, Michael. *Regions and Regionalism in Europe*. Cheltenham: Elgar, 2004.
Komjathy, A. T. and P. Stockwell. *German Minorities and the Third Reich*. New York: Holmes and Meier, 1980.
Lampe, John R. *Yugoslavia as History: Twice There Was a Country*. Cambridge: Cambridge University Press, 2000.
Lazar, Zsölt. *Vojvodina amidst Multiculturality and Regionalization*. Novi Sad: Mediterran Publishing, 2007.
Macartney, C. A. *Hungary and Her Successors: The Treaty of Trianon and Its Consequences (1919–1937)*. Oxford: Oxford University Press, 1937.
Mach, Zdzislaw. *Symbols, Conflict and Identity*. Krakow: Krakow University Press, 1989.
Magocsi, Paul Robert. *Historical Atlas of Central Europe*. Washington, DC: University of Washington Press, 2002.
Mc Garry, J. and B. O'Leary. *The Politics of Ethnic Conflict Regulation: Cases of Protracted Ethnic Conflicts*. London: Routledge, 1993.
Open University Subotica. *Essays on Regionalization*. Subotica: Agency for Local Democracy, 2001.
Paris, Edmond. *Genocide in Satellite Croatia (1941–1945)*. Chicago: The American Institute for Balkan Affairs, 1961.

- Paris Peace Conference (1919–1920). *The Hungarian Peace Negotiations: An Account of the Work of the Hungarian Peace Delegation at Neuilly s./S. from January to March 1920*. Budapest: Royal Ministry of Foreign Affairs, 1920 (reprinted in 1975).

Pavlowitch, Stevan K. *Yugoslavia*. London: Ernest Benn Limited, 1971.

Pavlowitch, Stevan K. *Serbia: The History behind the Name*. London: Hurst & Company, 2002.

- Pogonyi, Szabolcs. *Extra-Territorial Ethnic Politics, Discourses and Identities in Hungary*. London: Palgrave Macmillan, 2017.

Ramet, Pedro. *Nationalism and Federalism in Yugoslavia (1963–1983)*. Bloomington: Indiana University Press, 1984.

Review of International Affairs. *Kosovo: Past and Present*. Belgrade, 1986.

Rokkan, Stein and David Urwin, eds. *The Politics of Territorial Integrity: Studies in European Regionalism*. London: Sage, 1982.

Seton-Watson, H. *Eastern Europe between the Wars (1918–1941)*. New York: Halper Row, 1967.

- Seton-Watson, R. W. *The Southern Slav Question and the Habsburg Monarchy*. London: Constable and Co, 1911.

Shoup, Paul. *Communism and the National Yugoslav Question*. New York: Columbia University Press, 1968.

Singleton, Fred. *Yugoslavia in the Twentieth Century*. New York: Columbia University Press, 1976.

Smith, Anthony D. *Myths and Memories of the Nation*. Oxford: Oxford University Press, 1999.

Smith, Anthony D. *The Nation in History: Historiographical Debates about Ethnicity and Nationalism*. Oxford: Oxford University Press, 2000.

Stjepanović, Dejan. *Multiethnic Regionalisms in Southeastern Europe*. London: Palgrave Macmillan, 2018.

Szabad, G. *Hungarian Political Trends between the Revolution and the Compromise*. Budapest: Akademia Kiado, 1977.

Thomas, Robert. *Serbia under Milosevic: Politics in the 1990s*. London: Hurst & Company, 1999.

Tomašić Dinko. *Personality and Culture in East European Politics*. New York: George W Stewart Publisher Inc., 1948.

Union of Jurists' Association of Yugoslavia. *The Constitution of the Socialist Federal Republic of Yugoslavia (A Preliminary Draft)*, English language edition. Belgrade: Union of Jurists' Association of Yugoslavia, 1962.

Union of Jurists' Association of Yugoslavia. *The Constitution of the Socialist Federal Republic of Yugoslavia*, English language edition. Belgrade: Union of Jurists' Association of Yugoslavia, 1974.

Various authors. *Guide through Electoral Controversies in Serbia*. Belgrade: CESID, 2000.

Articles published in books/academic journals and papers (published and unpublished)

Ashbrook, John. 'Locking Horns in the Istrian Political Arena: Politicized Identity, the Istrian Democratic Assembly, and the Croatian Democratic Alliance'. *East European Politics and Societies* 20, no. 4 (2016): 622–658.

Aspalagh, Robert. 'Trianon Dissolved: The Status of Vojvodina Reconsidered?' *Yearbook of European Studies* 5 (1992): 124–128.

Batt, Judy. 'Transcarpathia: A Peripheral Region in the "Centre of Europe"' (unpublished paper). Birmingham: CREES, 2001, 1–35.

Bek, Stevan. 'Vojvodina's Economy Today'. *Review of International Affairs* 29, no. 666 (5 January 1978): 35–37.

Brubaker, Rogers. 'National Minorities, Nationalizing States and External Homelands in the New Europe'. *Daedalus* 124, no. 2 (Spring 1995): 107–132.

Brubaker, Rogers. 'Ethnicity without Groups'. *Arch. Europ. Social.* XLIII, no. 2 (2002): 163–189.

Brubaker, Rogers, M. Loveman and P. Stamatov. 'Ethnicity as Cognition'. *Theory and Society* 33 (2004): 31–64.

Craiutu, Aurelian. 'A Dilemma of Dual Identity: The Democratic Alliance of Hungarians in Romania'. *East European Constitutional Review* 4, no. 2 (1995): 43–49.

Džankić, Jelena and Christina Isabel Zuber. 'Serbia and Montenegro: From Centralization to Secession and Multi-Ethnic Regionalism'. In *Regional and National Elections in Eastern Europe: Territoriality of the Vote in Ten Countries*, edited by Arjan H. Schakel. London: Palgrave Macmillan, 2017.

Elazar, Daniel J. 'The Role of Federalism in Political Integration'. In *Federalism and Political Integration*, edited by Daniel J. Elazar, 13–57. Jerusalem: Jerusalem Institute for Federal Studies, 1979.

Escobalherrero, Patricia. 'Territorial Organization of the State'. In *Essays on Regionalization*, Open University Subotica, 25–42. Subotica: Agency for Local Democracy, 2001.

Gianfreda, Stella. 'Politicization of the Refugee Crisis? A Content Analysis of Parliamentary Debates in Italy, the UK and the EU'. *Italian Political Science Review* 48, no. 1 (2018): 85-108.

Giordano, Benito. 'A Place Called Padania? The Lega Nord and the Political Representation of Northern Italy'. *European Urban and Regional Studies* 6, no. 3 (1999): 215-230.

Giordano, Benito. 'The Contrasting Geographies of "Padania": The Case of the Lega Nord in Northern Italy'. *Area* 33, no. 1 (2002): 27-37.

Judah, Tim. 'A History of the Kosovo Liberation Army'. In *Kosovo: Contending Voices on Balkan Interventions*, edited by Buckley William Joseph, 108-117. Cambridge: Eerdmans Publishing, 2000.

Komšić, Jovan. 'Unitary or Asymmetric Regionalism? - An Insight into the Autonomy of Vojvodina within the Concepts of Regionalization in Serbia'. In *Essays on Regionalization*, Open University Subotica, 157-175. Subotica: Agency for Local Democracy, 2001.

Komšić, Jovan. 'Autonomism in Vojvodina'. *Südosteuropa* 61, no. 3 (2013): 332-362.

Korhecz, Tamas. 'The Rights of National Minorities in Vojvodina: Legal Norms and Practice' (unpublished work), Novi Sad, 1998, 1-23.

Kovačević, Boško. 'Preconditions of Regionalization'. In *Essays on Regionalization*, Open University Subotica, 9-14. Subotica: Agency for Local Democracy, 2001.

Lang, Nicholas R. 'The Dialectics of Decentralization'. *World Politics* 27, no. 3 (April 1975): 309-335.

Lazar, Zsölt and Marinković Dušan. 'Regional Identity: Vojvodina's Urban Public Research Survey'. In *Essays on Regionalization*, Open University Subotica, 177-186. Subotica: Agency for Local Democracy, 2001.

Lederer, I. J. 'Nationalism and the Yugoslavs'. In *Nationalism in Eastern Europe*, edited by P. Sugar and I. J. Lederer, 396-438. Washington, DC: University of Washington Press, 1969.

Léphaft, Áron, Ádám Németh and Péter Reményi. 'Ethnic Diversity and Polarization in Vojvodina'. *Hungarian Geographical Bulletin* 63, no. 2 (2014): 135-157.

Maliqi, Sqhelzen. 'The Albanian Movement in Kosova'. In *Yugoslavia and After: A Study in Fragmentation, Despair and Rebirth*, edited by D. A. Dyker and I. Vejvoda, 138-152. London: Longman, 1996.

Miley, Thomas Jeffrey. 'Against the Thesis of the "Civic Nation": The Case of Catalonia in Contemporary Spain'. *Nationalism and Ethnic Politics* 13, no. 1 (2007): 1-37.

Miller, Henry (et al.). 'Language Policy and Identity: The Case of Catalonia'. *International Studies in Sociology and Education* 6, no. 1 (1996): 113–128.

O' Duffy, Brendan. 'British and Irish Conflict Regulation: From Sunningdale to Belfast. Part I: Tracing the Status of Contesting Sovereigns, 1968–1974'. *Nations and Nationalism* 5, no. 4 (1999): 523–542.

Palairet, Michael. 'Economic Retardation, Peasant Farming and the Nation State in the Balkans: Serbia 1830–1914 and 1990–1998'. In *Economic Change and the Building of the Nation State in History*, edited by A. Teichova and H. Matis. Cambridge: Cambridge University Press, 2000, 197–218.

Palairet, Michael. 'The Economic Consequences of Slobodan Milosevic (Industry Overview; Statistical Data Included)'. *Europe-Asia Studies*, September 2001, 1–19.

Paxton, Roger V. 'Nationalism and Revolution: A Re-Examination of the Origins of the First Serbian Insurrection 1804–1807'. *East European Quarterly* VI, no. 3 (1972): 337–362.

Petsinis, Vassilis. 'The Refugees in Vojvodina: Prospects for Social Integration and Alternative Options'. Paper delivered on the occasion of the Center for Southeast European Studies seminar series at SSEES, UCL, London, on 12 February 2003, 1–15.

Petsinis, Vassilis. 'Vojvodina's National Minorities: Current Realities and Future Prospects'. *Spaces of Identity* 3, no. 1 (2 August 2003): 1–37.

Petsinis, Vassilis. 'Cross-border Cooperation in Southeastern Europe as Prelude to European Integration: The Case of Serbia'. Paper presented on the occasion of the SSEES Fifth Postgraduate Annual Conference, *Four Empires and an Enlargement*, London, 6–8 November 2003, 1–18.

Petsinis, Vassilis. 'The Banat Euro-Region: Prospects and Obstacles'. In *The Borders of Europe*, 97–126. New Europe College and Goethe Institute Bucharest. Bucharest: University of Bucharest Publishing, 2007.

Petsinis, Vassilis. 'Minority Legislation in Two Successor States: A Comparison through the Lens of EU Enlargement'. *Baltic Worlds*, no. 1 (2012).

Pettai, Vello. 'Explaining Ethnic Politics in the Baltic States: Reviewing the Triadic Nexus Model'. *Journal of Baltic Studies* 37, no. 1 (2006): 124–136.

Poulton, Hugh. 'The Hungarians, Slovaks, Romanians and Rysyns/Ukrainians of the Vojvodina'. *Minorities in Central and Eastern Europe*, 27–31. London: Minority Rights Group International, 1993.

Radosavljević, Duško. 'Autonomy of Vojvodina: Challenges and Perspectives'. In *Essays on Regionalization*, Open University Subotica, 151–156. Subotica: Agency for Local Democracy, 2001.

Segre, D. V. 'Regionalism in Italy – An International Conflict Internalized'. In *Federalism and Political Integration*, edited by Daniel J. Elazar, 133–142. Jerusalem: Jerusalem Institute for Federal Studies, 1979.

Sekelj, Laslo. 'Parties and Elections: The Federal Republic of Yugoslavia – Change without Transformation'. *Europe-Asia Studies*, January 2000, 1–17.

Serrano, Ivan. 'Just a Matter of Identity? Support for Independence in Catalonia'. *Regional and Federal Studies* 5 (2013): 523–545.

Smith, David. 'Framing the National Question in Central and Eastern Europe: A Quadratic Nexus?' *The Global Review of Ethnopolitics* 2, no. 1 (2002): 3–16.

Stanković, Slobodan. 'Yugoslavia's Census-Final Results'. *Radio Free Europe Research Report*, 10 March 1982.

Teokarević, Jovan. 'Neither War nor Peace: Serbia and Montenegro in the First Half of the 1990s'. In *Yugoslavia and After: A Study in Fragmentation, Despair and Rebirth*, edited by D. A. Dyker and I. Vejvoda, 179–190. London and New York: Longman, 1996.

Tomić, Pavle and Jovan Romelić. 'Industry in the Yugoslav Part of the Banat'. In *Geographic Monographs of European Regions: Banat*, edited by University of Novi Sad, West University of Timisoara and Jozsef Attila University Szeged, 148–156. Novi Sad: GIS Institute, 1997.

Vucinich, Wayne S. 'The Serbs in Austria-Hungary'. *Austrian History Yearbook* 3, no. 2 (1967): 3–47.

Reports and official documents

Amnesty International. 'Collateral Damage or Unlawful Killings?' AI INDEX EUR 70/018/2000, 6 June 2000.

Ana and Vlade Divac Foundation. *The Attitudes of Serbian Citizens towards Refugees: Key Findings of the Third Wave of Survey*. Belgrade: USAID/Ana and Vlade Divac Foundation, 2016.

Belgrade Centre for Human Rights. *Human Rights in Serbia*. Belgrade: BCHR, 2015.

Centre for Development of Civic Society. 'Ethnic Incidents in Vojvodina after Internationalization', May 2004, 1–6. http://www.cdcs.org.yu/docs/internat_engl.doc.

Council of Europe Publishing House. *Framework Convention for the Protection of National Minorities*. Strasbourg: COE, 1994.

Council of Europe Publishing House. *Draft European Charter on Regional Self-Government*. Strasbourg: COE, 1997.

European Commission. *Serbia 2009 Progress Report*, SEC (2009), 1339.

European Commission. *Serbia 2010 Progress Report*, SEC (2010), 1330.

European Commission. *Serbia 2018 Progress Report*, 17 April 2018, SWD (2018).

Human Rights Watch. 'Civilian Deaths in the NATO Air Campaign', vol. 12, no. 1 (D). New York: (February 2000).

Human Rights Watch. *Failure to Protect: Anti-Minority Violence in Kosovo (March 2004)* 16, no. 6 (July 2004).

United Nations Economic Commission for Europe (UN/ECE), *International Migration Bulletin*, no. 3. Geneva (1993).

Jobbik-The Movement for a Better Hungary. *Radical Change: A Guide to Jobbik's Parliamentary Electoral Manifesto for National Self-Determination and Social Justice*. Budapest: Jobbik, 2010.

Project on Ethnic Relations. *Vojvodina: The Politics of Interethnic Accommodation*, Central European University Archives: Budapest, Vienna September, 23/25, 1999; Athens February, 13/15, 2000.

Serbia Bulletin. *National Minorities in the Federal Republic of Yugoslavia* (exclusive issue), September 1996.

Transparency International Group. *1999 Transparency International Corruption Perceptions Index (CPI)*, 1999.

United Nations Economic and Social Council. *Situation of Human Rights in the Territory of the Former Yugoslavia: Special Report on Minorities*, E/CN.4/1997/8, 25 October 1996.

United Nations High Commission for Refugees. *Census of Refugees and Other War-Affected Persons in the Federal Republic of Yugoslavia*, UNHCR High Commissioner for Refugees in the Republic of Serbia. Belgrade: UNHCR High Commissioner for Displaced Persons in the Republic of Montenegro, 1996.

United Nations Security Council. *Resolution 1208*, adopted by the Security Council at its 3945th meeting, on 19 November 1998, Distr. GENERAL, S/RES/1208 (1998).

United Nations Security Council. *Resolution 1244* (including annexes 1 and 2), adopted by the Security Council at its 4011th meeting on 10 June 1999, Distr. GENERAL, S/RES/1244 (1999).

Venice Commission. *Opinion on the Constitution of Serbia*, Opinion No. 405/2006.

- VMDK. *Memorandum on Self-Administration of Hungarians Living in the Republic of Serbia.* Novi Sad, 1992.
- VMSZ. *Proposal for an Agreement on the Self-Organisation of Hungarians in Vojvodina (The Concept of the Alliance of Hungarians in Vojvodina).* Novi Sad, 18 January 1996.

Serbian language sources

Monographs, doctoral theses and dissertations

Bačević, Liljana (et al.). *Jugoslavija na kriznoj prekretnici.* Belgrade: Institut društvenih nauka, 1991.

Bačić, Zoran, Boško Mijatović, Aleksandar Simić and Zorica Radović. *Regionalizacija Srbije.* Belgrade: Centar za liberalno-demokratske studije, 2003.

Bilandžić, Dušan. *Istorija SFRJ.* Zagreb: Školska Knjiga, 1979.

Boarov, Dimitrije. *Politička Istorija Vojvodine.* Novi Sad: Matica Srpska, 2001.

Boban, Ljubomir. *Sporazum Cvetković-Maček.* Belgrade: SANU, 1965.

Božić, Ivan, Sima Cirković, Milorad Ekmečić and Vladimir Dedijer. *Istorija Jugoslavije.* Belgrade: Prosveta, 1970.

Bubalo, Milka. *Najnovije demografske promene u Novom Slankamenu* (Diplomski rad). Novi Sad: GIS Institute Library (University of Novi Sad), 1994.

Dedijer, Vladimir. *Novi priloži za biografiju Josipa Broza Tita.* Rijeka: Mladost, 1981–1984.

Džuverović Borislav (et al.). *Izborna upotreba medija.* Belgrade: Institut društvenih nauka, 1994.

Đurđev, Branislav. *Problem izbeglistva u Jugoslaviji* (monografska publikacija). Novi Sad: Matica Srpska, 1997.

Đurić, Vladimir. *Najnovije naseljavanje Bačke kolonistama iz Hrvatske.* Novi Sad: Matica Srpska, 1960.

Erić. M. *Agrarna reforma u Jugoslaviji (1918–1941).* Sarajevo: Akademija Nauke i Umjetnosti Bosne i Herčegovine, 1958.

Gaćeša, Nikola L. *Agrarna Reforma i Kolonizacija u Bačkoj.* Novi Sad: Matica Srpska, 1968.

Gaćeša, Nikola L. *Agrarna Reforma i Kolonizacija u Sremu (1919–1941).* Novi Sad: Matica Srpska, 1975.

Goati, Vladimir. *Izbori u SRJ od 1990 do 1998 – Volja građana ili izborna manipulacija.* Belgrade: CESID, 2001.

Golubović, Zagorka (et al.). *Društveni karakter i društvene promene u svetlu nacionalnih sukoba*. Belgrade: Filip Višnjić, 1995.

Helsinski Odbor za Ljudska Prava u Srbiji. *Ljudska Prava u Srbiji 2000*. Belgrade: HOLPS, 2000.

Ilić, Vladimir. *Manjine i izbeglice u Vojvodini*. Belgrade: Helsinki Committee for Human Rights in Serbia, 2001.

Ilić, Vladimir and Slobodan Cvejić. *Nacionalizam u Vojvodini*. Zrenjanin: Ekspres, 1997.

Kačavenda, Petar. *Nemci u Jugoslaviji (1918-1945)*. Belgrade: Institut Za Savremenu Istoriju, 1991.

Kasas, Aleksandar. *Mađari u Vojvodini (1941-1946)*. Novi Sad: Matica Srpska, 1996.

Kerčov, Sava, Jovo Radoš and Aleksandar Raić. *Mitinzi u Vojvodini 1988. godine – rađanje političkog pluralizma*. Novi Sad: Matica Srpska, 1990.

Komšić, Jovan. *Vojvođanska iskustva i savremene dileme*. Novi Sad: Matica Srpska, 1998.

Končar, Ranko. *Opozicione partije i autonomija Vojvodine 1929-1941*. Novi Sad: Matica Srpska, 1995.

Matić, M. *Republički i nacionalni sastav kadrova u organima Federacije*. Belgrade: Radnička Štampa, 1969.

Mesaros, Sandor. *Položaj Mađara u Vojvodini (1918-1929)* (monografska publikacija). Novi Sad: Matica Srpska, 1981.

Mesaros, Sandor. *Mađari u Vojvodini (1929-1941)* (monografska publikacija). Novi Sad: Matica Srpska, 1989.

Mirnić, Josip. *Denacionalizorska politika mađarskog okupatora u jugoslovenske zemlje-1941*. Novi Sad: Matica Srpska, 1967.

Mirnić, Josip. *Nemci u Bačkoj u Drugom Svetskom Ratu*. Novi Sad: Matica Srpska, 1974.

Molnar, Aleksandar. *Osnovna Prava Čoveka i Raspad Jugoslavije*. Novi Sad: Visio Mundi Academic Press, 1994.

Nikolić, Goran. *Društvena obeležja nemačke nacionalne manjine u periodu 1918-1929 godine* (magistrarski rad), Matica Srpska archives. Novi Sad: Matica Srpska, 1992.

Petranović, Branko and Čedomir Štrbac. *Istorija Socijalističke Jugoslavije*. Belgrade: Radnička Štampa, 1977.

Petrović, Nikola. *Svetozar Miletić*. Belgrade: SANU, 1958.

Petrović, Ruza. *Etnički procesi u Vojvodini danas*. Novi Sad: Matica Srpska, 1989.

Pijade, Moša. *Agrarna Reforma*. Zagreb: Školska Knjiga, 1948.

Plenča, D. and A. Đonagić. *Jugoslavija u Drugom Svetskom Ratu*. Belgrade: Institut za Savremenu Istoriju, 1967.

Popov, Čedomir and Jelena. *Autonomija Vojvodine – Srpsko Pitanje*. Novi Sad: Matica Srpska, 1991.

Popović, Dušan J. *Srbi u Vojvodini*. Novi Sad: Matica Srpska, 1959.

Radonić, Jovan and Mita Kostić, eds. *Srpske privilegije od 1690 do 1792*, in *Posebno Izdanje*, no. 225. Belgrade: SANU, 1954.

Rotbert, Vladislav. *Jugosloveni u mađarskim zatvorima i logorima (1941–1945)*. Novi Sad: Matica Srpska, 1988.

Samardžić, Miroslav. *Položaj manjina u Vojvodini*. Belgrade: Centar za Antiratnu Akciju, 1998.

Tomić, Jaša. *Krajnje je vreme da se razumemo*. Novi Sad: Matica Srpska, 1919.

Articles published in books and academic journals

Bahtijarević, Stefica and Goran Milaš. 'Reakcija javnost na mere i politiku SIV-a'. In *Jugoslavija na kriznoj prekretnici*, edited by Ljiljana Bačević. Belgrade: Institut Društvenih Nauka, 1991.

Bašta-Posavec, Lidija. 'Ustavna demokratija i (ne)demokratska konstitucija društva'. In *Raspad Jugoslavije – Produžetak ili Kraj Agonije?*, edited by R. Nakarada, L. Bašta-Posaveć and S. Samardžić. Belgrade: Institut za Evropske Studije, 1991.

Čečez, Momir. 'O efikasnosti društvenih sredstava u privredno nedovoljno razvijenim područjima'. *Pregled* 70, no. 1 (January 1980): 34–35.

Dimković, Borislav J. 'Neki aspekti sociološkog proučavanja starosedelaca i kolonista u Rumi posle Drugog Svetskog Rata'. *Zbornik za Društvene Nauke*, broj 48 (1967): 126–139.

Gaćeša, Nikola L. 'Privreda Vojvodine između dva svetska rata'. *Zbornik za Istoriju*, broj 22 (1980).

Gaćeša, Nikola L. 'Jedan document o sprovođenju kolonizacije u Jugoslaviji posle Drugog Svetskog Rata'. *Zbornik za Istoriju*, broj 28 (1983): 161–200.

Hrabak, B. 'Borba demokrata za samosvojnost Vojvodine (1919–1928)'. *Zbornik Istorijškog Instituta Slavonski Brod*, broj 1 (1982).

Janča, Dejan. 'Regionalizam, regionalna država, i problemi regionalnog uređenja Srbije'. In *Ustavno-Pravni Okvir Decentralizacije Srbije i Autonomije Vojvodine*, Centar za Regionalizam, 28–36. Novi Sad: CZR, 2000

Jovičić, Miodrag. 'Parlamentarni sistem nasuprot predsedničkom i skupštinskom sistemu'. *Arhiv za Pravne i Društvene Nauke* LXXXVIII (1992).

Ilić, Vladimir and Slobodan Cvejić. 'Vojvođani i nacionalizam'. *Sociologija* XXXV (1993): 533–547.

Kasas, Aleksandar. 'Ekonomske mere vojne uprave za Banat, Bačku i Baranju (17 oktobar 1944 – 15 februar 1945)'. *Zbornik za Društvene Nauke*, broj 47 (1967): 173–183.

Katić, Vesna. 'Savremene promene običajnog života kolonista iz Bosanske Krajine'. *Zbornik za Društvene Nauke*, broj 80 (1986): 161–171.

Končar, Ranko. 'Ideja o autonomiji Vojvodine i KPJ'. *Istraživanje*, broj 1 (1971): 29–52.

Kovačević, Milivoj. 'Normativna Funkcija Autonomne Pokrajine Vojvodine u Razdoblju 1945–1968 Godine'. *Zbornik za Društvene Nauke*, broj 58 (1973): 87–118.

Lazar, Zsölt and Radivoj Stepanov. 'Odnos Vojvođana prema ustavnopravnom statusu Vojvodine. In *Kultura u proćesima razvoja, regionalizacije i Evrointegracije Balkana*. Niš: University of Niš (Institute of Sociology), 2003.

Madžić, D., S. Petaković, D. Malobabić and V. Solarević. 'Utičaj izbegličke populacije na kretanje nataliteta u Sremu'. *Zbornik za Društvene Nauke*, broj 91 (1997): 201–203.

Mihajlović, Srečko. 'Od dobrih podanika ka pluralizmu'. In *Pregled Rezultat Istraživanja*, edited by Bogdanović Nadezda. Belgrade: Savez Socijalističke Omladine Srbije, 1990.

Milosavljević, Milivoje. 'Kolonizacija Banatskog Aranđelova, Malog Sigeta i Podlokanja (1921–1941)'. In various authors, *Priloži za poznavanje naselja i naseljavanja Vojvodine*, 45–106. Novi Sad: Matica Srpska, 1974.

Mitrović, Mirko. 'Naseljavanje i kolonizacija Vojvodine (1690–1945)'. *Godišnjak Društva Istoričara SAP Vojvodine* (1982): 195–247.

Nikolić, Vera. 'Progon i Prihvatanje Srba iz Hrvatske 1991. Godine'. *Zbornik za Društvene Nauke*, broj 88 (1994): 189–204.

Obradović, Marija. 'Vladajuća stranka: Ideologija i tehnologija dominacije'. In various authors, *Srpska strana rata*, 472–500. Budapest: CEU Press, 1999.

Pihler, Stanko. 'Autonomija Vojvodine u Regionalizovanoj Evropi i Demokratskoj Srbiji'. In *Ustavno-Pravni Okvir Decentralizacije Srbije i Autonomije Vojvodine*, Centar za Regionalizam, 5–8. Novi Sad: CZR, 2000.

Popov, Jelena. 'Jedno svedočanstvo o problemima Vojvođanske poljoprivrede neposredno posle oslobođenja 1945'. *Zbornik za Društvene Nauke*, broj 48 (1967): 175-186.

Popov, Jelena. 'Poljoprivredna kampanija u Vojvodini u prvoj polovini 1945'. *Zbornik za Društvene Nauke*, broj 47 (1967): 39-71.

Popov, Jelena 'Prilog proučavanju pomoći Vojvodine ratom opustošenim krajevima Jugoslavije (Novembar 1944-Novembar 1945)'. *Zbornik za Društvene Nauke*, broj 48 (1967): 53-67.

Popov, Jelena. 'Glavni narodnooslobodilački odbor Vojvodine 1939-1945'. *Istraživanje*, broj 4 (1974): 405-413.

Radojčić, Đorđe S. 'Arsenije III Carnojević'. In *Enciklopedija Jugoslavije*, vol. 1. Belgrade: SANU, 1955.

Radojčić, Đorđe S. 'Arsenije IV Jovanović Sakabenta'. In *Enciklopedija Jugoslavije*, vol. 1. Belgrade: SANU, 1955.

Radojčić, Nikola. 'Sava Tekelija'. In *Istorijski Časopis*, vol. XII-XIII. SANU, 1963.

Radović, Zorica. 'Srbija kao država regiona'. In *Prinčipi ustavne deklaracije*, Forum za Etničke Odnose, 30-48. Belgrade: FZEO, 2000

Sirački, Jan. 'Slovaci u Vojvodini kao Istorijsko-Etnografski Fenomen'. *Zbornik Za Istoriju*, brojevi 102-103 (1997): 109-117.

Veg, Sandor. 'Sistem okupacione vlasti u Banatu (1941-1944)'. *Zbornik za Društvene Nauke*, broj 35 (1963).

Vinaver, Vuk. 'O Jugoslovensko-Mađarskoj Trgovini (1933-1941)'. *Zbornik za Istoriju*, broj 1 (1970): 37-78.

Vrkatić, Lazar. 'Srbi u Vojvodini i njihov državno-pravni osnov'. *Sociološki Pregled* XXXIV, nos. 3-4 (2000): 109-131.

Živkov, Sava N. 'Oblici socijalne integracije u dva kolonistička sela u Banatu: Stajićevo i Lukićevo'. In various authors, *Priloži za poznavanje naselja i naseljavanja Vojvodine*, 107-167. Novi Sad: Matica Srpska, 1974.

Reports, party-declarations and other official documents

Ana i Vlade Divac Fondacija. *Stavovi građana Srbije prema izbeglicama.* Belgrade: USAID/Ana and Vlade Divac Foundation, June 2016

Ana i Vlade Divac Fondacija. *Stavovi građana Srbije prema izbeglicama.* Belgrade: USAID/Ana and Vlade Divac Foundation, December 2016.

Arhiv APV Sremski Karlovci f. GNOOV-a- Odeljenje građevinsko-tehniko. *Pregled ostecenih zgrada u Vojvodini*. Sremski Karlovci, 4 October 1944.

Demokratska Stranka Srbije. *Osnovna načela za novi Ustav Republike Srbije.* Belgrade, 2001.

Friedrich Ebert Foundation (Serbia). *Studija o Izbeglicama: Srbija 2016.* Belgrade: Friedrich Ebert Stiftung, 2016.

Liga Socijal-Demokrata Vojvodine. *Republika Vojvodina: Put mira, razvoja i stabilnosti.* Novi Sad, March 1999.

Novosadska Novinarska Škola. *Nacionalistička vrednosna orijentacija kao faktor otpora prema autonomiji Vojvodine.* Novi Sad: NNS, 2001.

NVO Diferentija Niš. *Istraživanje o stavovima građana regiona Srbije prema toleranciji, suočavanju s prošlošću, decentralizaciji, i prepoznavaju osnovnih demokratskih vrednosti.* Niš, 2009.

Pokrajinski Zavod za Statistiku. *PSDS 1981. godine,* Knjiga III. Novi Sad, 1983.

Puzigaca, Milka and Aleksandar Molnar. *Istraživanje javnog mnenja: Autonomija Vojvodine.* Novi Sad: SCAN, 2001.

Republički Zavod za Statistiku. *Prevremeni izbori za narodne poslanike u Narodnoj Skupštini Republike Srbije.* Belgrade, 1994.

Republički Zavod za Statistiku. *Opštine u Republici Srbiji.* Belgrade, 1996.

SAP Vojvodina. *Ustav Socijalističke Autonomne Pokrajine Vojvodine.* Belgrade: Savremena Administracija, 1974.

Savezni Zavod za Statistiku. *Jugoslovensko javno mnenje,* A-3. Belgrade, 1964.

Savezni Zavod za Statistiku. *Statistički Godišnjak (1947–66).* Belgrade, 1968.

Savezni Zavod za Statistiku. *Popis stanovništva Jugoslavije.* Belgrade, 1971.

Savezni Zavod za Statistiku. *Statistički Godišnjak Jugoslavije.* Belgrade, 1972.

Savezni Zavod za Statistiku. *Statistički Godišnjak Jugoslavije.* Belgrade, 1981.

Savezni Zavod za Statistiku. *Popis stanovništva 1991,* knjiga 3. Belgrade, 1991.

Savezni Zavod za Statistiku. *Izbori '92.* Belgrade, 1992.

Savezni Zavod za Statistiku. *Nacionalni sastav stanovništva po opštinama.* Belgrade, 1992.

Savezni Zavod za Statistiku. *Statistički Bilten 1993. godine.* Belgrade, 1993.

Savezni Zavod za Statistiku. *Statistički Godišnjak Savezne Republike Jugoslavije.* Belgrade, 1993.

Savezni Zavod za Statistiku. *Statistički Godišnjak 1996.godine.* Belgrade, 1996.

Savezno Izvršno Veće. *Šta Misli Jugoslavija.* Belgrade, 1990.

Socijal-Demokratski Front Vojvodine. *Autonomija Vojvodine Danas.* Novi Sad, 1993.

Socijalistička Partija Srbije – Pokrajinski Odbor SPSa u Vojvodini. *Vojvodina 2000. Korak u novi vek-Izveštaj.* Novi Sad, 1996.

Srpska Napredna Stranka. *Bela Knjiga Programom do Promena.* Belgrade: SNS, 2011.

'Statut Autonomne Pokrajine Vojvodine'. *Službeni List AP Vojvodine*, br. 17/2009.

'Statut Autonomne Pokrajine Vojvodine'. *Službeni List AP Vojvodine*, br. 20/2014.

UNHCR. *Izvestaj sa istraživanja javnog mnenja: Stav građana Srbije prema tražiocima azila*. Belgrade: UNHCR/CESID, September 2014.

'Ustav Kraljevine Jugoslavije'. *Službene Novine*, 3 September 1931.

Ustav Kraljevine Srba, Hrvata i Slovenaca. Zagreb: Prosvjeta, 1923.

'Ustav Republike Srbije'. *Službeni Glasnik Republike Srbije*, broj 1/90, January 1990.

'Ustav Republike Srbije'. *Službeni Glasnik Republike Srbije*, br. 98/06, 2006.

'Ustav Savezne Republike Jugoslavije'. *Službeni List Savezne Republike Jugoslavije*, 27 April 1992.

Ustav Socijalističke Republike Srbije. Belgrade: Savremena Administracija, 1974.

Yugoslav Committee for the Investigation of War Crimes. *Zločini okupatora u Bačkoj 1941–44*. Novi Sad, 1948.

Yugoslav Committee for the Investigation of War Crimes. *Zločini okupatora u Sremu 1941–44*. Novi Sad, 1948.

Vojvođanski Arhiv. *Fond 184*, Sremski Karlovci 1953: Statistical information on the postwar colonists in Vojvodina.

'Zakon o informisanju'. *Službeni Glasnik Republike Srbije*, 1991/19.

'Zakon o izboru predsednika republike'. *Službeni Glasnik Republike Srbije*, 50/1992.

'Zakon o osnovnoj školi'. *Službeni Glasnik Republike Srbije*, 50/1992.

'Zakon o radio-televiziji'. *Službeni Glasnik Republike Srbije*, 1991/48.

'Zakon o službenoj upotrebi jezika i pisama'. *Službeni Glasnik Republike Srbije*, 45/91.

'Zakon o srednoj školi'. *Službeni Glasnik Republike Srbije*, 50/1992.

'Zakon o univerzitetu'. *Službeni Glasnik Republike Srbije*, 50/1992.

'Zakon o ustavnotvornoj skupštini'. *Službeni List DFJ*, 63/1945.

'Zakon o visokom školstvu'. *Službeni Glasnik Republike Srbije*, 50/1992.

'Zakon o zaštiti prava i sloboda nacionalnih manjina'. *Službeni List Savezne Republike Jugoslavije*, broj 11, 27 February 2002.

AJ, A-CK KPJ 1944/389: The report of the Communist Party of Yugoslavia on the confiscation of the properties that formerly belonged to Vojvodinian Germans (1 November 1944).

AJ, F 153, k.25, III-3/138: The Yugoslav state report on the treatment of the Vojvodinian German inmates in the Communist concentration camps (late 1944).

AVII, VO, k.1661, f.1, d.1: The Yugoslav state report on the treatment of the Vojvodinian Hungarian inmates in the Communist concentration camps (late 1944).

IA PK SK Inv. Br. A.K. Reg. Br. 7388, 7913: The report of the Yugoslav committee for the investigation of the war crimes committed in Alibunar (Banat) in April 1941.

IA PK SK Vojvodine Fond A.K. br.7991: The report of the Yugoslav committee on the Logor-Svilara Nazi concentration camp.

IA PK SK Vojvodine, Novi Sad, br. A.K. 7992, 4: A Yugoslav state report on the war crimes committed in the Banat in April 1941.

Istorijski arhiv PK SK Vojvodine, Novi Sad, br. A.K. 7992. 3–21: The report of the Yugoslav committee for the investigation of the war crimes committed in the Banat in April 1941.

Istorijski arhiv PK SK Vojvodine, Novi Sad, inv. br. 14.678/5: The request of the *Kulturbund* leader in Eastern Srem to the occupation forces for the establishment of a Reich's southeast department comprising the Banat, Bačka and Eastern Srem (3 May 1941).

Monographs in other languages

Hungarian

Lorinc, P. *Hacban a Foldert*. Budapest: Akademia Kiado, 1981.

Newspapers and Magazines

Serbian language newspapers and magazines

'Autonomaški apetiti'. *Velika Srbija*, February 2002.

Bartos, Juraj. 'Izbori 2000: I Slovaci su rekli DOSta'. Centar za Multikulturalnost, *Reflektor*, nos. 13–14 (2001).

Boarov, Dimitrije. 'Podrivanje Vojvodinu: U Ustavnom Tunelu'. *Vreme*, 1136 (11 October 2012).

Borba, 18 January 1993: The OSCE report on the December 1992 federal elections in Serbia.

Borba, 3 May 1992: A statement by Vojislav Šešelj on the Vojvodinian Croats.

Danas, 20 March 2002: The reactions of the Reformist Party of Vojvodina in regards to the inauguration of the '*Omnibus Zakon*'.

Dnevnik, 16 October 2009: A statement by Nenad Čanak on the new statute for Vojvodina.

'DS: Novi statut Vojvodine,' *Dnevnik*, 21 August 2008.

'DSS i SRS nude svoje verzije Statuta'. *Radio-televizija Vojvodine*, 15 October 2008.

'Govor Svetozara Pribićevića na kongresu jugoslovenskih profesora u Zagrebu'. *Narodna Riječ*, 5 October 1921.

Gruhonjić, Dinko. 'Gde je Vojvođanska tolerancija išla?' *Građanski list*, 21 October 2003.

Jovičić, Miodrag. 'Konfederacija vodi u haos'. *Stav*, 2 November 1990.

'Kad jaganci utihnu'. Vojislav Koštunica interviewed by Bogdan Ivanišević in *NIN*, 3 April 1992.

'Klali vola za kilo mesa'. *Bulevar*, 8 February 2002.

Mikavica, Dejan. 'Vojvodina kao Politički Program'. *Srpska Atina*, February 2002.

Novi List, 3 June 1941: A statement by Milovan Zanić, a member of Ante Pavelić's apparatus, on Srem.

'Novi Statut Vojvodine'. *BBC Srpski*, 15 October 2008.

'Odbor za Statut Skupštine Vojvodine: Na Redu Vojvođanski Ustavni Akt'. *Dnevnik*, 11 December 2001.

'Omnibus Vojvodina, Srbija u Evropi'. *Dnevnik*, 23 January 2002.

'Omnibus Zakon neće oboriti Vladu Srbije'. *Dnevnik*, 14 January 2002.

'Omnibus Zakon za sada je dovoljan'. *Glas Javnosti*, 10 December 2001.

Osmica, 22 April 1992: A statement by Vojislav Šešelj on the Vojvodinian Croats.

Pašić, Nikola. 'Ko parčelira državu?' *Samouprava*, 5 June 1921.

Pašić, Nikola. 'Radikalima i radikalnim organizacijama'. *Samouprava*, 9 September 1921.

'Poslanička većina podržala statut Vojvodine'. *Građanski List*, 15 October 2008.

Politika, 31 July 1988: The statement of the Federal Presidium on Novi Sad's 'yogurt revolution'.

Politika, 7 December 1993: The results of an independent survey conducted by the Belgrade Centre for Politics and the Media in winter 1993.

'Prošla autonomija'. *Večernje Novosti*, 30 November 2009.

'SPS protiv omnibus zakona: Korak za razbijanju Srbije'. *Glas Javnosti*, 20 January 2002.

Stankov, Dubravka. 'Kretanja ka socijalno-klasnoj i nacionalnoj strukturi SKJ'. *Komunist*, 1 January 1990.

Valić, D. and B. Kostić. 'Samo budala veruje'. *Nezavisni*, broj 40, January 1993.

'Više od sto amandmana na "omnibus" zakon'. *Glas Javnosti*, 22 January 2002.

'Vojvodina je dobra vest za Srbiju'. *Dnevnik*, 5 February 2002.

Newspapers and magazines in other languages

Hungarian

Szekeres Laszlo. 'VMDK-s voltam'. *Magyar Szo*, 28 May–7 July 1995.

Internet sources

English language

https://www.aer.eu/: The website of the Association of European Regions (Brussels).

http://www.aimpress.org: The website of AIM PRESS (an informative electronic magazine on issues of a Balkan interest).

http://www.amnesty.org: The official website of Amnesty International.

http://www.coe.int: The official website of the Council of Europe.

http://criticallegalthinking.com/: The website of *Critical Legal Thinking* (an academic blog with a leftist orientation).

https://dailynewshungary.com/: The website of *Daily News Hungary* (an informative outlet).

https://www.euractiv.com/: The website of *Euractiv* (a London-based informative platform).

http://ec.europa.eu/: The website of the European Commission.
http://www.gallup.com/home.aspx: The website of the *Gallup* international polling agency.
http://www.theguardian.com: The website of *The Guardian*.
http://www.hhrf.org/kosovo.htm: The 'Statement by the Presidium of the Alliance of Hungarians in Vojvodina Regarding the Situation in Kosovo', 24 March 1999, at the website of the Hungarian Human Rights Foundation (an American-based NGO that focuses on the ethnic Hungarian minorities in Central and Eastern Europe from a Hungarian perspective).
http://www.hrw.org: The website of Human Rights Watch.
https://inserbia.info/: The website of *InSerbia* (an informative outlet).
https://www.jobbik.com/: The official website of Jobbik (English language version).
http://www.legislationline.org/: An accumulation of international legal texts under the auspices of the OSCE/ODIHR.
https://eng.lsm.lv/: The website of Latvia's Broadcasting Agency (LSM).
https://www.opendemocracy.net/author/vassilis-petsinis: The author's section on the website of *Open Democracy*.
http://www.osce.org: The official website of the Organization for Security and Cooperation in Europe.
http://www.pewresearch.org/: The website of the *Pew Research Centre*.
http://www.politico.eu: The website of *Politico*.
http://www.spacesofidentity.net: The website of *Spaces of Identity* (an electronic journal, published by the History Department at the University of Vienna, that focuses on the politics and society of Central and Eastern Europe).
https://visegradpost.com/en/home/: The website of the *Visegrad Post* informative outlet.
http://www.vmsz.org.yu: The official website of the Alliance of Hungarians in Vojvodina (VMSZ).

Serbian language

https://www.b92.net/: The website of *B92* (a Belgrade-based media outlet).
https://www.blic.rs/: The website of *Blic* (an informative outlet).
Boarov Dimitrije. 'Ustavnoj poveli susret: Ima neka tajna veza', July 2002, at: http://www.helsinki.org.yu (the website of the Helsinki Committee for Human Rights in Serbia).

http://www.cesid.org/predsednicki2002: The results of the 2002 presidential elections in Serbia at the website of the Centre for Free Elections and Democracy (CESID), a Belgrade-based NGO that monitors the electoral procedures in Serbia.

http://www.demokrata.org.yu/srpski/program/politicki.htm: The political program of the Democratic Party (DS) hosted in one of the party's websites.

http://www.dkmt.regionalnet.org: The official website of the Danube-Kris-Maros-Tisa Euro-region.

http://www.dss.rs: The official website of DSS.

'Ekonomski i socijalni program SRS (1992)', at: http://www.srs.org.yu (the official website of SRS).

Mikavica Dejan. 'Kome treba Vojvođanski Komunistički Ustav?', Novi Sad 2002, at: http://www.dssns.org.yu (the official website of the DSS Novi Sad branch).

Mikavica Dejan. 'Simboli za Pokrajinu', 20 June 2002, at: http://www.dssns.org.yu.

Mitrović Milovan. 'Politika Demokratske Stranke Srbije u Vojvodini', 22 April 2002, at: http://www.dssns.org.yu.

'Osnove programa Socijalističke Partije Srbije', Drugi Kongres (23–34 oktobra 1992. godine, Beograd), at: http://www.sps.org.yu (the official website of SPS).

'Politički Program Demokratske Stranke', at: http://www.ds.org.yu (the official website of DS).

'Politički Program Demokratske Stranke Srbije', at: http://www.dss.org.yu (the official website of DSS).

'Programske osnove Socijalističke Partije Srbije', Prvi Kongres (16 jula 1990. godine, Beograd), at: http://www.sps.org.yu.

'Program Srpskog Pokreta Obnove', at: http://www.spo.org.yu (the official website of SPO).

'Program Srpske Radikalne Stranke', at: http://www.srs.org.yu.

Putnik Milena. 'Omnibus Zakon ili vraćanje autonomije: Prenete nadležnosti ali ne i novac', 24 December 2001, at: http://www.aimpress.org.

'Referendum i u Vojvodini', 4 February 2002, at: http://www.medijaklub.cg.yu (the homepage of Medija Klub, a Podgorica-based NGO that monitors the Serbian and Montenegrin press and media).

http://www.politika.rs: The website of the Serbian daily *Politika*.

http://www.rts.rs: The official website of *Radio-televizija Srbije*.

http://www.rtv.rs/: The official website of *Radio-televizija Vojvodina*.
http://www.srs.org.yu/izbori/ns.htm: Tomislav Nikolić's speech in Novi Sad (9 May 2004).
'Umorni od lidera', at: http://www.medijaklub.cg.yu.
'Ustavna Povelja Državne Zajednice Srbija i Crna Gora, 2003', Srbija i Crna Gora: Direkcija za Informisanje at: http://www.gov.yu (the official website of the government of Serbia and Montenegro).
http://www.vesti-online.com/: The official website of *Vesti* (an informative outlet).
http://www.vojvodina.com/prilozi/omnibus.htm: A full text-version of the 2001 '*Omnibus Zakon*' on Vojvodina at: http://www.vojvodina.com (a website of general Vojvodinian interest).

List of research interviews

March 2001: General Manager of the Humanitarian Centre for Integration and Tolerance, Novi Sad; Lecturer in Sociology, University of Novi Sad; Lecturer in History, University of Novi Sad; Vice President of the Executive Council of the Autonomous Province of Vojvodina – member of the organizational committee of the DSS Novi Sad branch; Director of the Novi Sad School of Journalism, Novi Sad; Monk at the Serbian Orthodox monastery of Kovilj; Vice President at the Executive Council of the Autonomous Province of Vojvodina – member of the organizational committee of the Reformist Democratic Party of Vojvodina; Secretary for National Minority Issues at the Executive Council of the Autonomous Province of Vojvodina

April 2002: President of the SRS Committee in Novi Sad; General Manager Assistant at the Museum of Vojvodina in Novi Sad; Vice President of the SPS Committee in Novi Sad; Producer of the Roma language informative programme at RTS Novi Sad; Producer of the Ruthene language informative programme at RTS Novi Sad; Producer of the cultural programme in the Hungarian language at RTS Novi Sad; Producer of the Romanian language informative programme at RTS Novi Sad

November 2005: Sociologist at the University of Novi Sad; Academic expert in ethnic relations at the University of Belgrade

April 2008: Academic expert in ethnic relations at the Hungarian Academy of Sciences (Budapest)

Index

Albanian nationalism 78, 92
Aleksandar, King 39, 42
Alliance of Hungarians in Vojvodina
   (VMSZ) 150–6, 158–65, 168,
   172, 177, 204–5, 212–13, 217,
   221, 233
Ana and Vlade Divac Foundation 229
ancestral territory 5–6
Anti-Fascist Council for the National
   Liberation of Yugoslavia-
   AVNOJ 51–2
Arpasy, Ildiko 153 n.123
Arsenije III Carnojevič 30
Arsenije IV Jovanovič Sakabenta 31
Assembly of European Regions
   (AER) 193, 225
Aulic Court for Transylvania 33
Aulic War Council 32
Ausgleich ('Compromise') of 1867 37
Austria-Hungary 11, 38–40
Austrian Succession War 33
Austro-Prussian war 37

Bajatović, Dušan 213
Banać, Ivo 41 n.24, 44 n.31
Basque country (autonomous region
   of Spain) 25, 27
Batt, Judy 17 n.19, 57 n.71
Bechev, Dimitar 235 n.57
Bečkerek Programme 38–9
Bilandžić, Dušan 71 n.101
Bogaroški, Branislav 213
Bosnia-Herzegovina
   collective rights 94
   colonist segment 112
   constitutional framework of
      Yugoslavia 58, 81, 204
   landless peasants 48
   1995 'Operation Storm' 205

Partisan movement 68
   refugees 3, 117, 121, 123, 201
   reprisal attacks 57
   territorial division 97–8
Bosnian Serb Republic (*Republika*
   Srpska) 97, 112, 122, 210–11
Brubaker, Rogers 8, 8 n.10
   theoretical matrix 10
   triadic nexus theory 10–11
Buckley, William Joseph 155 n.125
Bugajski, Janusz. 155 n.125
Bujošević, Dragan 170 n.133
Bulatović, Momir 132
Burg, Stevan L. 61 n.75

Čanadanović, Mirko 65, 145
Čanak', Nenad 136, 138 n.101, 140–2,
   176, 182, 184, 188, 194 n.43,
   212, 222, 225
Charles III (1713) 32
Civic Alliance of Serbia (GSS) 98
   n.42, 100, 104–11, 136
Civic Group for a Better Serbia 169
Cluj Declaration 150
Cohen, Lenard J. 79 n.3
Communist era
   regional and ethnic identities 17
   Vojvodina's regional character in 1
Communist Party of Yugoslavia
   (CPY) 59, 63, 68, 70, 74, 140
Connor, Walker 7
constituent regions 19
   myths 4–7, 13
   core group/ethnos 5
Ćosić, Dobrica 97
Council of Europe
   Draft European Charter on Regional
      Self-Government 189, 195
   ethnic minorities, definition 12

Count Rakoczi's rebellion (1703–11) 32
Croatian crisis of 1967–72 61–2, 65, 69
Croatian Democratic Community
    (HDZ) 17 n.20
Croatian Peasants' Party (CPP)
    41–3, 46
Croatia-Slavonia 29, 38, 40, 43
cultural–ideological myths 5–6
Cvetković, Dragiša 43

Dačić, Ivica 212
Danube-Maros-Tisa (or 'Banat')
    Euroregion (DKMT) 190
Deak, Leo 53
decentralization process 19–20, 24
deconcentration 20
Democratic Alliance of Hungarians
    in Romania 10
Democratic Community of
    Vojvodina's Hungarians
    (VMDK) 100–1, 103–11,
    113, 150–4, 158–64, 168–9,
    204–5, 213
Democratic Party (DS) 81, 99–111,
    113–14, 135, 141, 165, 172,
    178, 181, 188, 190–1, 205, 210,
    212–13
Democratic Party of Serbia (DSS) 81,
    99, 101, 103–11, 113, 135, 141,
    158, 172–3, 176–82, 186, 191,
    194, 210, 212–13, 230 n 52
democratization 17, 27
Đinđić, Zoran 177
displacement/deportation,
    migration 14
Djilas, Aleksa. 40 n.21, 59, 63 n.79
Djilas, Milovan 59
'Draža' Mihailović, Dragoljub 52
Drašković, Vuk 80, 141, 165
Đukanović, Milo 89, 132–3
Đukić, Đorđe 177

Ecological Party of Vojvodina 168
Elazar, Daniel J. 21 n.26, 24 n.29

election. *See also specific parties*;
    Milošević, Slobodan
    proportional electoral system 23
Enlightenment 35–6
ethnic group/ethnicity. *See also
    specific regions*
    conflict 8–9
    ethnicity without groups,
        Brubaker's 8–11, 8 n.10
    ethno-cultural heterogeneity 16, 23
    ethno-symbolism 4, 7–8
    minorities 3–4, 10, 11–13, 18–19
    multi-ethnic cohabitation 3–4
    relations in Serbia 1–2, 4
ethnopolitics
    theoretical approaches in 4
    triadic configurations of 8–11
European Commission 17
European Union (EU) 10–11
    federalism 20
    inter-regional forums 22 n.27
external national homeland
    (kin-state) 10–11

federalization 20–1, 23, 27
Fico, Robert 227
First World War 40, 43, 68
fixed identity 4
forced migration 14
'Four Motors of Europe' initiative
    22 n.27
France 18 n.22
    regional agencies in 20
French Revolution 36
Friedrich Ebert Foundation 229
functional decentralization 19–20

Galantai, Jozsef 49 n.46
Garašanin, Milutin 6 n.5
Germany 20, 49, 56, 194
    Budensrat (second legislative
        chamber) 21 n.25
Glenny, Misha 112 n.49
Gojković, Maja 213

Index

'golden age' 5-6
Gonzalez, Felipe 26 n.33
groupism/groupness 4, 8-9

Habsburg Serbs
   administrative system 31-8
   collective status 31-3
   first *'Velika Seoba'* ('Great
      Migration') 30-1
   Leopoldine Privileges 31-2
   migration 30
   modern nationalism 29, 36-40
   monarchical centralism 29-39, 42
   natio Illyrica 34
   Privilegium 32, 38
Helsinki Committee for Human
   Rights in Serbia 127 n.86
Hungarian Autonomous District 150
   n.116, 152
Hungarian Civic Alliance (FIDESZ,
   Hungary) 218-19
Hungarian revolution 37
Hungarians ethnic group 4-5, 10-11

identity. *See also specific regions*
   -construction process 4
   -formation process 4, 11-13
   grassroots perceptions 3, 28
Independent State of Croatia (NDH)
   54, 56
intercultural cohabitation 2
Islamic State 226
Italy
   regional agencies in 20
   regionalization 24-5, 24 n.30

Jakšić, Đurađ 213
Janjetović, Zoran 57 n.68
Jashari, Kaqusha 89
Jeftić, Branislava 213
Jobbik Magyarországért Mozgalom/
   Movement for a Better
   Hungary 218-19, 221, 230, 233
Joseph, Franz 37

Joseph I (1706) 32
Jovanović, Čedomir 212
Jovanović, Ljuba 88
Judah, Tim 78 n.1, 155 n.125

Kann, R. H. 37 n.18
Karadžić, Radovan 189
Karađorđević, Petar I 39
Kardelj, Edvard 59
Karlowitz, Treaty of 30-1
Keating, Michael 16 n.18, 18 n.21, 21
   n.23, 23-4, 25 n.31, 26 n.32
Kertes, Mihalj 83, 85
Koalicija Vojvodina 101, 139, 157-65
Komjathy, A. T. 48 n.43, 50 n.49,
   53 n.55
Korhecz, Tamás, 125 n.77, 126 n.83,
   213
Kosovo
   radicalization of the Albanians 128
   Serbian nationalism 89-94
   Serbia's bombing 132
   UN Declaration 1224 134
Kosovo and Metohija (Kosmet) 62-4,
   71, 149
Kosovo Liberation Army (KLA) 9
Kosovo: Past and Present
   (Garašanin) 6
Kosovo Polje battle 90
Kozić, Svetlana 213
Koštunica, Vojislav 81, 135-6,
   170, 212
Krunić, Boško 82
Kurdish Workers Party (PKK, Turkey)
   9, 98 n.42, 133, 153, 205
Kurds ethnic group 9

Lampe, John R. 65 n.84, 79 n.3
Lazar, Zsölt. 188 n.32, 199 n.45
League of Communists (LC) 61,
   65-6, 78-9, 82-5, 89, 91, 101
League of Communists of Yugoslavia
   (LCY) 62, 65, 71, 78-9, 83,
   91, 184

League of Vojvodina's Social-
    Democrats (LSDV) 100-2,
    114, 136, 140-1, 172, 182-4,
    212-15, 222-3, 225 n.31
Leopold I 30

Macartney, C. A. 43 n.29, 48 n.42,
    50 n.50
Mach, Zdzislaw 7 n.7, 13 n.15, 15
    n.16, 138
Maček, Vladimir 43
Mao Tse-tung 7 n.9
Maria-Theresa 33-4
Matić, Petar 82
McGarry, J. 92 n.30
migration 14-15, 34
    Serbs 30-1
    Social integration process 121-3
Mihajlov, Dejan 176-7
Mihajlov, Vojislav 135
Milan, King 39
Miletić, Svetozar 38
Milošević, Slobodan
    anti-bureaucratic revolution 27-8,
        77-9, 82-5, 88-9
    December 1990 election 81
    December 1992 election 98
    fall of 132, 134-6, 217, 234
    indictment 134
Milutinović, Milan 134
minority group(s). See also refugees
    individuals relation with nation-
        state 12
    irredentism 11
    national 10, 12
    radicalization of 12
    unreliable 13
    modern nation. See nation-state
modus vivendi 23
Montenegro 145-8
Morina, Rahman 89-90
Most-Híd/'Bridge' party 217
multi-ethnic cohabitation 3-4

'nationalizing state' 10, 17
national minority 10, 12
National Peasants' Party (NPP) 100,
    104-11
National Radical Party (NRP) 39,
    41, 44
nation-state 1, 4, 27
    European 11
    function of modern 12
    socio-psychological components
        of 4-8
Nemanjid dynasty in Serbian
    nationalism 6
New Communist Party of Yugoslavia
    168-9
Nikezić, Marko 65
Nikolić, Pavle 185-6
Nikolić, Tomislav 135, 205, 209, 212,
    228

'old Serbs' 2
O'Leary, B 92 n.30
Omnibus law (Omnibus Zakon) 28,
    171-7, 185
Orbán, Viktor 218, 227, 230 n 51
Organization for Security and
    Cooperation in Europe
    (OSCE) 98 n.41, 133, 153, 205
origin, myths
    biological continuity 5
    constituent 4-7, 13
Ottoman Empire 2, 30-4, 36, 47, 146

Pajtić, Bojan 191
Panić, Milan 97
Paris, Edmond 56 n.65
Parliamentary Party of Kosovo 155
    n.125, 156 n.127
Partisan movement 59, 67-8, 86-7
Party of Democratic Socialism
    (Montenegro, DPS) 132-3,
    146-7
Party of Natural Law 168

Pašić, Nikola 39, 41 n.23, 168–70
Passarowitz, Treaty of 31
Pásztor, István 212–13, 217 n.15, 221
Pavkov, Radovan 83
Pavlowitch, Stevan K. 47 n.40, 48, 72 n.104
Periclean Athens in Modern Greek nationalism 6, 6 n.3
Pijade, Moša 63
Pogonyi, Szabolcs 221 n.22
Polit-Desančić, Mihajlo 39
Popov, Čedomir 88
Popular Unity Candidacy (CUP, Spain) 224 n.29

Radić, Stjepan 41
Radovanović, Ivan 170 n.133
Ramet, Pedro 61 n.76
Ranković, Aleksandar 59
Reformist-Democratic Party of Vojvodina (RDSV) 100–2, 104–11, 113–14, 136, 140, 183 n.27, 184
refugees
    Bosnia-Herzegovina 3, 117, 121, 123, 201
    demography 117–22
    integration, legal complications 122–3
    international provisions 123–7
    UNHCR definition 117
regional identity. *See also specific regions*
    and regionalism 15–18
    of Vojvodina 1–2, 4, 28
regionalization 1
    asymmetric and symmetric 21–4
    Italy 24–5, 24 n.30
    Serbia 28
    Spanish 25–8
Republican Left of Catalonia (ERS, Spain) 223, 224 n.29
Rokkan, Stein 15 n.17

sacred territory 5–6, 11
second legislative chamber (*Budensrat*), Germany 21 n.25
Second World War 24, 55, 67, 138
Sekulić, Tomislav 90
Serbian Democratic Movement (DEPOS) 98–101, 103–11, 113–14, 164
Serbian Democratic Opposition (DOS) 135–6, 149, 167–70, 172–3, 176, 182
Serbian National Liberal Party 38
Serbian parliamentary elections 1992 99–103
Serbian Progressive Party (SNS) 209–17, 232
Serbian Radical Party 81, 97–102, 104–13, 121, 140, 157–72, 188, 191, 194, 205, 209–10, 212–13, 230
Serbian Radio-Television (RTS) 51 n.51, 93, 126 n.82, 129 n.91, 174–5
Serbian Renewal Movement (SPO) 80–1, 98, 102, 135, 141–2, 149, 158–65, 168–70, 210
Serbs of Vojvodina 1–3
Šešelj, Vojislav 81, 121, 212, 230
Seton-Watson, R.W. 38
Silesia, Polish region 15 n.16
Singleton, Fred 68 n.92, 74 n.112
Sipovac, Nedeljko 83
Smith, Anthony D. 4, 7
    myths of origin 6–7
Socialist Autonomous Province (SAP) 66
    of Kosovo 17
    of Vojvodina 17
Socialist Federal Republic of Yugoslavia 1, 3, 17, 27
Socialist National Party (Montenegro) 133, 147

Socialist Party of Serbia (SPS)
  79–81, 93, 97–101, 103–14,
  132–3, 135–6, 140, 143, 148–9,
  157–72, 212–13
Socialist Republic (SR) 17, 63, 65–6, 72
Šogorov, Milovan 82
Spain
  Andalusia 26, 26 n.33
  autonomous provinces 25–7
  Catalonia 25, 27
  'historical regions 25–6
  SPS–SRS condominium 97–9
Stambolić, Ivan 78–9
Stjepanović, Dejan 2, 234 n.56
Stockwell, P 48 n.43, 50 n.49, 53 n.55
Stojšić, Đorđe 82
Šuvar, Stipe 84
symmetric regionalization 21–4
Szávay, István 219

Tadić, Boris 188, 210, 212
third war (1737–9) 31
Thomas, Robert 79 n.2
'Tito,' Croat Josip Broz 51, 59, 85
Tomašić, Dinko 6 n.4
Tomić, Jaša 39
Topola, Bačka 83
triadic nexus theory 10–11
Trianon Treaty 49

Union of Jurists' Association of
  Yugoslavia 60 n.74, 62 n.77
unitary state 1, 18–19, 18 n.22, 21
United Nations High Commission
  for Refugees (UNHCR)
  117–18, 122 n.70, 122 n.72,
  228, 229 n.42, 231 n.53
UN Resolution 1244 177
Urwin, David 15 n.17

Vance-Owen Peace Plan 98
Vasin, Miroslav 213
Visegrad Four group of states 226–8,
  230

Vllasi, Azem 89–90
Vojvodina, current development
  administrative system 232–5
  European regionalisms, impact
    on 221–6
  interethnic relations 216–21
  refugee crisis 226–32
  2012 elections 212–15
Vojvodina in the 1990s
  against Milošević 136–42
  anti-bureaucratic revolution 82–9
  anti-SPS opposition 148–9
  autonomy, termination of 77
  colonists and refugees (1948–
    1996) 119
  economic crisis 114–16
  electoral results 104–11
  ethnic Hungarian parties 149–54
  ethnic minorities 1996 120
  forced migration 121–2
  interethnic relations 123–32
  Kosovo, comparison 154–6
  local elections 1996 158–64
  Montenegro, comparison 145–8
  multiparty landscape 78–82
  new constitutional order of Serbia
    95–6
  political preferences 103–14
  regional identity (*Vojvođanski
    identitet*) 142–5
  Serbian parliamentary elections
    1992 99–103
  Serbian-Montenegrin rift 132–6
  social integration of newcomers
    122–3
  sociopolitical aspects 94–5
  UN embargo 114–16
  Vojvodinian Central Committee
    82, 84–5
  'third' Yugoslavia 95–6
  Yugoslav elections of 1996 157–70
Vojvodina in 2000s
  administrative status 197–8
  autonomy 199

Index

ethnic incidents 204–7
interethnic relations 196–204
major national communities 202
new statute in 2009, political significance 190–6
Omnibus Zakon (Omnibus law) 171–8
provincial budget, denial 198
regionalization policies 178–84
Serbian Constitution of 2006 185–90
status within Serbia 200
Vojvodina's Academy of Sciences (VANU) 193–4
Vojvodina under Axis occupation
administrative system 52–4
Bihać manifesto 51–2
Chetniks' aim 52
interethnic relations 54–7
Magyarization 55
mass execution 55
Yugoslavia 1941–5 51–2
Vojvodina, within the first Yugoslavia 40–3
administrative system 43–5
annexed lands 43
Croatian Peasants' Party (CPP) 41
Democratic Party 41, 45
German bond 49–50
interethnic relations 49–51
National Radical Party (NRP) 41, 43–4
'Novi Sad Resolution' 45
political clash with *Srbijanci* Serbs 40, 44, 46
socio-economic condition 47–8
'Sombor Resolution' of July 1932 45
'Vojvodinian Front' 46–7
Yugoslav Constitution (1921) 41–2

Vojvodina within the Socialist Federal Republic of Yugoslavia
administrative system 62–6
constitutional framework 58–62
Constitutional Law of 1953 60
interethnic relations 72–5
'Law on the Constituent Assembly' 63–4
Socialist Alliance of the Working People of Yugoslavia 60
socio-economic system 67–9
Vojvodinian Party Committee 70–1
Vojvodinian Coalition for Yugoslavia 168
Vojvodinian Radicals 39, 46
voluntary migration 14
Vrkatić, Lazar 87
Vučić, Aleksandar 209–14, 232
Vulin, Aleksandar 228

Walker, Connor 7
Wolczuk, Kataryna 17 n.19
Workers Party of Kurdistan (PKK) 9

yogurt revolution 86
Yugoslavia. *See also specific parties;* Vojvodina within the Socialist Federal Republic of Yugoslavia
Bosnia-Herzegovina and 58, 81, 204
Constitution (1921) 41–2
elections of 1996 157–70
in 1941–5 51–2
parliamentary elections 100, 167–9
'third' 95–6
Yugoslav National Army (JNA) 126
Yugoslav United Left 135, 140, 157–65, 167–70

Zagreb National Council 47
Zajedno 157–65

Lightning Source UK Ltd.
Milton Keynes UK
UKHW010306070921
390157UK00008B/213